WATER THICKER THAN BLOOD

T0265563

IN THE SERIES *Asian American History and Culture*,
EDITED BY Cathy Schlund-Vials, Shelley Sang-Hee Lee, and Rick Bonus.
FOUNDING EDITOR, Sucheng Chan; EDITORS EMERITI, David Palumbo-Liu, Michael Omi, K. Scott Wong, and Linda Trinh Võ.

ALSO IN THIS SERIES:

Long T. Bui, *Model Machines: A History of the Asian as Automaton* (forthcoming)

erin Khuê Ninh, *Passing for Perfect: College Impostors and Other Model Minorities*

Martin F. Manalansan IV, Alice Y. Hom, and Kale Bantigue Fajardo, eds., *Q & A: Voices from Queer Asian North America*

Heidi Kim, *Illegal Immigrants/Model Minorities: The Cold War of Chinese American Narrative*

Chia Youyee Vang with Pao Yang, Retired Captain, U.S. Secret War in Laos, *Prisoner of Wars: A Hmong Fighter Pilot's Story of Escaping Death and Confronting Life*

Kavita Daiya, *Graphic Migrations: Precarity and Gender in India and the Diaspora*

Timothy K. August, *The Refugee Aesthetic: Reimagining Southeast Asian America*

L. Joyce Zapanta Mariano, *Giving Back: Filipino Diaspora and the Politics of Giving*

Manan Desai, *The United States of India: Anticolonial Literature and Transnational Refraction*

Cathy J. Schlund-Vials, Guy Beauregard, and Hsiu-chuan Lee, eds., *The Subject(s) of Human Rights: Crises, Violations, and Asian/American Critique*

Malini Johar Schueller, *Campaigns of Knowledge: U.S. Pedagogies of Colonialism and Occupation in the Philippines and Japan*

Crystal Mun-hye Baik, *Reencounters: On the Korean War and Diasporic Memory Critique*

Michael Omi, Dana Y. Nakano, and Jeffrey T. Yamashita, eds., *Japanese American Millennials: Rethinking Generation, Community, and Diversity*

Masumi Izumi, *The Rise and Fall of America's Concentration Camp Law: Civil Liberties Debates from the Internment to McCarthyism and the Radical 1960s*

Shirley Jennifer Lim, *Anna May Wong: Performing the Modern*

Edward Tang, *From Confinement to Containment: Japanese/American Arts during the Early Cold War*

Patricia P. Chu, *Where I Have Never Been: Migration, Melancholia, and Memory in Asian American Narratives of Return*

Cynthia Wu, *Sticky Rice: A Politics of Intraracial Desire*

Marguerite Nguyen, *America's Vietnam: The* Longue Durée *of U.S. Literature and Empire*

Vanita Reddy, *Fashioning Diaspora: Beauty, Femininity, and South Asian American Culture*

A list of additional titles in this series appears at the back of this book.

Uba family, January 1954 (Courtesy: George Uba)

WATER THICKER THAN BLOOD

A Memoir of a Post-Internment Childhood

GEORGE UBA

TEMPLE UNIVERSITY PRESS *Philadelphia • Rome • Tokyo*

TEMPLE UNIVERSITY PRESS
Philadelphia, Pennsylvania 19122
tupress.temple.edu

Library of Congress Cataloging-in-Publication Data

Names: Uba, George Russell, author.
Title: Water thicker than blood : a memoir of a post-internment childhood /
George Uba.
Other titles: Asian American history and culture.
Description: Philadelphia : Temple University Press, 2022. | Series: Asian
American history and culture | Summary: "Utilizing narrative prose,
impressionistic poetry, and retellings of Japanese myth and legend,
George Uba's memoir examines post-internment life and generational
trauma among Nisei and Sansei across the United States"— Provided by
publisher.
Identifiers: LCCN 2021051892 (print) | LCCN 2021051893 (ebook) | ISBN
9781439922576 (cloth) | ISBN 9781439922583 (paperback) | ISBN
9781439922590 (pdf)
Subjects: LCSH: Uba, George Russell—Childhood and youth. | Japanese
American children—Biography. | Japanese Americans—Forced removal and
internment, 1942–1945—Psychological aspects. | LCGFT: Autobiographies.
Classification: LCC PS3621.B3 Z46 2022 (print) | LCC PS3621.B3 (ebook) |
DDC 811/.6 [B]—dc23/eng/20211228
LC record available at https://lccn.loc.gov/2021051892
LC ebook record available at https://lccn.loc.gov/2021051893

Printed in the United States of America

9 8 7 6 5 4 3 2 1

To the generations past and present damaged by camp

and injured by ideologies of belonging

CONTENTS

PART III   TRAUMA

PART IV   LIKE CHILDREN BICKERING

PART V   DEPTH PERCEPTIONS

PART VI   REQUIEM FOR YESTERDAY

ACKNOWLEDGMENTS

As I BEGIN the happy task of acknowledging those who have aided me in bringing this project to completion, I find myself pausing. Eight people have been shot to death in Atlanta, six of them Asian spa workers. An Asian woman walking her dogs in Riverside, California, has been stabbed to death. An elderly Asian man in the Bay Area has died from a violent, unprovoked street assault. Returning from her husband's burial service, an Asian widow has been greeted by an unsigned hate letter in her retirement community in Seal Beach. The letter gloats over "one less Asian to put up with in Leisure World" and warns the woman to "go back to your country where you belong." All this and more, much more, in the space of seven weeks.

There is nothing new about hate crimes and hate incidents directed at members of the AAPI community, and certainly those incidents are not limited geographically. But this is a telling historical moment all the same. Today's numbers and frequency of event are staggering—more than 3,800 reports of hate incidents in the year or so since the start of the pandemic; hate incidents increasing in the nation's largest cities by 145 percent in 2020 alone; anti-Asian comments on Twitter surging by 900 percent.

Yes, words matter too. Even using the term "Japs," which for the sake of historical accuracy I find myself obliged to do at various junctures in this book, most notably in Chapter 1 and in the Epilogue, brings painful reminders of its vengeful (and at the same time casual) deployment during and after World War II. Similarly with the drill instructor's racist slur for Vietnamese, which I cite in Chapter 16. Of course, I do not use these terms to grant them license but rather to serve as forcible reminders of how virulent speech is itself a type of hate act, which frequently correlates with other hateful acts, both individual and national. (Note: Profanity is used sparingly in this text, but its occasional appearance is for the sake of verisimilitude and to register accurately the varying levels and intensities of feeling at a particular moment.)

Although in this memoir I elect to use terminologies most closely associated with my childhood, I readily acknowledge the inadequacies of descriptors such as "camp," "relocation," and "assembly center" and the contestations over and imprecision of the words "internee" and "internment."

I am one who does not easily lose hope for the future. I remain steadfast in my faith in America's democratic principles. Nevertheless, every day I am reminded of how citizenship still operates on multiple, uneven tiers. How starkly I can recall how, as a child, I once wanted so badly to fit in with the dominant American culture, even if that state of belonging came with an asterisk. My hope is that this book helps illuminate some unexamined corners of midcentury childhood affected, and afflicted, by the long shadow of internment, itself an extension of an even longer racial shadow the nation continues to grapple with.

On a much brighter note, I wish to express my sincere gratitude to the editorial staff at Temple University Press and to the university's Faculty Advisory Board. Their warm support of my project and their recognition of its potential educational worth are much appreciated. I am thankful too for the commentary from my outside reviewers and from the series editor. Their valuable suggestions and observations guided my revisions and helped me in reconfiguring various chapters. Thank you to expert copy editor Jamie Armstrong. Very special thanks to editor Shaun Vigil, who oversaw the manuscript's vetting and production.

I wish to acknowledge the journal *Ploughshares*, which first published the poem "Dawn in the Internment Camp at Heart Mountain"; and Turning Point Books, which published my volume of poetry *Disorient Ballroom*, in which the poems "The Threat of Canned Spinach," "Family Album," and "Teaching the Stroke Victim" first appeared.

To my many cousins and relatives, thank you for the vital family connections you keep alive and for the memories you do so much to sustain. I think of each one of you often. Particular thanks to Larie Akashi Izumo, who provided me with a trove of photographs and materials relating to her mother, to our mutual grandparents, and to the prewar Issei community in the Imperial Valley; and to Michael Odanaka, who provided me with valuable documentation and letters shedding light on the prewar activities of the Uba family and yielding special insight into his remarkable mother, Fukiko, and his father, Fred, who served in America's Military Intelligence Service in the Pacific during the war.

My professional colleagues and good friends Anthony Dawahare and Ian Barnard expressed timely interest and strong encouragement at key moments when my momentum on this project threatened to stall. I am indebted to them for their support and goodwill.

Thank you to my brother, Bryan Uba, who stimulated my memory via lengthy telephone conversations, and to my sister, Laura Uba, who provided me with a wealth of family materials and memories, while taking the time to pore over the manuscript with a keen attention to detail.

Deep thanks to my mainstays over so many years—Janice, Tracy, Eric. I have learned so much by observing and honoring how each of you expresses your individual self. And thank you always to my wife, Alice Ho, who keeps me grounded and fulfilled day after day and year after year.

WATER THICKER THAN BLOOD

PROLOGUE

Mother-of-Pearl

Los Angeles, Mother's Day, 1961

"I WILL NOT accept this from you."

A rejection rooted in grief. Grudges are grievances grown adamant. I will not accept this from *you*.

Her lips narrowed, unlike my own, which rounded like a vowel. They say if you get mad, you lose your looks. It's true.

She held the letter opener, its handle fashioned in mother-of-pearl, the colors iridescent. For as long as I could recall, Mother had used this letter opener, its blade leaving an identical slit along the head of each envelope, but the handle changing colors, depending on the angle of light.

We were gathered in the formal dining room, where in lieu of wallpaper, a stencil ran above the wainscot and looped around three walls. In Japan, the walls of a traditional home moved, their sliding panels, called *fusuma*, often accented with mountain landscapes. But this was not a traditional home and not located in Japan. Here, silhouettes of revelers in masks cavorted, brandished multicolored streamers. A jester juggled balls. A horse lifted its hooves, gaily pulled a cart. The carnival was in town.

One by one, the remaining cards slid out of their jackets. Cards embossed with hearts, soft with sentiments. Mother murmured thank-yous, but her letter opener looked sharp enough to puncture platitudes, to extract blood from those hearts. Outside the room's west-facing windows, the crows collected on the lawn like a cluster of dark notes at the start of a requiem.

In the fables, special occasions are marked by lavish feasts attended by nobles, not by a family lunch at a local diner. When the feast occurs at the end of the story, it is a sign of ever after. When it comes at the start, it is a warning that the good times won't last.

Today's lunch was off. It was off, so there. Get back. The rest of the day was a fist with hard knuckles. Chew on those. In the kitchen, a fork scraped at a can. Stand back. At the cutting board, the hands were swift. Onions. Celery stalks. Tomatoes trucked in from Oxnard. Chop and chop and chop.

Later, Father spoke to her in a way that was not done in the fables. "Why don't you ease up?" He called her "Florence," which meant that he was not speaking in his customary way. By then, her rage had softened. But as usual, as always, her will had hardened, had set. Quietly, she released a sob into his embrace. She only wanted what was best for the children. She repeated her mantra. *I didn't have a mother!*

In Japanese folklore, the *ubume* is the ghost of a mother who has died prematurely, leaving young children behind. When she returns, she brings them sweets to wash away bitterness.

Father paused just outside the door leading to the bedroom Bryan and I shared. Laura remained secreted in her bedroom; the youngest was wise enough to steer clear of all the fuss. "Why do you always have to react? Let things go and they won't get out of hand." He was Solomon dispensing wisdom to a second son. No, he was a father awkwardly blocking the entry light from the hallway. "It makes no sense to fight with her. She's not going to change. Use your common sense."

The words contained nearly the whole of Father's philosophy. The advice was reassuring, sort of. Like an insurance salesman informing a client that his current policy was better than nothing at all. Or a dentist advising a patient that if he brushed regularly, he could save the rest of his teeth.

Were Father a mean spirit, which he was not, he might easily have crushed a hypersensitive teenager like me. How can you fight with your own mother when she is ill? And on Mother's Day. What's wrong with you? You're no son of mine.

Instead, he credited me with common sense. Exercising it sounded doable, like juggling balls with both hands. Like exhaling sounds soft as vowels.

Yet somehow, even back then, I guessed that my failure to use common sense in the presence of Mother's volatility was not the key to unlocking what was wrong with me year by year—what was wrong with me, with her, with our family. We were still all together. Blood ran thick. It would prevail over all else, would it not? But I struggled to grasp the depth of Mother's anger, its length and breadth. How was it that her care and gentleness, what I remembered and cherished from my early childhood in the Midwest, was so utterly changed? Her illness accelerated the change, no doubt, but some other torment preceded it, something had lain in wait until that age when each of her children first exhibited signs of independence.

No, that was too strong a word, independence. A failure to submit. A failure to heed, to yield, to obey. Not to follow the right pattern, not to reproduce the correct image—it was too dangerous to contemplate. Lessons wrought from camp, that dark period of exile, I understood, but the camp experience itself I had heard little of, just as I had learned little of the historical factors, which in affecting my mother's and father's families before the war, helped produce those lessons in their particular expressions afterwards. What would be the effect of my learning of pasts about which my parents seldom spoke? Would I be enlightened by the discovery that some tensions are never relieved, or would I be overwhelmed? I did not formulate the questions in exactly this way. Not back then. But I felt their presence. Their heft. Their weight.

In some tellings of the folklore, the ubume has lost her infant during childbirth. In a common version, she hands her baby to a passerby to hold. When the ubume disappears, the baby grows heavy, eventually turning into stone.

Pasadena, California, 1941

FLORENCE FUNAKOSHI leaned over the sewing tray beneath the dining room window. Home was the compact rental in Pasadena, its yard consisting of two pockets of grass joined by a seam of cement. Behind the house stood an elm and a shed protected by a chain-link fence. Blocks away, boxcars with names like Santa Fe branded on their flanks gathered at the railroad station. In the kitchen, Freddie adjusted the radio.

Florence knotted the thread, snipped the loose ends. The shirt button was secure. Around the neighborhood, people were awake, her friends headed off to the Buddhist temple. Papa remained Buddhist, as did Ne-san. But Florence hoped to convince her brother to attend Christian church. It was Mr. and Mrs. Carew who had guided her conversion, and recently she had counseled Freddie on the matter of salvation. He had taken communion once, nibbling on a square of cracker, sipping grape juice from a chalice.

Since summer, when Mary wed David Akashi, Florence had had a bedroom all to herself. Before going up the Central Coast on her honeymoon, Mary had warned Florence to keep the house clean. Older sisters, Ne-sans, were like that.

Freddie wore a white tee and sporty trousers, standard gear for guys barely out of high school. His thick black hair held just the right amount of natural wave. It looked good, it usually did. A slight touch of pomade had done the trick. Yes, her brother was a nice-looking guy, and he had a pleasant disposition. Several of Florence's girlfriends had noticed. "Cradle robber!" they needled one another. Florence just laughed. She liked doing favors for Freddie.

"Did you hear?"

A formal look for church was best, especially with Christmas approaching. Urge him to wear the wool suit, the navy-blue tie.

The voice came from the kitchen, where occasional bursts of static marred the radio transmission.

Into the sewing cabinet went the thimble, the pin cushion, the spool of thread. "Where did you say?"

It was Sunday morning, the sun streaming through the elm tree. At the railroad station, the boxcars browsed peacefully. Freddie raised his voice in reply.

BEFORE FLORENCE had slipped into the dental chair, she had stolen a second glance. This had been, what, two weeks and two days ago? The dentist was above medium height for a Nisei. His face lacked the pleasing oval shape that declared a man to be handsome, but it was honest-looking, and his hair looked washed and well-groomed. Nisei are Americans of Japanese ancestry; their parents are Issei, who constitute the first-generation immigrants from Japan. *Open.* His dental instruments had picked and probed efficiently, without wasted movements. The man's glasses had round, thick lenses. He had to be nearsighted. *Close.* No caries, the voice had declared, as if the discovery marked a minor medical miracle.

She had laughed up her sleeve, she could not help it. He looked like a young man struggling to say something not directly related to tooth decay. In the rail yard, the locomotives assumed a similarly stiff, motionless stance. They looked dependable, if not exciting. In need of a conductor.

As she left the office, Florence had said, "Thank you, Doctor." Just before that, "Where did I put my hat?"

It was a bold hat, a statement hat, a social confidence hat with a clipped brim, not her style, but Ne-san insisted that she wear it. Mitzi, her girlfriend at the hair salon, had set this thing up. It was her bright idea. It's at the edge of J-Town, his office. Trust me, Mitzi confided, he's available.

Last night was their first date. The dentist did not say a lot after he arrived at the house and proceeded to guide her to his car. He shared that he was the one who taught his brother to play ball. That was what he had taken her to, a Nisei basketball game at a local gymnasium. His brother Hideo was the star player of the winning team. The dentist was not boasting, just making small talk.

Afterwards, at her front door, he politely shook her hand. She was relieved that he did not try to get fresh. Not like that one Nisei guy who kept trying to steal a kiss on a first date. Terrified, she had managed to push him away at last. When he finally gave up, he muttered, "Whatsamatter with you? You're just a cold fish!" Repeating the story years later, she mimicked the disdain in the man's voice. As if keeping her virtue was wrong. As if the whole thing was her own darn fault.

The question of a second date arose. She hesitated, thinking it meant another basketball game.

Once home, Florence had had time to reflect. Papa had gone to bed. Freddie was out with friends. He's nice, the dentist, but awfully quiet. A dentist with lockjaw, that's a good one.

Why not? had been her actual reply. Next time, if there truly were a next time, perhaps she could suggest a movie, maybe one with Ginger Rogers. The dentist said he liked the French actor Charles Boyer. How funny, since Katsumi Uba was anything but cosmopolitan or suave. He talked easily about golfers like Walter Hagen and Bobby Jones but said not one word about government, about politics. Another thought. Should she have insisted that he charge her for that office visit? If not, would she not be under an obligation to him?

Her mind sorted through these matters the next morning as she finished mending the shirt button for Freddie, who had turned up the volume on the radio. Outside, the dew had evaporated. Barely months ago, Florence had turned twenty-one. Her birthday also fell on a pleasant day, the weather sunny and mild. Like today, December 7.

In the kitchen, Freddie turned up the radio.

PART I

DISLOCATIONS,
RELOCATIONS

1

CAMP TOWN, RACE TRACK

IT ALWAYS STARTS before you are born. Always starts with preceding generations, their hardships, perils, traumas, which in your early years you believe are simply yours to hear about, to collect in fragments, to wonder at, to sympathize with, until gradually you realize that your life connects to that past in ways you had not foreseen. Though its events may be long gone, the past is a living network through which a current still moves. Still moves the way the common blood courses through the veins, the way DNA pronounces its verdict inside the cells and bones and upon the surfaces of skin, reminding you where you come from and where you do or do not fit in. I thought my life began in Chicago. I was mistaken. That is where my body first made its appearance, but the contours of my life, just like the contours of my brother's and sister's lives, had their start much sooner.

ABOUT EIGHT MILES EAST of the old railroad station in Pasadena lies the Santa Anita Race Track, a landmark in Arcadia, California, one of the municipal jurisdictions founded by the late-nineteenth and early-twentieth-century real estate magnate Lucky Baldwin. Baldwin gained fame for his entrepreneurship, as well as notoriety for his marriages and affairs. To the dismay of many, he hired minority workers, including blacks and Chinese, whom he found reliable and willing to work for low wages.

The racetrack symbolized an appropriate social circuit for the horse racing set, whose association with the real Lucky Baldwin was at times tenuous.

In 1941, newlyweds Mary and David Akashi passed by the splendid grounds while on a shopping excursion. The grassy infield and lush seasonal floral gardens always pleased Mary, who was drawn to lovely scents and pretty things. Recently, the couple had started negotiations for a florist's shop in Hollywood. They did not know it yet, but this marked the last time they would regard Santa Anita in the same appreciative way.

Everything happened too fast to absorb all at once. On the evening of December 7, Mary and David Akashi maintained their busy social calendar. Mary, the older sister Florence referred to as her Ne-san, had been the domestic mainstay of the Funakoshi household ever since the mother's death and until her own marriage earlier in the year. The young Akashi couple did not cancel their planned get-together with friends. They served tea while their friends helped themselves to bite-sized *sembei*. Someone broke out the playing cards. Everyone expressed shock and dismay over the brazen attack at Pearl Harbor—two words that in less than twelve hours were etched indelibly in the nation's consciousness. Over the card table, they talked about America's probable entry into war, but they did not yet deliberate, at least not fully, on the war's potential impact on them. They said, "Whose deal?"

By the start of 1942, the florist shop was put on hold. In the aftermath of the attack, Japanese living in and around Los Angeles and up and down the West Coast were left stunned and fearful but also uncertain and perplexed. Although they lived in their own neighborhoods and although some Nisei children had been relegated to separate, segregated schools, others attended public schools with Caucasian children, where they had felt free to join most clubs and to participate on most athletic teams. Their honesty and courtesy had been repaid with honesty (as far as they could tell) and courtesy. Never before had their devotion to the country of their birth been challenged or, as far as they knew, even considered. But in one brutal instant, every fiber of their presumed security had come undone.

GET OUT! GET OUT, DIRTY JAPS!

The hatred spewing across the newspaper headlines and blaring daily from the radio reverberated with a frightful intensity through Japanese American communities everywhere in the weeks and months after the attack. Friendships were dissolved. Business dealings came to an abrupt halt. Snappy quotes from legislators ensued, along with menacing stares from people who once treated Japanese with civility.

General DeWitt, head of the Western Defense Command, insisted that "a Jap's a Jap." He wanted them gone, all of them, wanted them "wiped off the map." The absence of a single instance of sabotage, he argued, was evidence that such sabotage was imminent. The farmers and the unions joined the chorus of fear and hate. Patriotic associations like the Native Sons and Daughters of the Golden West and the American Legion were no allies of Japanese Americans. Most people wanted them gone, vanished, all of them. During time of war, the country united. One nation. Indivisible.

GET OUT, JAPS. DON'T COME BACK. EVER.

The crude hand-printed signs appeared in windows. Chinese and Koreans got targeted too. Those living near downtown faced threats and property damage. It did not matter to white Americans that Imperial Japan had invaded and ravaged Asian countries. In desperation, the people wore newly minted lapel buttons proclaiming, "I am Chinese" or "I am Korean," which Florence, however unreasonably, resented.

When the federal government issued Executive Order 9066, Japanese up and down the West Coast learned that they were to be uprooted and placed in internment camps. The horse races at Santa Anita were suspended indefinitely and the grounds transformed into a temporary assembly center. The infield was decimated. Rows of barracks sprang up like overnight mushrooms. Most occupants remained for periods of four or five months in this and other designated assembly centers, until each of the ten internment camps in more remote parts of the country was completed and ready for occupation of longer durations.

Black-and-white photographs capture the moment when the suitcases and trunks held together with twine lay strewn across the lawns of neighborhoods just south and southwest and northeast of Little Tokyo and along the streets and corridors of East Los Angeles, as if the country's largest rummage sale were about to take place. In actuality, a convoy of trucks and cars conveyed many of the items to the assembly centers. In the photographs, the men wear white shirts and the women dresses and hats because the occasion was public. Children mill about or sit on suitcases. Even with the help of vernal rains, it would take weeks for the lawns to fully recover their sheens.

MOKICHI "JOE" FUNAKOSHI was a wiry man who applied muscle, sinew, and bone to his work. A padlock secured his gardening and handyman tools in the backyard shed. Each day was like that padlock. It clicked open at dawn, clicked shut at night. In between spun the clock hands, hour upon hour, day after day, year after year, whatever the place, whatever the job. Decades of toil left their mark. His thick black hair whitened and thinned, his muscles took longer to recover. The lawn mower pushed and pulled across the winding expanses of Pasadena lawn, the pruning and shaping of bushes running like fortified hedge rows along the perimeter, the sweeping and scraping and gathering and raking and shoveling—all of it took its toll, especially at night when Papa slipped into the easy chair.

Where he was going, he would not need the lawn mower or shears or even a shovel or rake. He gestured at a small equipment box.

"No, Papa," said Florence. "There won't be room. Leave it."

The youngest of a succession of boys and the only one who crossed the ocean to a foreign land, Mokichi Funakoshi subscribed to an unflagging Japanese work ethic and to *gaman*, the principle of perseverance, or as I came to understand it, of endurance, relentless endurance. Perhaps that was why his skull looked chiseled from granite, why with each passing decade his face, handsome in his youth, looked more humorless, why it appeared so unflinching and stern.

Now Papa listened as Florence tried to explain what lay ahead. From the time she was a child, she was the one with worry teetering in her eyes, her eyes like saucers. The one who did not often go out with friends, unlike Mary and Freddie. The child who preferred to nestle at her father's feet after supper as he leafed through the Japanese-language newspaper, the child assiduously explaining what she learned in school that day. On those evenings, she soothed herself with the belief that Papa valued her presence as much as he did that of anyone else.

Florence advised him to destroy their Japanese possessions, the things linking them to the enemy and potentially placing them under suspicion with the authorities. Many Nisei burned letters and pictures, destroyed woodblocks and ceramics. Even disposed of valuable kimonos. Mary said otherwise. We'll find someone to store things for us, she declared, thinking ahead.

Other items, bulky items that could not be stored with a trusted neighbor, had to be sold. Freddie helped Papa move the easy chair to the front yard. For Sale. Cheap. The chair looked out of place, floating on the cement walkway between the twin clusters of grass. Out of place and forlorn, like a vessel already consigned to another owner, its family history unsalvageable.

Like that chair, the four of them had managed to stay afloat through the long yesterday, despite Florence's fears of capsize. "Nothing better happen to me," Papa had declared after the children's mother died. *Nothing better happen to me* resounded in their heads once the Great Depression began. He said everything in Japanese. *Wakatta?* Of course the children understood. What's not to understand?

The indigent often succumbed. But the wealthy white people in Pasadena still needed laborers. They knew nothing, cared nothing, about "Joe" the gardener's present circumstances, even less about his Japanese college education or his skill with calligraphy or the businesses he ran in the Imperial Valley, where he held membership in the Chamber of Commerce, but they liked the fact he rolled up his sleeves and worked all day without taking a break.

At one residence, a pleasant maid helped Joe communicate with the homeowner, and Joe and the maid were able to strike up a cordial relationship. The maid, Mallie, was originally from Georgia, where her family worked as sharecroppers, her parents having been born into slavery. Two of her sons exhibited rare athletic ability. One was an exceptional sprinter. Mack Robinson ran all the way to a silver medal at the Olympic Games in Berlin. The other son excelled at every sport—football and basketball and track and field and baseball and tennis. His name was Jack.

By the time the war broke out, Mokichi, or Joe, had seen none of his birth family in over three decades. Were they to pass by each other on a street or in a marketplace, they would scarcely have recognized one another. Maybe his brothers' sons or grandsons were enlisted in the Imperial Japanese Army, cutting a heartless swath across the Korean peninsula or into the Chinese mainland.

"Ooh, it stinks."

The infield having reached capacity, the Funakoshi family, along with hundreds of other families, was hurriedly directed to the horse stables, where Florence recoiled at the smell. Workers had hosed the stables and here and there laid planks of wood lengthwise to create walkways across the alleys of mud. But the lingering odors of horse piss and dung and animal sweat penetrated the wood, filled the air. Smells were the permanent, unwashed residents, the people temporary guests.

Elderly Issei with ambulatory problems remained stuck inside the smells even during the long hours of daylight. Others found respite outdoors, free to meet friends or, like Papa, to wander up and down the rows of converted stables. Most of the time was spent in lines, long lines for the mess halls and the laundry and the restrooms. Everything was shared, including food shortages. Mary hated that there was just one shower for every thirty residents. It was embarrassing to everyone that the *obenjo* were also communal. Like the showers, those bathrooms were separated only by sex, just as they would be in each of the internment camps.

At night, the racetrack village shut down, a gigantic clamp placed on all outside activity. As many as three families squeezed into each stall, each family bedding down on tick-filled mattresses. Each detainee was issued one blanket. Florence offered hers to Papa, who, having started his family rather later in life, was now into his late sixties. At night the odors collected, filling the nostrils. From random stalls, the occasional whiff of cigarette smoke provided relief. Everyone was in limbo, each day as aimless as the one before, as empty as a vacated house.

Homeowners in Arcadia were willing to do their part for the war effort. But they were not pleased. Theirs was a grassy, tree-lined city, whose name memorialized the region in Greece associated in Western art with untrammeled nature and utopian ideals. In Greek mythology, Arcadia is the home of Pan.

By order of municipal law, the residents of Arcadia were white, exclusively so. Realtors were prohibited from selling homes to non-Caucasians. Arcadia was scarcely the only city in the region with such a housing covenant. Before the attack on Pearl Harbor, at least the city's residents did not object when Mary and David Akashi passed through their streets before sundown. They did not prohibit them from patronizing their retail shops. But most did not favor Orientals of any type actually inhabiting their city, let alone nearly eighteen thousand of them invading their prized civic landmark like squatters, like refugees.

AT THE POMONA ASSEMBLY CENTER located on the grounds of the annual Pomona County Fair, Toshio turned to his big brother. "You popped the question?" he asked. Toshio was just nine, and already he had developed a habit of saying whatever came to mind. Katsumi did not reply. In April 1942, Katsumi Uba, D.D.S., had accompanied his mother Misao and brother Toshio to their assigned assembly center.

Soon his sister Miyeko and her husband Ken, a carpenter, joined them. Likewise his other sister Fukiko, energetic and athletic and another of the family's nearly straight-A children. Fukiko and a friend having organized the Nisei Women's Athletic Union before the war, it was logical that camp officials should appoint her head of the women's recreation program at the assembly center. Luckily, their brother Mahito was attending medical school away from the West Coast. But Hideo, the star athlete, would join them here and at Heart Mountain until he was able to secure an early release by gaining a college admission in Chicago. As for Florence Funakoshi, Katsumi's main worry was that the War Relocation Authority would send her family to a different internment facility.

At first, Mama remained silent too, following Toshio's indelicate question. After putting Toshio to bed, she confided her reservations to Katsumi. *You barely know her.* Mama spoke with a quiet conviction, in Japanese, of course. By now, she had met the girl twice. *With all that is going on, we don't know what the future holds.* When Katsumi deigned a reply to Mama, it was in an impatient patois of conversational Japanese and English, he fully aware that she picked up only scraps of the latter.

There is something about this girl, Mama insisted. She sensed that the girl was not truly complaisant, not gentle and easygoing and tender. Not *yasashii.* To be sure, she had enough schooling, possessed some intelligence, but she tried too hard to leave a favorable impression. She used big words, and her compliments sounded effusive. Mama doubted her work ethic. Unlike Miyeko, unlike Fukiko, she seemed like a talker rather than a doer. Those were not desirable traits in a daughter-in-law, particularly in the wife of an eldest son. What would it be like to live with such a one? She did not mean for her son. She meant for herself.

Katsumi declared that the matter was settled. It was settled. It was his life, and he would decide for himself. How American his attitude was! Still, even a Japanese mother dare not disrespect her eldest son. Even were she not— over the last eight years—a widow.

THEN THEY WERE OFF. The train with its string of passenger coaches clattered and roared through barren landscapes and along mountain divides, wheels clutching the tracks. It was in a hurry to reach its destination and to repeat its circuit as many times as possible. It raced, it raced like mad, like the mother of all mayhem, like Seabiscuit galloping down the homestretch, straining for the finish line. But inside the coaches, little stirred, including time, except when the train passed through a town and the passengers were ordered to lower the window shades.

Human sweat worked its way through the wool overcoats and layers of clothing, and odors from people packed close together permeated the close air. The children grew restless. They scrambled up and down the aisles like chickens, their identification tags flopping from their necks. When the children tired, they settled into a lassitude that expedited the transition into luxurious sleep. Infants woke, squalled, pooped, slept.

Make no mistake, Florence Funakoshi and Katsumi Uba sided with the Nisei majority. They sided with the Japanese American Citizens League, agreed that cooperation was paramount. No one wanted to leave their homes. No one welcomed removal for who-knew-how-long to who-knew-where. But they would cooperate fully with the federal government now that the internment camps were ready for habitation, and by cooperating prove loyalty to the country of their birth, the country they believed in, the only country they knew. Always make the best of a bad situation. *Shikata ga nai*, Florence repeated. *It can't be helped.*

Not that "internment" was a term Florence ever used. She no more uttered that word than the words "incarceration" or "imprisonment" or "concentration camp." She referred to the time period as "relocation," the forced removal from home as "evacuation," and the internment center located deep in the nation's interior as "camp."

However softened the terminology, it was the watershed moment for all Japanese in America. Their immigration history was aborted, their rights as citizens denied, their identity cast into doubt. And that was what they found so queer. It was not a moment of self-questioning or self-doubt. Not for Nisei like Florence and Kats. They never ceased to know exactly who they were. It was the others who changed in their perceptions of them. Their perceptions, their attitudes, their conduct.

Confounding too, that moment when Japanese Americans had to view themselves through the eyes of white people, as if all along they had existed only in abstraction until the morning the bombs fell and they materialized as the enemy, the tangible foe, until just as quickly dematerializing into an obscene, buck-toothed caricature played out in newspapers and newsreels. It was as if a curtain had been lifted, and each one stood in full view of a thousand thousand hostile eyes.

"What gives?"

Toshio sat across the aisle. To dramatize his point, he pinched his nostrils with the fingers of his right hand. Katsumi glanced past his kid brother, past Mama, who looked tired. Through the window, whose shade was now open, the landscape rushed by. In the near distance were throngs of cattle, permitted to stare at the train's cargo, if they were so inclined. They greeted the train with a dense wave of methane gas.

A fellow in the next row was less restrained.

"What kind of shithole are we heading to?"

2

———

WOMEN WITH BRIGHT IDEAS

IT WAS THE CENTURY'S MIDPOINT, and Mother was in charge of the move. I learned about this much later. Later, when I was old enough to attend school, old enough to blow my own nose and master the alphabet and then old enough to pick up bits and pieces of family lore and to start to wrestle with notions of bloodline and with all the answers to how come and the fleeting sensations of how sad.

Katsumi Uba and Florence Funakoshi had wed on a hot summer afternoon in 1943. They had waited patiently, the dentist having proposed much earlier—actually on only their third date. But back then, in the days and weeks following the attack at Pearl Harbor, there was no time for long deliberations. He possessed the instincts of an athlete. When the pressure was on, you moved fast or you lost the game.

Fortunately, the couple had been sent from their respective assembly centers in California to the same internment camp at Heart Mountain, Wyoming. Not fortunately. It had taken considerable maneuvering with the government. The spare, simple wedding ceremony had taken place with a few family members and close friends in attendance, the ageless mountain the presumptive state witness. No fuss. No record of a bouquet toss. One modest wedding photograph had commemorated the event. Afterwards, the newlyweds had been assigned to a raindrop-sized "apartment," which threatened to evaporate among the dusty rows of tar-paper barracks.

On May 30, 1944, the couple left Heart Mountain for good, having secured an early release. They would start over—but not in Los Angeles. The

War Relocation Authority had issued stern warnings to the former internees not to return to the West Coast and not to congregate with other Japanese. The word it had employed was "resettle." It was code. It meant don't go back. Don't go back to where your families had roots, to where most of your kind were born. It meant disperse, assimilate, turn for God's sake invisible. As a result, Nisei settled in numbers in the dense urban centers of the Midwest—Chicago, Cleveland, Detroit, Minneapolis, or Denver high in the Rockies.

Years later, my brother was able to recall that first cramped apartment on Chicago's South Side. Bryan also remembered that Mother was in charge of moving, while Father stayed busy fixing people's teeth, his office on the second floor of a building set within a warren of other buildings catching the rumble of the El in the distance and in the evening the glow of white lights from Comiskey Park. Neither Bryan nor I absorbed the whispers relating to all the black people moving into the area. *Kuro-chan*, the Nisei called them, a term that was not a hate word but nevertheless held a pejorative edge. Looking back, it seems odd. It seems odd since black people had nothing to do with the racial hysteria during the war or with the camps. In fact, the NAACP was one of the few national organizations issuing a formal statement of protest against the internment.

If on some days, Mother felt daunted as she rode the El or boarded the bus, she did not let on. She visited two realtors and then a third and a fourth and a fifth. They took her name and phone number. Weeks passed without a single call back. Recently, she had begun to experience nausea, wondered if it might be morning sickness, but she fought through it, made breakfast for us. She cleaned the apartment, waited for the call that did not come.

She had scoured the listings for the North Side and beyond. New highways had sprung into existence. They were arteries carrying people to and from the previously remote suburbs. Before the war, Japanese Americans were too clannish; they did not allow Caucasians to get to know them, and by knowing them, learn to trust them and have faith in their patriotism and loyalty. Mother was not the only Nisei to believe this.

As soon as we children were old enough to understand, Mother started telling us that Japanese Americans must strive for "acceptance." That was her preferred term. She meant acceptance by *hakujin*, which was the neutral Japanese term for Caucasians. To her, the white world was shape making and authoritative. After all, weren't hakujin the ones who built this great country? Her young family must seek the accepting embrace of a benevolent white community, something to last through life's changing seasons. Camp had altered everything. Survival and success were nothing without acceptance. Nothing at all. When at last the telephone rang, Mother believed that her patience had been rewarded.

"Listen," the voice confided, "I've got a three BR on a corner lot. A quiet residential area, peaceful. That's right, s-k-o-k-i-e, you've heard of it. The town's growing but still keeps its village appeal. Good schools, lots of children. Great family atmosphere." Florence listened, excitement growing despite her efforts to keep her hopes in check. "Truth is," the realtor continued, "it's a property that's been a little bit slow. You can get a good price. They've just lowered the asking. Did I mention it's got a nice yard?"

Her spirits buoyed, Mother secured a sitter for Bryan and me and boarded the bus to the realtor's office. The weeks and weeks of "checking in" (*Terribly sorry to keep troubling you, yes, it's me again, I must be such a bother*) had paid off.

The realtor drove her to the site. He had not lied about the house. It was lovely, nestled on a gentle ribbon of road that would fit into a rural landscape. "Harms Road, with an s," the realtor declared. A convenient cinder alley ran behind the property. There were three two-story houses all in a row, and further up the street stretched pleasant one- and two-story houses with flower beds gracing the front yards. There were two or three well-kept houses directly behind but facing in a different direction from the one for sale.

Of course, Mother also saw what the problem was, what the realtor had forgotten to mention.

A bit slow? Ha! No one short of a vampire seeks a home directly across the street from one cemetery and paralleled on the side by a second! One cemetery immediately to the east, another immediately to the south. The realtor scratched his chin. His pink face reddened.

"I'm not the superstitious type," he murmured. "I'm guessing you're not either."

She was not. Or if she ever was, she was not now. The brick two-story was a beauty. Compact but refined. She inspected the kitchen, the dining and living rooms, which included wall-to-wall carpeting and curtains. Upstairs was the master bedroom, and down the hall, a room for a baby and one for the boys. A quick glance to take in the bathrooms.

The realtor looked relieved. He looked relieved, and from a briefcase he hauled out page after page of documents. He had brought them all with him, just in case. He had experience with people; he knew that this nice Oriental lady was not going to quibble over price. At the very least, she'd sign a promissory.

He was surprised, then, when the lady hesitated.

MISAO UBA'S FACE WAS ROUND AND SOFT like a muffin. She looked kind and gentle, which is how Japanese women should be. Yasashii. That was how I was to remember my grandmother year after year. But that was appearance only. For Misao was not one to endure insult. She was no one's trembling pet poodle, even if she sprang from a litter of fourteen children of Iiku and Yoshitaro Abe. As a picture bride, Misao Abe vowed to herself that if her groom-to-be's appearance and demeanor did not satisfy her, she would promptly turn around and swim back to Japan. Or at least swim as far as the nearest ship capable of ferrying her home.

As it turned out, she rewarded Senpachi Uba with four sons among their six children. Give him credit. The man had worked hard. But he had had no idea how risky it was, the method he had improvised for stains and spot removals at work. It was fast, effective, and, with spritzer bottles unavailable, simple—take the cleaning solvent, which came in five-gallon cans, and fill an empty pop bottle. Take a swig. Cast a spray onto the shirt or blouse spread out before him. One mouthful was sufficient for a large garment, half a mouthful for a small one. Spray. Clean. Rinse. Spray. Clean. Rinse. At his feet stood a small bucket. Every few minutes, he spat out the remnants of the taste.

Misao knew that the sun would set long before her husband left the steaming interior of the cleaning establishment. The big black sedans and the Pacific Electric streetcars would be heaving their ways through busy 1st Street and 2nd Street between San Pedro and Alameda, as he found his way home in the dark. Misao prepared his *ochazuke*, his mixture of green tea poured over white rice. He slurped it contentedly. It was sufficient, almost, to wash away the acrid flavors of the long workday. Still, sometimes his throat felt swollen, as if it had been flushed with mechanical waste. He noticed when several teeth began to loosen.

Year by year, Senpachi Uba, who had immigrated to America just after the turn of the century as an energetic youth in his twenties and who worked relentlessly at his job as a Fancy Spotter, successfully coated his internal organs with a petroleum-based chemical used for cleaning. Before he reached his fifty-fourth birthday, before the country managed to climb fully out of the sinkhole that was the Great Depression, and before his family was uprooted and forever dispersed, he was dead, and Misao knew that she was on her own.

She did not hesitate. She knew where to focus her primary attention, starting with her eldest son. Grief she suppressed, even were such a goblin of misadventure to dare rear its head in her vicinity. She wore her face like a mask, like Okame, the Goddess of Mirth, with the large round face and smiling eyes, the one associated with good fortune. Misao devised a plan intended to produce, and reproduce, good fortune.

The first thing was the life insurance. Life insurance was comparatively new around Little Tokyo. Senpachi had declared the idea a waste of money.

Plenty of other Issei also were reluctant to part with their hard-earned cash on the mere promise of a payout when you died. Besides, it was bad luck to forecast your own death. The sales guy popped up one day, like a new branch on an office tree. But he was not easily brushed aside. Senpachi promised to think about it. But he had no intention to purchase death insurance. It was Misao who had gotten it into her head that a policy made sense. Finally, her husband had given in. The guy in the suit returned, happy. Misao would have the last laugh, although that was not how she phrased the result to herself.

She feared that collecting on the insurance policy would prove complicated. The hard times had hit everywhere. They showed no signs of letup. Plenty of Caucasians, hakujin, lined up for bread. Kids peddled apples on street corners. The family was fortunate that for years both Miyeko and Fukiko, the two eldest, the daughters, contributed their entire work salaries to the family coffers. Misao persevered, signed forms, produced the death certificate, signed more forms. And finally, there it was, her eldest son's future in her hands.

Now she implemented her long-term plan. The money would go toward Katsumi's education. She supported his idea of leaving the new UCLA campus and transferring to USC, which was closer to home and offered an accelerated predental track. Yes, she would use the life insurance, every bit of it if necessary, to support her eldest son's education. He would be the first but not the last "Dr. Uba." He could help Mahito further his education, and Mahito could then assist Hideo, and Hideo in his turn, young Toshio.

Her sons embraced the plan. She consulted with her daughters too. Both Miyeko and Fukiko were ready to help. Misao became the target of gossip. Some people thought that she was a hardheaded woman with too-lofty ideas. That's right—she was. The Uba name would move forward. Her sons would all occupy professional positions in America. They would climb that ladder of success, gain notice in the Japanese American community for something beyond their athletic prowess. Misao would see to it.

About herself, she did not worry. She could manage on her own. For a while, the widow Misao Uba had worked in a perfunctory fashion as a housekeeper. Eventually, she turned her remarkable sewing skills into a cottage industry, producing an array of plump stuffed animals—rabbits, ducks, and her specialty kangaroos—each well-nourished, each with a distinct personality. They made splendid Christmas presents. People wanted to purchase them (how precious!), even advance-order them. It took much effort, and not a little skill and patience, to hand sew a single animal, to bring the figure to life.

By the time her six children and the passing years turned her once slim figure stout and her hair, which she tied back in a bun, gray, Misao Uba had become the grandma who each and every Christmas stitched together marvelous stuffed kangaroos, which she distributed to her grandchildren, whose numbers multiplied year after year. Mama kangaroos squatting upright on generous hips and broad tails, and each with a pouch holding a plush baby kangaroo. For Bryan and Laura and me, there were many babies, including ones we named Reddy and Pinkie and Bluey and Junior. Christmas after Christmas, the postman delivered kangaroos in a big box, sent from the best grandma ever.

MOTHER'S EXCITEMENT WAS REAL but constrained, entangled in a net of thought. There remained the one vital task to complete before she signed anything. Years later, when she told me exactly what she did that day, she spoke without a hint of embarrassment. That day, the task stood before her like a granite boulder blocking the entrance to a throughway. It had to be moved in order for her to proceed.

An advantage, to put it bluntly, of having so many neighbors already resting in the ground was that Mother paid just one visit to one house. The one directly to the north, where the peonies and lush pansies bloomed cheerfully along both sides of the front walkway. She summoned her courage, as the realtor obligingly retired to his automobile.

Mother approached the door, the door to the neighboring house. But not the front door. Like a maid in the Hollywood movies, or like a gardener tending to a rich person's grounds in Pasadena, she automatically retreated to the rear of the house, where, if there had been servants, they would have entered.

The lady heeding the knock at her back door was fair-haired, with a pleasant, pretty face. She expected to see only bottles of milk standing in their milk rack on the back porch, the drop-off point for the twice-weekly deliveries. But the shadow standing outside the door was not a man in a rumpled uniform and cap, but a young Oriental woman in a dark dress and short-heeled pumps.

The woman introduced herself, then asked the hard question, the one she had repeatedly turned over in her mind, mulled over for many nights before she received the call back from the realtor. The question the answer to which might send her brain reeling, her hopes shattered like a porcelain vase.

Did they have any objections to her and her family moving in next door? Would it be all right with you?

Objections? Mrs. Ione Gebuhr, wife of the physician Dr. Carl Gebuhr, hastily wiped her hands on her apron and stared at the stranger, who appeared to be about her own age and whose face looked earnestly into her own. What was it this nice young woman had asked? How did one process such a question? Mechanically, Ione reached for the metal handle of the container holding the bottles of milk. The milk would be cold and fresh.

For goodness sakes! She invited the woman inside.

IN THE EARLY YEARS, there were handfuls of business owners achieving prosperity in Brawley, a town located in the Imperial Valley, some 130 miles east of San Diego and directly southeast of the Salton Sea. With water secured through a diversionary canal from the Colorado River, the naturally arid region started to flourish with agriculture at the turn of the twentieth century. I only heard of the place because Mother mentioned having lived there before the war. Brawley. I wondered what kind of town would be called by such a bare-knuckled name. It sounded rugged—like a place covered in bruises.

As I was to learn much later, prior to the Great Depression the state enlisted migrant workers by the dozens, by the hundreds, from Mexico. A substantial colony of Issei immigrants also moved into the Imperial Valley to farm, to cultivate onions and broccoli and lettuce, cantaloupes and other melons, and to operate family-run businesses. They called the area Teikoku Heigen, which translated roughly into Prairie Empire.

The Nisei children were American-born. They attended public schools in the city of Brawley alongside the hakujin children, and with little conflict, although each socialized with their own kind. The Brawley Buddhist Church was established. Several times a year—during Obon, or for Boys' or Girls' Day, or for Oshōgatsu, the new year—the residents gathered for photographs, the men in dark suits and the women in western-style dresses and Sunday hats. In one photo, Mokichi Funakoshi stands almost midcenter behind several Buddhist priests, his wife Haruko in the row behind him. Mary stands in the front row, her hair dangling in Mary Pickford locks. Florence's hair is cut short, in the *chawan*, or rice bowl, style.

Mokichi Funakoshi's hiring of a flatbed truck to haul lumber from San Diego County was Haruko's idea. Already the couple operated a boarding house. But the plan was to build a bathhouse. They could work around the laws prohibiting Issei property ownership by renting the land and applying for modifications and improvements. Mokichi showed his certificate of registration as an alien, which the law required he maintain on his person at all times. He acquired the permits.

The plumbing, the drainage, the aeration—they figured it out. Buildings in the area were apt to look nondescript, even dilapidated, with exterior walls that were neither plumb nor finished. Haruko and Mokichi's bathhouse bulged at one end, which appeared to be covered with sapling-like brush, perhaps for ventilation. It resembled a yurt. Inside, the small entry was well-swept, the interior bath area tidy. Buckets, mops, scrub brushes stood ready.

Mokichi and Haruko got along well with the Mexican workers, who were scattered throughout the agricultural camps in the valley. They joked with each other in words neither side understood. But the Mexicans were hard-working. Hard work was the common denominator, sweat and grime the shared product. The workers trooped in. Some Japanese did not like the idea of a bathhouse where non-Japanese could enter. But the workers liked it, and anyway they paid in cash.

Quickly, they learned the protocol. Wash and scrub at the faucets. Wash first. It was okay to laugh. Fart. Curse. Sing. Whatever. This was not rule-bound Japan. Once clean, use the communal bath, the water heated not from a natural hot spring (the *onsen* type of bathhouse) but from the boiler room directly behind a divider wall. Muscles relaxed. Even scraps of conversation died down. It was bliss.

Both boarding house and bathhouse prospered. The couple added a laundry. The laundry boasted a long countertop and a conspicuous sign along the wall—LAVANDERIA. Along another wall hung a smaller sign urging patrons to "drink orange Kist," which Mokichi, by now renamed "Joe," sold by the bottle. For patrons who really tired of waiting, their pockets perhaps laden with coins, there was a one-armed bandit, a slot machine, placed conveniently in the center of the counter. Haruko was full of ideas.

Business prospered, Joe and Haruko getting it done, operating three businesses at once. Joe Funakoshi became a notable in the Imperial Valley. In the Chamber of Commerce photograph, he is seated at a table alongside a long row of white businessmen, everyone in western suits. In all of Brawley, they became just the third family to own a telephone with a private line.

For some occasions, Haruko still wore a kimono, but Joe always wore western-style clothes. Every few weeks he took a day off. When he did, he went fishing. First, he checked his fishing permit, which he renewed annually. He secured a driver's license. In 1927, he purchased an automobile, a top-of-the-line Imperial Landau Chevrolet.

The Chevrolet was the harbinger of bad luck. Soon Mummy was admitted to the hospital. That is what Florence called her mother as she tagged along after her. Mummy. Even as the medical staff debated Haruko's exact ailment, her condition deteriorated. Shortly before she died, she urged her husband not to remarry, a fact recounted years later in Mary's diary. How odd. As if, in dying, Haruko was thinking only about herself and not her children.

Except that Haruko knew Mokichi, and she knew how avarice floats through the world. The family's prosperity left the children vulnerable should he marry the wrong one. Her husband was absorbed in hard work, single-minded in its pursuit. His focus had left him little time and even less inclination to study people. He did everything by the book, and he thought everyone else did too. Haruko knew better. People were not all alike.

That was why she gave Mary space to socialize with her friends, why she let Florence take voice lessons with a music teacher after noticing how she carried a tune. Freddie? Well, he was still quite young, but easygoing, willing to follow directions. When she admonished her husband not to remarry, she was thinking about her children's welfare. There was no reason to suppose that Mokichi should get lucky in marriage twice. *Kodomo no tame ni* would become a collective refrain on the eve of internment, though scarcely a slogan Mokichi would ever be inclined to use. *Kodomo no tame ni* already filled the heart of the dying woman. *For the sake of the children.*

Within three years, a cascade of misfortune began anyway—and without the assistance of a grasping new wife. First, the stock market panic, and in the long aftermath of the crash, the Mexican laborers vanished. As residents of the Western Hemisphere, Mexicans previously had been exempted from the quotas contained in the Immigration Act of 1924, which had effectively barred any further immigration from Asia. But by 1930, with a prolonged depression and an abundance of unemployed Anglo workers looming on the horizon, the agricultural industry had joined forces with politicians, hate-mongers, and nativists urging deportation of Mexican farm workers, deportation of Mexicans in general. No longer were they welcome, despite the fact that many had established homes and families throughout the region and indeed through much of the United States. By some estimates, hundreds of thousands of Mexican migrants—perhaps 60 percent of them American citizens—were "repatriated" to Mexico. It was a forced exodus.

Now the Funakoshi family's hopes for the future were kept on a short leash. Seldom were they let out for a walk. When the county swooped in, clutching regulations in its bureaucratic fists, it was all over. By late 1933, as the family prepared to leave Brawley for good, it already had surrendered the boarding house and the lavanderia, abandoned the bathhouse, the water having been shut off. Another flatbed truck arrived, this one intent on salvaging reusable lumber. Joe Funakoshi gathered his brood into the Chevrolet. He headed off in the direction of Los Angeles with three children in tow, a pair of chickens, and one ebony-colored box containing ashes.

3

IN HONOR OF GERMAN COOKIES

WHEN OUR FAMILY MOVED into the house on Harms Road, we were, as far as any of us knew, the first Japanese Americans, quite possibly the first Orientals, to purchase a home in Skokie. Many of the early European settlers in the area had been of German descent. Back then the village, which lies west by southwest of Evanston and about fifteen miles north of Chicago's Loop, was called Niles Center. After the war, substantial numbers of Jews settled in Skokie. By 1977, when the American Nazi Party sued to stage a parade through its streets, nearly one in six residents was identified as a Holocaust survivor.

Our next-door neighbors, the Gebuhrs, welcomed us with enthusiasm. Soon we met and grew comfortable with the other neighbors—the Baldwins, the Adams, the Plettners, the Ritzmans. By the time Mother had given birth to her third child, Laura, who was named after Mrs. Harold Carew, she had proved something important to herself—that our family could successfully gain acceptance in an all-white community. In our own small way, we were advancing the cause and telling the story, the right story, of Japanese in America. Her idea, which had had its stirrings in the internment camp, was to strive doubly hard to be law-abiding citizens while maintaining an overall low profile, a shadow profile. In that way, we Japanese could fit in. If we were never exactly the same as hakujin, we could at least pass for what we were—Americans.

Mrs. Gebuhr and Mother clicked immediately. Ione was like a sister who had time for her. Like an attentive friend. She was the one who shared with "Ubi" her "secret recipes" for German Christmas cookies. In the Gebuhrs' kitchen, the two of them labored, thick as thieves. Together they rolled dough, created magic. There were the *Spekulatius*, cut in shapes of angels and Christmas trees and stars, and the horns, tiny crescent-shaped moons steeped in buttery goodness, dusted with vanilla sugar, and hinting of almond. Yum! Buried in their avalanche of powdered sugar, pecan fingers left a snowy residue on the plate, while rum balls added depth and contrast to the array of sweet and savory delights. Store-bought cookies seemed ordinary by comparison, although dutifully I consumed them as well, experimentally biting into a frosting-laden arm or leg of a gingerbread soldier.

For nearly four years, and particularly in the year and a half before I started school, my life was inexpressibly satisfying. For that I had our neighbors and my parents to thank. Our neighborhood was rooted in stability, it was sturdy as a brick house, undisturbed as a cemetery, as two cemeteries. In later years, when I was beset with turmoil, my mind would hasten back to that brief period when it felt as if well-being had been served to me whole. Eventually that wholeness split into pieces and crumbs, but for a long time my appetite for it remained intact.

The Color of Rum

Each morning began bright as an apple, the neighborhood children munching time to its core. My earliest outdoor memory was of boys in an open field. We did not organize our play, just heaved the ball and caught and ran in an unsynchronized pas de deux, quarterback to split end. Dickie Baldwin to Carl Gebuhr. Go out for a long one! The football was well scuffed across its pebbled skin.

The littlest boy, maybe four, got caught between hurtling bodies and started to bawl. It was me. Jackie Baldwin rushed to my side to check. "You're okay, right? Aren'tcha?" Yes, I was all right. Back to the game. C'mon, throw it here!

I would remember all of them, the neighborhood boys. Not their faces but their first and last names—Dickie and Jack Baldwin, Dean Adams (who would die young), Paul and Carl Gebuhr, Jon Ritzman, Lanny Isaacs, Billy Plettner—all of them engraved in my memory as surely as cemeteries preserve the names of the dead.

It was a neighborhood of boys tossing a football the color of rum, of fathers driving to work and mothers providing for everything else.

Angel Shapes

Mother rounded the corner carrying a large basket. She wore a crisp blouse and skirt and brown loafers. All mothers are angels, especially my own, who was at my side whenever a bad dream disturbed my sleep. She set down the clothes. Each shirt and sock and pair of pants having passed through a wringer consisting of stiff rubber rollers, they emerged as flat impressions of their prior selves, as if a steamroller had had fun running over them.

The clothesline sat atop a shoulder of grass that proceeded to bump down a slope before leveling out into a full backyard bordered at the far end by a cinder alleyway. The mogul was good for sliding after a late spring rain. Mother always recognized the crunch along the cinders as the patter of my feet. Having momentarily deserted the field where the other boys were at play, the feet clambered up the slope.

"Do you need to go the bathroom?"

"No, just checking."

How nice to be the sun with its confident smile, envying nothing! Beneath it, the breeze picked up, and the shirts and trousers waved greetings across the neighboring clotheslines. There were no fences separating yard from yard. I stayed by her side. She was the song, I the accompaniment.

My hand reached and grasped a clothespin by its wooden legs. I squeezed the legs to open the jaw, revealing the serrated teeth. The clothespin's legs were in conspiracy with its jaws. Release the legs and the jaw shut. Open, shut, open, shut. The clothespin snapped and bit but never swallowed. It had no stomach and therefore stayed hungry forever. Mother held one, two clothespins in her mouth as she hung a shirt. She looked funny, as if she had sprouted teeth. It was a funny thought, a mother with fangs.

I offered her a clothespin.

"Why, thank you!"

Before hurrying back to the playing field, I offered her another.

Gingerbread Warriors

Paul Gebuhr and I were the same age, although he would soon attend a local Catholic school rather than the public school I was bound for. He liked to spread the columns of plastic soldiers across his front porch. They were his summer soldiers, so he had final say over where each one went. Once in place, both of us proceeded to mimic the sounds of rifle fire (*pop pop pop*), machine guns (*rat-a-tat-tat*), and artillery shells (*bhhooo! kkrrgghh!!*). During the bombardment and intense fire, some of the figures did not survive. The dead ones we flipped on their sides. When the wind picked up, the flowers lining the walkway turned their panic-stricken heads toward the street, desperate to flee the clamor and devastation. But their stems held them fast. They were safe after all, rooted in place.

My brother wandered the neighborhood, content, adrift, pursuing random angles of solitude, obeying an internal command to keep moving. For now, the one who one day would serve in the real U.S. Army, perched atop the jungle gym, at the eagle's aerie, then clambered down, his attention as divertible as a squirrel. When the wind commenced, it raked through the pants and shirts, which flapped noisily on the clothesline, as if scolding the socks, every cloth tongue going at once. Bryan stepped through the hours, his fists pounding his pockets. He was a mystery, a clock without hands. At night he put shoes on the moon. He was one eye of the crow.

The Moon and the Stars

In the bedroom, where the second-floor windows were left ajar at night to catch the breeze, Bryan and I scanned the dark for the Big Dipper. We mimicked crickets and owls, aimed noises in the direction of next door, waiting to see if Paul and Carl Gebuhr answered with weird sounds of their own. When Bryan fell into his nightly snore, I observed the crisp autumn moon through the window. It was savory as a cookie.

Heaven is a cookie made from a secret recipe. To get there, you mount steps carved from butter. Heaven is filled with melt-in-the-mouth delights. The reason you clasp your hands when you pray is to preserve every crumb.

Figure Covered in Snow

The base of the snowman provided strength and durability. Even when the weather warmed and the sun reappeared as a pale disc, the base remained in place for a long time. The head was finished off with a carrot nose and two fist-sized prunes for eyes. We never thought to call it a snowwoman. It was a neighborhood still filled with boys. But in truth, it could just as easily have been a woman made of snow. In Japanese legend, the Snow Woman, *yuki onna*, is a fearsome, shape-shifting wraith equally capable of acts of mercy or revenge.

There was not enough time to loop the scarf between the trunk and the head because the battle broke out. Carl Gebuhr was strong-armed and accurate, but Bryan was skillful too. I kept packing and repacking snowballs, not realizing that they had grown too bulky for my hands. When I tried to hurl them, they were thick as tires, and they fell yards short of their target. But it was fun to duck and dodge—hah! missed me!—and take cover behind a small rampart of snow erected for defense.

The battle done when someone's mother called someone home, we scurried off in every direction. In the service porch, which served as a mudroom,

I removed my mittens, unstrapped my boots. Kick! Kick them off! Mother helped me undo the layers of clothing she had bound me in, extra protection from the cold. A bowl of Campbell's Chicken Noodle Soup or a cup of Ovaltine awaited. The living room smelled like fresh tree; it was expectation draped with tinsel. Hurry, turn on the Christmas lights! The lights, how bright and cheerful they looked! Even the tombstones in the cemeteries looked satisfied.

Storytelling

At night, Mother let me choose from the Childcraft books. There were many volumes, including the ones with short stories and poems and folk and fairy tales. We nestled together on the sofa, I in my pajamas, the book resting between us. I grasped one half of the binding, she took the other. Laura slept. Babies were boring. They were governed by the sleep command. Bryan existed somewhere in the house, playing with his Erector Set or Lincoln Log cabin, experimenting with novel disproportions. Outside, the rain tapped confidently against the window, as the barometric pressure fell. Each raindrop carried an ounce of learning. Nothing surpassed her children's education. Let it pour.

At my signal, Mother turned the page. Ready. My favorite illustration was of the amphibious air clipper, which had to wend its way through a fierce storm. Fortunately, it could set down safely either on sea or on land, which doubled its chances of survival. The scariest illustration was of the mounted Highwayman, who looked stern and unforgiving in his ebony hat and cape. He sat astride a coal-dark horse, whose eyes filled with nervous fury, both man and horse lashed by a storm. I peeked but turned away lest the Highwayman and his phantom steed, rising from their hiding place in the dark cemetery, ride furiously into my dreams.

Public Enemy

It was many years later that I learned about the real highwayman. His corpse was found outside a cemetery in Niles Center in 1934. Exactly which cemetery is uncertain. Some reports stated that the body was left near the front entrance to St. Paul's Lutheran Cemetery, while others maintained that it had been deposited near the St. Peter Catholic Cemetery. At least one account affirmed that the body was found outside Saint Peters Cemetery. What *is* certain is that Lester Gillis, aka George "Baby Face" Nelson, notorious bank robber and cop killer and recently named the FBI's Public Enemy No. 1, was no saint at the time his body was discovered in the near vicinity of where a

Japanese American dentist and his family would occupy a brick two-story residence a few years after the war.

I recalled St. Paul's Lutheran Cemetery as the "white cemetery" because the sunlight splashing over the light-colored grave markers once reminded me of a cup of cream. The other cemetery, the one lying directly to the south, I remembered not as Saint Peters but as the "dark cemetery" because of its iron railings and thick fortress of firs.

Two days before the discovery of the body, Nelson had engaged in the last of his notorious gun battles with police. During the shootout, the diminutive but fearless bank robber had managed to kill two FBI agents, rushing directly toward them rather than attempting to flee, despite suffering multiple gunshot wounds. This brought his total slaying of law enforcement officers to at least four. His murderous rampage also included a stockbroker, a witness in a federal mail fraud case, and a paint salesman, whose aggressive driving Nelson had found annoying.

At first reaching a safe house, the grievously wounded killer had succumbed on the following day. His wife, who sometimes worked the getaway car during his heists, carefully wrapped the body in a blanket before it was dropped off. As she later explained to police, her husband always hated feeling cold.

Fare Thee Well

Every morning, Father took the highway to go to work. One evening he did not return. Mother did not express worry or concern. Weeks later he came back. He came back as a uniform. The uniform was a deep woolen cordovan, no, it was milk chocolate, and we children could taste its significance. It was adorned with insignia, brass buttons, and a shoulder patch identifying its wearer as a member of the United States Fifth Army. Bryan was all grin beneath the hat. Laura was content to climb onto Father's lap. Mother declared that he was "serving our country." I beamed with pride.

Father left for additional training at an army base in Texas, returned home, then departed once again. This time Mother set to work, applying labels to cardboard boxes and to crates: Overcoats and Gloves; Blankets and Sheets; Armoire—downstairs; China—fragile. To my dismay, I learned that Father was not finished performing his duties. Father had answered the military draft, and now the rest of the family would have to march in step, following mysterious highways onto an army base far from our home.

But I like it here.

Bring me that lamp.

Why do we have to move?

Not that one. The other one.

When will we come back?

Put your finger there. Where the strings meet. Good. Press down.

I fretted. I fretted that things would be different when we got back. No one mentioned that the red brick house on Harms Road with the backyard that sloped down to the jungle gym and the play log cabin would be sold. Or that never again would Mrs. Gebuhr stop by, as she did that first Christmas with her array of yummy German butter cookies for "Ubi" and her family. Never again would I bear witness to the gray-haired ladies in polka-dot dresses navigating the white cemetery's gravestones, while bearing flowers to their dead, the quiet obedient dead, who would never be forced to move. Naively, I had thought that life could stand still. I was wrong. It had merely drawn leisurely, motor still running, to the curb.

Farewell, Skokie, Illinois, USA.

PART II

FITTING IN NICELY

4

THE INDIANS OF ROLLO STREET

ON July 4, the military base showcased its weaponry, including rocket launchers, howitzers, the mobile M4 Sherman Tanks, and the M48 Pattons with their powerful 90 mm guns, which surely were manned by Paul Bunyan–sized recruits. During the evening, cannons went off, their exploding rounds adding earsplitting depth to the fireworks punching holes in the sky. In the motor pool, two-and-a-half ton cargo trucks and rows upon rows of jeeps stood idle in the darkness yet managed to convey readiness. They were the mechanical horses of the modern-day cavalry, which awaited the command to saddle up and move out.

To get here, the newly commissioned major had saddled up his own mechanical horse in the form of a gray Chevrolet, loaded up family and suitcases, and ridden south then west past miles of farmland and empty space, until the Eads Bridge conducted us over the broad M-I-S-S-I-S-S-I-P-P-I, the river spilling out its letters naturally, like a story moving toward a happy end. We were delivered into boisterous, sweltering St. Louis. From there we followed another trail of cement, this one situated well below the long river named after the Missouria, a tribe once known as the "big canoe people."

Had we continued westward, we would have reached Independence, once the starting point for legions of wagon trains in the decades after the Lewis and Clark Expedition. Instead, near Jefferson City, our party of five swung south once again, through miles and miles of woods and countryside, the Chevrolet eventually panting in the heat, its radiator longing for a draught of fresh water.

THE HOUSE AT 506 ROLLO STREET lay pinched in a hollow at the end of the first of a double row of homes built hastily for the families of officers and NCOs stationed at Fort Leonard Wood, Missouri. They were residential barracks, private and separated from their fellows but each one of uniform dimensions. The road ran like a flattened ridge above the houses, while gravel provided a crunchy shoulder, along with space for parking. Here and there, segments of oversized logs dappled with tar were set lengthwise to serve as parking curbs, and various LaSalles and Hudsons and Pontiacs hunched expectantly over the houses below, transformed from grazing horses into metallic birds of prey.

Mother did not balk at the cramped living conditions. She and Father had faced much worse in camp, although they still did not talk about that experience to us children. About some things, Nisei in the years following the war stayed silent. About the years of incarceration, the years of camp, Nisei didn't talk. They just didn't. All of us Sansei kids were to learn that much. Even ten or fifteen or twenty years afterwards, when Mother and Father conceded a reply to questions we kids would ask, it was partial and not whole, like a set of random numbers retrieved from an abandoned memory bank or a partial entry torn from a diary. Brevity would hint at things purposely unremembered. It wasn't that they were reconciled to what they had gone through—the indignities, humiliations, distrust, losses. It was just, well, what was there to say?

The houses on Rollo Street were each an exact rectangle except for a compact front porch with an unfinished railing. Inside were two bedrooms set at opposite ends, and in the middle a kitchen and dining table, which vied for space. Here and there an artful housewife had broken the exterior monotony with a flower garden bursting with irises, daisies, and calla lilies. Mother quickly dubbed the house "the Shoebox." It was an apt label, and it was easy to imagine a phalanx of storybook women in aprons with their tiny offspring living contentedly within.

In actuality, we kids found the living conditions unpleasant, particularly due to the rigors of the climate. Winters were frigid, the thermostat and the extra blankets of little use. The summers were worse, far worse—hot, sweltering, the days marked by intense, strength-sapping humidity, which even Father found barely tolerable outside the dental clinic. The occasional thunderstorm made things worse. His back crawling with beads of sweat, Father joked that the humidity had earned Fort Leonard Wood several nicknames, including "the hell-hole of the army."

Mother frowned when she heard the H word. Neither Father nor Mother smoked or drank or had other bad habits, like cursing. But she smiled bravely at the seasons, ran errands, shopped at the PX, washed clothes, prepared meals. Fortunately, she did not perspire easily. Unlike Father and the rest of us, including Laura, who even as a toddler looked uncomfortable in her sticky T-shirt.

CHILDREN ENTERED AND EXITED the shoeboxes, depending on when their fathers' tours of duty started and ended. More constant were the rolling hills, cavernous valleys, and dense woods. After a summer squall, one straw-haired boy emerged, the leader of Rollo Street. Restless and adventuring, nimble and daring, he was Tom Sawyer braving the rock-strewn gullies, tempting the dark woods beyond, as other kids trailed after, a small tribe of watching eyes and adventure-bearing feet.

We were an amorphous group, joining up or dropping out on a whim, the way glints of sunlight can break through gloom or just as suddenly vanish. The only constant was Tim. One day, a turtle was discovered at a small runoff near a muddy tree root and pulled from its hiding place. It resembled an army helmet. As an experiment, Tim flipped it over, revealing the mustard and slime-green camouflage across its vulnerable belly.

The turtle was unable to right itself without help. The rest of us stayed neutral regarding its life-or-death plight. Nevertheless, someone angled it near the bank of the stream, and we watched as gravity and its own wiggly feet and limber neck marking turtle determination combined to topple it right side over. F-l-i-i-p-p! Shell righted, the turtle lumbered off, as if treading on its knuckles. It evinced no memory or concern over what had transpired, no fear of becoming the main ingredient in someone's experimental soup. If Bryan were a turtle, he would be thus.

The hills behind the second row of houses on Rollo Street ascended gradually, then steeply, before fanning out toward a ravine. Even the foothills of the grand Ozarks are filled with intrigue. Kids climbed one hill, then inched their way down another, Tim leading the way. Overhead, the trees looked grim and humorless, and they cast long, grasping shadows. Their roots rose out of the soil like moldy fingers. Here and there the incline grew slippery, made worse from the rain-saturated leaves. There were rumors of copperhead snakes, which exactly resembled the mottled ground. Step on one, step on that thing you thought was a nothing patch of leaves, and *pffft!*, you were dead. So we moved stealthily, intently, alert to slithery sounds.

The actual snake seemed long ago. Like a movie scene spliced from a different reel. Pooled in front of the play log cabin, barely yards from the jungle gym, it had frightened me so! By the time Father arrived with a long broom, which he turned round and wielded like a kendo sword, the snake had crawled over the lip of the front entry of the cabin and trapped itself within its walls. It was not a small, slender snake. Unwound, it was a good three feet in length, maybe more, with an assortment of colors. What kind of snake it was, who could say?

Sensing that it was cornered, the snake started to move. It slid along the side of the cabin wall and toward the entrance. By then the commotion had aroused interest, and several neighborhood boys had hastened over to see what the fuss was about. I crouched behind Father, the guardian of public safety. I did not want to be there, but a dark fascination held me in place. Suddenly, the snake received a well-placed blow on its head. Stunned, defenseless, it made a wounded attempt to slide off. Two or three severe strikes later, the snake lay limp.

"Dad to the rescue!"

Those were my exact words. I felt elation and relief, as if the cavalry had swooped in to save the wagon train from marauding Indians. No one wanted to get too close to the thing, so repulsive, so recently full of slither. A snake lover would have commented on the beauty of its colors, no doubt would have chastised the man for killing a nonvenomous reptile in an unjustified act of violence. And on a Sunday!

But among this crowd there was no snake love. No one wanted to touch it, including Father, who advised getting rid of it. Dean Adams was among the kids gathered around. Dean found a stick (not the broomstick) and draped the snake's body over it. It's heavy, he commented. Then he led a trail of kids to the gully alongside his own house, where, leaning back, he used the stick to hurl the body into the bowels of the brush.

Were Father a Japanese upholding Japanese tradition, he might have dealt with the snake intruder in a different fashion, in a way the indigenous peoples of Missouri might well have understood. In ancient times, snakes were linked to the Japanese concept of *kami*, which is related to spirit or god or deity. Some snake kami were believed to protect whole regions, others were prone to wreak personal or family havoc if injured or destroyed. Some were thought to house the spirits of reincarnated ancestors. Even the venomous *mamushi* were not killed. Not in the old days. With the advent of Westernization, the old attitudes in Japan changed. If Father had been more Japanese, he would have handled the snake differently, perhaps instilled in his son a more pacific relationship with nature.

TIM DID NOT STEP on or crush a snake. Survival instincts guided him but not fear. He was the scourge of the grasshopper nation. The spindly creatures were numerous as fallen leaves, as disorderly as enlistees enduring their first week of basic training. They bivouacked atop the rock-strewn ground or between stands of trees. They lingered in the shade of flower gardens, lurked in the engine compartment of the family car, or conducted lazy surveillance from a window ledge. Judging from their numbers, few went AWOL, despite their obvious distaste for discipline.

With his teeth Tim experimented, with avidity he laid waste. To shock the timid and to test his own mettle, Tim first scoured the ground for well-fed, corpulent grandfather types, which were never green like Disney's Jiminy Cricket and not to be confused with that cosmopolitan relation, but different shades of brown. In some Indian legends, they are associated with tobacco, a crop to be shared and not hoarded.

Approaching the creature from behind, Tim cut off its escape, then bent over and scooped his wriggly meal in both hands. He proceeded to thrust the victim, raw, into the cavern of his grin. With a conspicuous show of chomping and gnashing of mealy-looking parts and torn limbs, he conducted a promiscuous carnival of carnivorism. I was among those transfixed by the grisly spectacle. Tim opened his jaw to reveal a salad of glutinous guts accented with splintery rum-colored limbs amid fragments of grasshopper skull—saturated with a pea-green vinaigrette. The onlookers offered tribute through mock gagging sounds. It was appalling, ghastly, marvelous. A mockery of survival but also its execution.

I pushed away the thought, the thought of having my body annihilated, my bones crushed. I pushed it away just as I did with the Indians in the movies, who got flung from their horses after a sharpshooter's bullet found its mark. Did that Indian have a family? Never mind, here comes the next one!

I also pushed away the other thought, the one that occurred outside the move theater following the Saturday matinees. The army post's movie theater was a short trek up Rollo Street, and during the summer months the matinees provided temporary relief from the oppressive heat. Inside, it was cool, dark, invisible, the children chattering between the double features, usually westerns. The movies culminated with a fierce battle between the cavalry, who maintained discipline and order, and various Indians, who lurked behind bush and rock or gathered in loose formation just behind a rise, plotting ambush. The Indians were treacherous savages except when they acquired English and started to become civilized.

Outside the theater, the children blinked in the sunlight before they all headed home. This was when the troubling thought raised its dangerous, reptilian head. Day by day under the malevolent sun, my skin had turned darker and darker. In the sunlight, I felt self-conscious. I had always known that my skin tone looked different from normal children, white children. But before attending matinees on the army post, I had never considered the possibility that I might resemble an Indian rather than an American. Even my hair color made me look Indian-like. I hurried down the road.

Once home, alone, I arranged my Nesbitt grape and orange soda pop caps across my bedcovers. The purple caps were the United States Cavalry, while the orange ones were the Indians. The purple cavalry maintained an orderly formation, two by two, but the Indians, devious and cunning, spread out randomly over the sheets and blankets newly bunched into hills and ravines. The grape bottle caps annihilated the savages. The grape bottle caps always prevailed.

I NEVER OBSERVED an actual Indian on or near the military base, only enlisted men, mainly young white fellows who gave officers smart salutes. I knew that before Tom Sawyer, before Lewis and Clark, before everyone but the grasshoppers and the turtles and the snakes there were Indians. But laboring under the impression that all Indians wore moccasins and feathered headbands, I believed that I would recognize an Indian at once if ever I saw one.

What I had yet to learn was that century after century the indigenous peoples of the region survived the sweltering heat and the game-bare blasts of winter, while safeguarding the land and its resources. Nature provided—and it was neither plaything nor foe. But the people were less successful in surviving the advances of explorers and pioneers, less successful at fending off the blue militia, who eventually controlled the waterways and even the forests and trails.

Perhaps young Meriwether Lewis was sincere in advising the native peoples he encountered upon starting out on his expedition in 1804 that they, the Indians, were "children" who henceforth could depend on physical protection and a more reliable system of trade from the Great Father far to the east in Washington. But repeatedly the Great Fathers to the east provided neither economic advantage nor defense. Well before the end of the nineteenth century, there were no tribes left intact in Missouri.

The formidable Osage once occupied the land on which my father's military base now sat. Once they did, but not now. Relocation on the North American continent, I was to learn, did not start with Japanese Americans. After Lewis and Clark's arrival, substantial numbers of Osage removed themselves from the region—to avoid further contact with European Americans. The ones remaining behind were forced repeatedly to cede large portions of land to the American government before they too had to relocate. The removal to the Kansas Territory came after the federal government began to supply arms and munitions to tribes hostile to the Osage, encouraging those tribes to wage war against them. Eventually, the Osage relocated again, this time to the Oklahoma Territory.

Having earlier merged with the Otoes, the Missouria saw their numbers continue to decline. Following an outbreak of smallpox in 1829, they numbered fewer than a hundred. In the late 1870s, the combined tribe split into two factions—one side seeking to preserve native traditions, the other pursuing assimilation. On four separate occasions during the nineteenth century, the federal government pressured the Missouria-Otoes to cede lands. The fifth time was to occur later, after oil was discovered, and many tribe members eventually surrendered their government land allotments. But long before then, and within decades of the Lewis and Clark Expedition, the only big canoes left in the region were the steamboats to the east, chugging up and down that other great river, the one memorialized in the writings of Mark Twain.

5

NOBODY BOY

TEACHERS SAY CHILDREN are colorblind.

The answer to that one is—False.

While I waited, nervous and alone, at the bus stop, the birds fussed invisibly in the trees. They fussed and fussed, as if it were *their* first day at the new school, and they were worried about being tardy. The bus would carry me several miles outside the military base to a town called Waynesville, a small black dot among dozens of other black dots on the map.

The bus stop was not far from the house on Rollo Street. Still, I had to remember the route in reverse in order to return home safely at the end of the day. Hansel and Gretel left a trail of breadcrumbs, a strategy foiled by a different set of birds. Their bigger challenge was facing day after day without their mother. Did she take sick before she died, struck down in the prime of her life like Mother's mother?

A station wagon pulled up to the bus stop, and a sweater and plaid skirt sprang out. Vermilion-colored curls cascaded wildly down their owner's back. Never had I seen such brilliance, like a girl with her hair on fire. A riot of freckles swarmed her neck and face, a contagion of pigment, an epidemic of color. The mother did not leave the car, but through the open window the two of them demanded goodbyes. Literally, they shouted at each other, as if competing for volume. Like braying donkeys. BYE!! BYE!!! Their love was spectacular.

I gripped my Roy Rogers lunch pail tightly, as Roy's golden palomino Trigger reared on its hind legs in fright. As soon as the station wagon raced off, the girl stamped her foot, as if her mother had forgotten to pack an item essential for wilderness survival. Frowning, she scrounged through her sweater pockets until she found what she was looking for. A large napkin. No, a tangerine scarf. She waved it in triumph. Like a magician.

At last, she noticed me standing there, mute, as nerveless as a misplaced street sign. For an instant her mind processed the uncanny sight.

"Hey, what are you?" she demanded.

I ALREADY KNEW ALL I ever needed to know about school. It was a device used to pry children from home. School was indoctrination, a set of commands, a summons to conformity. Keep to the right when passing in the halls. Use the door for BOYS or the one for GIRLS when you need to go wee-wee. Raise your hand before talking. Why did school separate a child from its mother? Answer me that. The best part of the day was the bell signaling its end. As the exact instant drew near, we children studied the tick-a-tick of the wall clock with the intensity of surgeons repairing the damage to a human heart.

For a Japanese American child, particularly one set down in the middle of the century in the middle of the country, school was a never-ending trial, a never-completed experiment whose results, even if satisfactory, had to be replicated again and again. As Mother kept insisting, "Everything you do reflects on the Japanese race." At home, Mother prepared us by chastising us when we made noises with our fork tines as we chewed, by chiding us when we did not properly close the toothpaste cap. It was for our own good. Still, we got away with nothing, literally nothing. Mother did not yell at us. Not yet. But we had to practice good manners and police our own conduct— "police" being a word she employed with frequency.

The schoolhouse stood atop a small rise overlooking several acres of pasture. Compact and grim, the building looked ready-made for dunce stools and rote learning. It stood at dreary attention, its rows of tall windows double daring anyone to peer inside. Nearby, trees prepared to sacrifice themselves for new fences for farm animals or for a palisade to ward off Indian raids. But there were no fences or palisades or Indians, just lots of dirt and open fields. The sturdier grasses ran down the rise into a meadow, where the cows grazed. When the school day ended, the animals were free to roam through the school grounds, as if nibbling for the pieces of learning they were otherwise denied.

Already what I most feared was being called on by Teacher to speak out loud in public. I was shy to begin with, but knowing that anything I blurted out might be used against Japanese made things worse. At my first school, the one in Skokie named after Abraham Lincoln, I learned to turn my face to the side and cast my eyes downward whenever the teacher glanced in my direction. That way, the only times I had to say anything were when the class recited the Pledge of Allegiance (which I quickly learned to repeat both forwards and backwards) and when Teacher took attendance. By now I had acquired the manner and presence of a mouse in a cathedral.

At the school in Waynesville, there were many, many substitute teachers. One positive effect of the slate of new names chalked week after week on the blackboard was that second grade got to do a lot of silent reading. Reading was so simple. I had grown my vocabulary ages ago. The words in the reader were printed in fat letters. Repeat the words in order. If you did not know a word, you moved your lips and sounded it out. It was Teacher's rule, but Mother said it first. If I were ever asked to read aloud in front of everyone, that was the one thing I could do. Like the story they told, the words in the reader belonged to somebody else.

Besides, reading aloud was just sound traveling through air, which was invisible, the way I wished to remain. The sounds led the listener here or there but most often to a park. Sometimes I wondered why the book did not move things along, picking up the pace the way Father did when striding to his car after buying a newspaper, the latest war tucked under his arm. Let's get Dick and Jane to the park. Let's get Spot to the park so he can run around and fetch sticks, chase calico cats up trees, wag his tail, scratch fleas.

On the playground, no one ever spoke to me first. The normal kids ran around, made silly noises and rude sounds. They sensed that I was different, silent, nobody they needed to reckon with. For my part, I merged into the shadows of the trees, became a shadow, while other boys drew circles in the dirt, shouting, "My turn!" and shooting marbles for keeps, and the girls paired off near the swing set to exchange secrets, holding hands when they wanted to exclude anyone from their tête-à-têtes. During recess, I shoved my fists in my pockets, letting my fingers unfurl the seconds one by one. Despite the tight configuration of the school, I never saw my brother. Not at recess or lunch. It was as if Bryan had darted down a rabbit hole and decided to remain there, munching a carrot of solitude, being hassled by no one.

In the classroom, I was also a shadow. The one time the shadow materialized into a voice, the one time it whispered to another kid in class, it got caught. The substitute teacher looked old and sleepy and talked like she was chewing grapes, but she was cannier and more alert than she appeared. You there! she shouted, the grapes suddenly moving in her mouth.

I took the walk of shame to the main office. Entering, I stopped in front of a second door. It was solid oak, but its upper half featured an opaque window in which a sheet of chicken wire appeared to be suspended. The words VICE PRINCIPAL glared in black from the window's bumpy surface. In the alcove outside the office were two chairs, where the bad boys had to sit and wait. I spent several moments pondering the effect of my disgraceful act on other Japanese Americans. I fretted, unsure whether to stand or sit. During recess, the older kids often spread rumors about the stockpile of sticks and paddles and other instruments of torture lurking within the vice principal's office. Spare the rod, spoil the child.

I had seen the vice principal stalking the school grounds, patrolling to and fro, occasionally drawing from a cigarette. He reminded me of the actor Richard Widmark, who starred with Spencer Tracy in *Broken Lance*, a film screened recently at the Saturday matinee. His hawklike stare belonged to someone paid to spot trouble and keep it cornered. His skin was pale, eerily so, like that of a man who had spent his entire life avoiding sunlight, peering through narrow apertures. Like that of a man rattling his baton against the iron bars of cells because he enjoyed the sound.

When the door moved, terror rose. A man with thinning blond hair, neatly groomed, emerged from the office. Over his starched white shirt he wore a dark tie affixed with a pin. The pin was unneeded, since the tie dared not stir without the man's consent. His fingers were thin, thin as a knife's edge but capable of squeezing a disobedient will into the size of a pea, then whacking it into two stunned halves.

Richard Widmark threw a brief glance at me, the sole occupant of an alcove chair. By now I was trembling. I stared hard at the floor, as if the day's lesson were written there. When I practiced capitals, F went with "Fear," as G with "God."

What's this? From Room 2, Mrs. What's-Her-Name? He was speaking to the clerk in the outer office, each word accented with impatience and the scent of tobacco. Briefly, he scanned my face. His time was precious. He knew exactly who the bad boys were, the troublemakers earning his attention. Not this one, whom he briefly glanced at as if observing a chip in a mirror for the first time. *Go back to your room. Don't talk in class.* That was it. Being a nobody came with an escape clause. I was neither cavalryman nor Indian but a piece of the background, harmless as sage brush.

That night I asked Father why he never smoked cigarettes.

"Because it smells," Father replied.

THE BIG TRIAL INVOLVED SMELL TOO, but it came later in the semester. It was all the fault of the cows, or rather of bovine carelessness. First came the odor, subdued yet distinct. Following recess, the children had returned to the classroom, wholly unaware of what lay in wait. I glanced at the child seated to my right, at the one to my left. Their heads were turned into their books. It was a stinky-sickly smell. Dropping my head, while casting a surreptitious look behind me to the left, behind me to the right, I finally looked down.

I looked down. It was as if one of the delicate jelly bean bombs I trailed from my crude drawings of B-24s had exploded right before my eyes. The smell came from my own shoe! Or rather from what newly lathered the shoe. As I looked, the smell seemed willfully to spread, like a slow radioactive leak. During recess, I had unwittingly stepped on a pile of fresh cow dung in the playground, and now I had tracked it into the classroom. Now it was here, clinging to my shoe, my right shoe, a mixture of greening ooze and brown slime.

How could this be? I was a statue through most of recess. I watched where I was going when forced to move. Now I had stepped into the middle of a mess, and it had fastened itself to my shoe the way exasperation overstays its welcome. When I whispered "cow shit" to myself, it immediately intensified the smell, as if I had offered insult to its bovine maker. With its windows shut, the classroom rapidly warmed. The contamination had to be removed, had to be scraped off and sent away. My shoe begged for relief, it suffocated with shame. No one could survive under such rank conditions. But the odor was a bully. Determined to mount the high ceiling, to hunker into the walls, it dared me to take action. Go ahead. Try something. I dare you.

The lunch bell was a billion hours away. Minute by minute, my shoe strained to hold its breath. It could not last. Each classroom was fitted with individual oak desks attached to metal runners. They were sleigh desks, which in a different context inspired memories of a sled containing two boisterous boys being lugged up a snowy avenue by their father in an overcoat and scarf. The metal runners along the bottom were good for one thing.

Slowly, surreptitiously, I slid my shoe along the edge of the right runner of my desk. The stuff came off, gradually, terrifyingly, with each movement offering new life to the poop, which peeled off not in inert brown chunks but as a sickening ooze. The world held its collective breath. The children read at their desks, their senses blunted by another pointless assignment from the latest substitute teacher. No one was watching. At last, my shoe was allowed a breath. The breath was slow and shallow, like the one coming the instant after the night sentry marches past the escapee crouching in terror.

Never did a lunch bell bring greater relief. I was the last child out of the classroom. Across the floor, there remained the original track left by my shoe, which was another thing I feared, more evidence leading directly back to the guilty party. Fortunately, the floor was dark and musty, just like the class-room, just like the hallway, and the track was hard to detect.

Safe outside, I slipped unnoticed into a concealed patch of shrubbery. There I ran my shoe over the root of a tree. Scrubbed and scrubbed. I dragged my shoe across the dirt, until its leather turned gritty. I returned to the tree root. I worked the shoe.

The assault on my shoe occurred on a Friday, a good thing. At home, I applied water from the garden hose and soap pilfered from the laundry, until an unpleasant wet-leather smell arose. The shoe dried out in the sun, its leather parched. By Monday it smelled stale, looked cranky and stiff. But at least it was free to start life over again.

What must it have thought, that shoe, when it discovered the remains of the previous Friday still stuck to the runner of the desk? Cow shit. Every bit of it, though its exterior looked different, all dried and crusted over. At least, the stink was gone. Or did noses just make peace with nasty smells the way grownups did with traffic snarls? But if a shoe, anyone's shoe, accidentally kick-ed the crust, who knew what might happen?

One thing was for sure. Having been subjected to torture and tribulation for an entire weekend, the shoe would stoutly declare its innocence. How on earth did that stuff get there? Who allowed some unsupervised cow to wan-der through the school? The classroom had not changed. The same finger paintings reached across the top of the blackboard, and just below them hung the same cardboard cutout ABCs. The same children sat at their desks. The next day came and went, and the day after, and the day after that. No careless shoe kicked the stuff, reopening it like a festering wound. It remained fastened to the runner, remained undisturbed, content in its increasingly dry neglect. Friday came, the weekend, and the next week.

For two weeks the stuff remained. With a merciful God overlooking me, I did not experience an air raid drill during all that time, did not have to hug the floor, seek shelter against the runner of my desk. Gradually, the stuff hardened, fossilized, married with the desk's runner.

No one cleaned this place? Who knew what other foul secrets lay buried beneath the accumulated dust and grime of an old schoolhouse, what smelly artifacts awaited tomorrow's archeological dig? It was a lesson on the deposits of history, the indignities that got overlooked or ignored, even as the appara-tus of learning, all its spokes broken, pretended to roll on.

At least no deed of my own had provoked painful consequences. I be-lieved myself guilty of another foul act, but I had gotten away with it. I was an animal without a scent, a being that left no mark. It was a relief to be no-body, a Nobody Boy.

BUT TIRESOME TOO.

It would have been nice to know everyone and to be known by everyone in advance. It would have solved my dilemma, the dilemma of not wanting to draw any attention to myself, but at the same time not wishing to remain nobody.

The opening of the new elementary school on the military base made things no easier, even though it meant no more jouncing bus rides over country lanes pitted by armored vehicles, only a short hike up the road and past the inverted triangular sign that commanded the passerby to YIELD, followed by the smaller three-word explanation—Right of Way. It was a sign the army post had recently invented.

The new school, which hunched low to the ground like a soldier in basic training ordered to eat dirt as the live rounds whistled overhead, did not bother Bryan, who was neither excited nor daunted at the prospect of changing schools midyear. He detached himself from all schoolyard tyrannies, inevitably yielded the right of way. Bryan never feared bullies, he just refused to be bothered by them. Shove him. Shove him hard, go ahead. He would walk away, looking neither fearful nor alarmed.

But I knew it would take effort on my part to become recognized as— somebody. I could not just paw the dirt or moo at the grass. I would have to initiate conversation. Pint-sized, nut-brown under the sun with itty-bitty shoulders accentuated by the suspenders employed to hold up my pants, I was shy and easy to overlook. Among a crowd of people, I was normally noticed by accident, the way shoppers browsing for Waterford crystal chanced upon an odd-shaped knickknack in a far corner of the display.

Talking-aloud-in-public-to-a-stranger was not easy without a topic sentence. But I reminded myself that there was no progress without effort. *No pain, no gain*, Father liked to say. Of course, Father was a military officer whom other people had to salute.

"Man, it's hot."

The boy nearest to me looked up.

"*Man*, it's hot."

It was a conversational gambit. Get it? Here was its variant. *Man, it's cold.* Or another. *Man, it's humid.*

Today was hot in a distinct voice. If I could be recognized by a single boy at school, I might become something other than a complete nobody. What a gain in confidence, what a foothold for the future!

The boy looked at me.

"What are you?"

The question, loaded with innocent curiosity, once again came as a direct inquiry, although over time it was occasionally delivered through a silent, questioning stare. I had answers prepared in advance, a short one and a long one.

"I'm Japanese American."

I am a Japanese American. I am an American of Japanese descent, which means I was born in America, even though my grandparents came from Japan. I am a Sansei, which means third-generation Japanese in America. My parents are Nisei, second generation. They were born in America too. These were things Mother repeated and I knew by heart. I liked the rhetorical elevation. It aligned with the patriotism the schools taught, the patriotism my family felt.

Perhaps also for rhetorical purposes, Mother referred to the "Japanese race." The only Japanese she excluded from this racial category were the "Hairy Ainu" of Northern Japan, who were light-skinned, with deep-set eyes, and quite hairy. The Ainu, Mother contended, are the only Japanese who are also Caucasian. I wondered if it were easier in the world to be an Ainu. I looked closely when Father stepped out of the shower. His legs were hairy, his skin complexion light. But his chest showed only a sprinkling of hair, almost few enough to count and not enough, I concluded, to qualify as an Ainu.

The full explanation of identity, the one Mother had supplied me with, never satisfied interlocutors, who returned quizzical looks, as if my answer were a trick. Why couldn't they just agree that it was hot out? "You can say that again" or "You got that right."

What are you?

To get out of their concentration camp, Mother and Father were required to answer a government loyalty questionnaire containing lots of questions. For the men, questions twenty-seven and twenty-eight provoked discussion among many, consternation among some. Question twenty-seven said, "Are you willing to serve in the armed forces of the United States on combat duty, wherever ordered?" In other words, are you willing to volunteer for service in the military or submit to the draft?

Question twenty-eight was more confusing and long-winded and had to undergo a rewrite. It basically asked the internee to swear unqualified allegiance to the United States and to foreswear allegiance to Japan. One problem was that Nisei had never sworn allegiance to Japan in the first place. After all, they were Americans. Also, what if they swore allegiance exclusively to the United States only to have their citizenship permanently revoked? Would they be left without any prospect for a country? Father had to answer yes and yes to secure release from the camp. Otherwise he became a No-No Boy, who would be hauled off to Tule Lake or thrown into a federal penitentiary.

Father did not struggle with his answers. Always Father knew who he was and where his allegiance lay. He knew these things when he was still in camp, and he affirmed them much later, after having answered the military draft and taken his family to an army post in Missouri. He knew who he was, even if others were stymied by his appearance.

Someday when a group of Americans stands as one, hands upon their hearts, pledging their allegiance to the flag of the United States of America, no one will even notice that an Oriental stands among them. They will all be recognized as Americans. Nothing else. Acceptance so deep that no difference is detectable. At seven, I believed this. I was eager to believe it. No difference. That day was on its way, loaded with hopes and promise. Even now it was chugging into the station. It would arrive soon. And when it did, there would be no need for trick answers since there would be no more trick questions.

6

FOREIGNERS MADE IN AMERICA

AFTER TWO YEARS OF SERVICE, Father declined the army's invitation to reenlist, resisting the lure of soaring in rank on colonel's wings. The day before Mother and Father's twelfth wedding anniversary, we set off in a brand-new two-tone Buick, which General Motors accentuated with a bold lemony body and a generous dollop of cream for the roof. We were eager to escape the bristling heat and humidity of Fort Leonard Wood. Further west, where the Mediterranean-like coastal climate promised to be temperate, childhood tantrums would be a thing of the past. California would mark a fresh start. I would eat well, bulk up, and require only a belt, not suspenders, to hold up my pants.

The timing was right, finally. In December 1943, two years after the bombing of Pearl Harbor, the *Los Angeles Times* conducted a survey of Southern Californians. The poll showed that residents favored a ban on all further immigration from Japan and supported permanent repatriation of all Japanese from the United States. The poll did not explain how American-born citizens of Japanese ancestry were to be "repatriated," but the margin of support was ten to one.

Now, ten years had passed since the atomic bombs ravaged the cities of Hiroshima and Nagasaki. By 1955, the federal government had ceased to track the whereabouts of former internees, no longer assiduously collected data on their gathering spots or monitored their types of industry, their cultural proclivities, their forms of worship.

The newspapers had ceased their daily headlines excoriating the "Japs." Occupied Japan was an ally in the Cold War. Nisei, their third-generation Sansei children in tow, returned as a trickle, then a steady flow, to sites up and down the West Coast, especially where the prewar Japanese American *nihonmachi* once flourished. The destinations included Seattle, Portland, San Francisco, San Jose, the farmlands around Fresno, around Clovis, around Merced, but most of all Los Angeles, the burgeoning metropolis where Father and his siblings were born and raised.

Not everyone returned. By now, lives had been established elsewhere. Uncle Fred and Aunt Fukiko, my father's sister, remained in Chicago, where school teachers, upon encountering the name Odanaka, immediately assumed that my cousins Susan and Erick and Michael must be Irish. During the war, Fred Odanaka had served in the U.S. military intelligence in the Pacific Theater, while Aunt Fukiko had been sent to Heart Mountain prior to gaining her release to serve as a housekeeper for one Colonel Rasmussen, Commandant of the Military Intelligence School at Camp Savage, Minnesota. Following the war, Grandma Uba moved to Denver with her physician son Mahito, who would later marry Ruriko and have four sons. Uncle Toshio served in the military and eventually settled in the Denver area too. After he married, he and his wife Jane raised two boys and a girl.

Before our shiny Buick turned west, it headed north toward Jefferson City, then east, Lewis and Clark in reverse. It was a blueprint for the future based on events of the past, Mother the architect of summer. Her idea was to tour the metropolitan areas of the Eastern Seaboard, stopping at civic monuments, federal landmarks, historic battlefields, museums, and cultural sites. We went as tourists not invaders, as Americans not enemy aliens. It was vacation and pilgrimage and patriotic reenlistment all wrapped into one. As if to emphasize the point, Father continued to wear his service uniform.

AT GETTYSBURG, where the combined Union and Confederate forces suffered nearly fifty thousand casualties in just three days of battle, Bryan and I leafed through pamphlets and studied wall maps of Cemetery Ridge and Little Round Top, as Mother held Laura's hand while exchanging pleasantries with the salesclerk at the Visitors Center. We children were photographed, squinting at the sun, arms at our sides, no slouching, in front of battlefield sites, monuments, and commemorative plaques. Click. It was the same everywhere. In Philadelphia, we stood before the Liberty Bell with its unholy crack. Click. In Washington, DC, on the steps of the Capitol Building, on the sidewalk outside the White House, at the top of the Washington Monument, at the base of the Lincoln Memorial, at the entrance to the Smithsonian. Click, click, click.

We children were respectful, well-behaved, subdued, never running around noisily like the hakujin kids on summer holiday. Our family was not merely collecting memories to gather dust in a musty family vault. We were leaving our own imprint, an indelible image of well-behaved and law-abiding Japanese Americans. Mother wielded the power of Thor, prepared to hammer our being into the shape of iron rectitude. We were modest, quiet, patriotic, entirely deserving to be regarded as loyal Americans. Sometimes Mother was included in the shot, sometimes Father, but seldom all of us together, since asking a stranger to take a photograph of all of us would have constituted an imposition.

In New York City, Mother snapped a photo of the Little Church around the Corner, where Mr. and Mrs. Carew were married, and of the Empire State Building, where Aunt Yuki, Father's cousin, worked on the thirty-second floor. It was hot and humid, and sometimes Father elected to wear trousers and short sleeves. That was what he was wearing when we toured the United Nations building and when we boarded a ferry boat on Staten Island intending to visit the Statue of Liberty. Our lungs catching the crisp salt air, we realized too late our mistake, winding up an hour later somewhere on the shoreline in New Jersey.

At the Automat, each food item slid neatly through coin-operated windows. Mother cautioned me to let other people operate the machines before I did. Japanese hold back, let others go first. They *enryō*. They enryō until it is second nature, sometimes comical. *You first. No, you first. Oh, no, you first, I insist. Please, after you. No, after you.* Here enryō was part of the bigger vision. Never do anything to hurt the Japanese race. In my personal experience, I knew three races: Caucasians, who were everywhere; Negroes, whom I occasionally had seen walking along big city streets or shopping at grocery stores; and Japanese, which for now consisted of my immediate family, several uncles and aunts, my Odanaka cousins, and Grandma Uba.

Mother was scarcely alone in her belief that the actions of one necessarily reflected on all. After Jack (now Jackie) Robinson broke the color barrier in major league baseball in 1947, Negro newspapers tracked his every move, heaping praise upon him when he stoically endured harassment and racial slurs, while criticizing him when he retaliated with a show of annoyance or a flash of anger, such actions reflecting badly on the Negro race.

Bryan argued that Japanese were a nationality, not a race. He liked to argue obscure points. But in this case, the books agreed. They categorized Japanese as Mongoloids, which sounded weird, like an infection. Mother neither pursued the point nor changed her phrasing. Among the children, I was the most resistant to being ordered about and therefore required the most frequent scolding. I must learn obedience, must demonstrate it, starting with the basics. I must do right. I must fit in inconspicuously. See George. See George misbehave. See George mess the hell up for everyone else.

BY THE TIME WE REACHED the whitecaps crashing the beach near the Santa Monica pier, our family had logged more than four thousand miles cross-country, traversed eighteen states. The drive itself was mile after tedious mile of cities and towns, networks of four-lane highways and two-lane roads, colossal iron bridges, endless stretches of field and forest, the occasional sequence of signs advertising Burma-Shave. During one thunderstorm, lightning struck the ground just a hundred yards or so off the Pennsylvania Turnpike, the brush suddenly leaping up in smoke and terror. We pled for stops at Howard Johnson's restaurants, and we relaxed in plush hotel accommodations in the city centers.

Father had the car's radiator filled before speeding through the plains of Kansas, had it filled again before starting the gradual ascent into mile-high Denver, where we stopped to visit Grandma and Uncle Mike. Father's brother had been named Mahito, but had adopted the familiar American name Mike. Grandma wore a navy-blue and white polka-dot dress and beamed in the tiny kitchenette, which sat adjacent to Uncle Mike's downtown medical office from which he received patients and made frequent house calls, particularly to poorer residents of the city and to those who were disabled. Rice steamed in a pot. Uncle Mike was tall and handsome, with thick, dark eyebrows. Both he and Uncle Hideo could sport a merry twinkle in their eyes. Between patients, Uncle Mike grabbed a broomstick and pretended to play cowboys and Indians with Bryan and me.

We dipped south into Albuquerque, hurried westward on Route 66, hurtling the continental divide and racing through Arizona and into California, by now the trip having consumed over a month. Traveling the country and exploring its history—"our history"—was like coming into an inheritance. Occasionally, Mother spoke to Father in Japanese. It was code. She used it when she did not want us children to understand what they were saying. Father answered briefly, often in monosyllables. His preference was for English. By trip's end, we had visited countless historical landmarks and cultural preserves.

Through the entirety of the cross-country adventure, we were surrounded by hakujin. That fact did not disturb, it reassured, even though I did not like it when complete strangers stared at us in frank curiosity. The secret of a post-internment childhood was to blend in behaviorally, to be inconspicuously normal while accepting the fact that you were not regarded in the same way. Be alert and on guard, lest you slipped or fell or failed to respect the divide between how you looked as a foreigner and what you thought and felt as an American.

So what if I and my family looked as out of place as green tea in a pantry stocked with condensed milk? That was not how I felt. I felt knowledgeable, worldly, deeply experienced in geographical locales, well armed with vast and important knowledge of government and history in America, land of my birth. I was two months short of turning eight.

WHEN I REACHED TWICE THAT AGE, would I know twice as much and have traveled twice as far? Maybe not. But when I was sixteen, I would participate in another moment of transit thick with historical significance. In recognition of the first-ever visit to America of the young Crown Prince of Japan and his wife, the Japanese consulate enlisted the aid of Sansei Explorer Scouts. Instructed to assemble at Los Angeles International Airport, we were to create a ceremonial chain of welcome for the scion of Emperor Hirohito, which meant that we Scouts would see in person Crown Prince Akihito, the future emperor of Japan.

We fidgeted beneath the airport terminal's bright lights until, at a prearranged signal, we formed two parallel lines and stood at respectful attention. Here was the moment when Japan, embodied in its thirty-year-old monarch, set foot on the American mainland. We did not realize that prior to the end of the war the vast majority of Japanese had never seen their emperor. Not even in photographs. They had never heard the emperor's voice, dared not utter his name. For many Japanese, to actually see the divine patriarch or his male heir would have marked an event of indescribable magnitude.

And then—how refined they were! How pale! Their hands delicate as chrysanthemums, their gait informal yet dignified as they wound their way through the airport terminal in the country their country lately engaged in bitter war with. Both Crown Prince Akihito and his wife Michiko smiled gently, moved with a butterfly grace between the welcoming lines composed of Sansei Scouts. We stood silently at attention. The Crown Prince and his wife looked pleasant. They looked nice. They looked Japanese.

Could they guess that we Sansei, many of us tanned like fishermen's sons and wholly lacking the soft, milky, sun-shielded skin of Japanese nobles, were the children of wartime internees? That during the last war, some of us, with our long, swept-back hair, had fathers or uncles serving in the U.S. military intelligence or fighting with the 442nd in Italy and France? Would they have been astonished to know that hardly any of us was fluent in Japanese?

In a few seconds it was over. They were gone. I was uncertain what to make of it all. For me, it was a memorable event but not a moment of fervent national pride, much less a moment of rapture. And then the thought occurred. As the Crown Prince and his wife walked through the airport terminal in Los Angeles and all at once found themselves greeted by a double row of teenaged boys who looked so recognizable yet so different, did they wish for just an instant that they had brought along a camera to snap a few keepsake photos of their own?

7

WATER THICKER THAN BLOOD

"*HIT THE BALL*, numbnuts!"

At Nora Sterry Elementary, the children played games with odd names like bat ball and kickball, and inside the classroom something called heads up, seven up, which could leave any new kid the unwanted center of attention. I managed to get on base in sock ball twice in a row by taking big windups and proceeding to bunt. On my third at bat, I received the greeting from one of the outfielders, who threw his hands up in exasperation to emphasize his point. A bunt was nothing. Deception was for sissies. *Hit the ball, numbnuts!*

Our family was staying in West Los Angeles with Aunt Mary and Uncle Dave, who years earlier had returned to Los Angeles, Papa and first child Alan in tow. On the weekends, Mother and Father searched for a more permanent place to live. Los Angeles had changed from the town they knew before the war. Vast and bewildering, with expanded roadways and with housing developments wedged into once-vacant plots of land, it was cluttered with intersections and traffic, with new businesses and billboards, with bulging apartment complexes invading once stately neighborhoods. The new and proposed freeways were balls of cement twine wildly unraveling and at the same time collecting in dense urban tangles and in suburban knots.

To reach school required crossing Mississippi (the avenue, not the river) and Missouri (the avenue, not the state). Not grassy pastures but a chain-link fence enveloped the playground, protecting it from the cars and delivery trucks speeding up and down the adjacent streets and rolling through the stop signs.

When safely removed from the confusions and alienation induced by the latest new school, I enjoyed a comfortable life, soft as a bubble. With four cousins, especially with the three younger ones being girls, I did not have to show how hard I could strike the white ball with my fist or how far I could kick the brown one with my foot. I enjoyed playing house with Larie and Candace, with Jennie and my sister Laura tagging along, even though it was a game I would have spurned in Missouri. With my cousins, it seemed natural, and I liked pretending to be the man of the house. We played board games too, including Monopoly and Clue, and even Bryan participated. Later, we fooled around with the Ouija board, which I found weird and unsettling when Candace proved that she and Larie were not manipulating the planchette.

Outside, there was room to play hide-and-seek among the rows and rows of plants that lined the length of driveway and extended all the way to the far edge of the property line. Uncle Dave owned a nursery and a landscaping business. Property owners in Brentwood and Bel Air and Beverly Hills remained convinced that Japanese possessed an inherent gift for cultivating plants, domestic and imported.

They forgot, or did not know, that during the prewar era, many Nisei men, including ones with college degrees, were only able to find work as gardeners or doing manual labor. During the postwar resettlement, more than two dozen Nisei-operated nurseries and florist shops opened or reopened along a corridor of Sawtelle Boulevard, eventually spawning boarding houses that allowed nursery and gardening apprentices to learn on the spot.

VISITING WITH MY RELATIVES quickly became my favorite pastime. Aunt Miyeko (Father's eldest sister) and Uncle Ken lived in the South Bay, in a city called Torrance, one of the few municipalities allowing Japanese Americans to purchase property even before the war. The house itself looked slightly cramped and rickety, but I scarcely noticed, since the backyard was thick with juicy strawberries, and my four Yokoyama cousins—Glenn, Naomi, Ailene, and Anne—enjoyed lives enriched with a mountain of comic books, which would take a lifetime to scale. It was a pleasant neighborhood. There were no street toughs around each corner, just comic book villains behind the next page.

Uncle Hideo and Aunt Lillian lived on a hillside far to the northeast in a place called Silver Lake. If I ran away from home, I would ask Uncle Hideo and Aunt Lillian if I could shelter with them for a while. They did not have children yet. As a runaway, I would have had to contend with the big, friendly boxer, John-L, whose mouth was a lake filled with drool, but navigating that lake still would have been preferable to living alone in the woods, hunting and trapping my food, or lurking in culverts and city parks while the police or park wardens happened by.

Aunt Lillian was vivacious and an excellent conversationalist, while Aunt Miyeko was quiet and subdued but friendly nevertheless. Somehow each managed to be the opposite of Mother. For one thing, they never got impatient or mad. For another, they were by nature generous, while Mother wanted acknowledgment for any act of giving. Neither aunt used complaint to get a conversation rolling. And only Mother had the habit of immediately comparing any troubling thing overheard to a personal tribulation she herself had experienced.

When it came to raising children, Mother had plenty to say. I flinched whenever I overheard my name mentioned among the grownups, my reputation already sullied by multiple acts of domestic misconduct. I noticed Mother's habit of handing out advice to Aunt Lillian for when the time came to raise children of her own.

Uncle Hideo used to be the famous Nisei basketball player and a high school track star who reportedly held all-city track records. But he never talked about such things or boasted. At his office, he said, "Which line is darker, this one or that one?" and patiently repeated the question when I was unable to decide. When he fitted me with glasses, he never said things like tsk, tsk, your eyes are really bad for someone so young! The word "optometrist" sounded like "optimist." Uncle Hideo was both. He was also the third Dr. Uba. Father was Dr. Uba. Uncle Mike was Dr. Uba. Uncle Toshio would become an engineer.

Of course, I was allowed to call my optometrist "Uncle Hideo." That was another lucky thing about having relatives—the forms of address were easy and familiar. It was different with other adults, particularly Caucasian men, whom Mother wanted me to address in a curious, stilted manner. She said, "George, this is Mr. Sam," or "George, I want you to meet Mr. Ronald." Evidently, Mother picked up the idea from the movies. In the movies, the black maid or the black butler referred to their white boss as "Miz Sally" or "Mr. Pete." Mother's form of address was disturbing, even for a boy who wanted to be obedient and good. In person, I chose to address the plumber as "Mr. Petersen" and the electrician as "Mr. Briggs."

But even with the hakujin women Mother eventually met through the PTAs, her voice and demeanor changed. She armed herself with makeup, offered bromides to white ladies. *You look like a million. Wish I had a corner on talent like you.* The PTA ladies looked pleased. They said, *thank you*, rather than demurred with a *No, no, not me!* At the meetings, the white women did the talking, made the announcements, the formal introductions, the kickoff speeches. They were the ones elected to office: president, vice president, secretary, treasurer, respectively. But the scut work fell to others. In private, Mother tried to make light of the situation, commenting in a jocular fashion on how the Nisei women did all the work and the hakujin women took all the credit.

I also overheard Mother offering advice to my other Aunt Lillian, Uncle Freddie's wife. They had a young son, Keats, and later on a second son, John. Aunt Lillian was soft-spoken and friendly. Like the other Aunt Lillian, she listened respectfully when Mother gave advice on childrearing. Mother had experience raising children. And she liked to share.

SOME OF THE ADVICE MOTHER DIRECTED AT US, her own children, was standard for the day. "Don't do anything to bring shame to your family's name," she warned. I was aghast at the thought that my temper tantrums and childish misbehaviors might negatively affect the name and solid reputation of my entire family, many of whom I had only recently gotten to know. A family name just like a family life was to be respected and held in esteem. Indeed, not just one but two families, one on my father's side, one on my mother's.

But one day Mother made a startling revelation. She explained that "Uba" was not the ancestral name of Father's family. The ancestral name, Mother asserted, was "Hara." That was why Father still had relatives back in Japan with that surname. A few generations ago, an elderly woman pleaded with a Hara to assume her last name, as it was in danger of dying out. Magnanimously, this Hara agreed to do so. So the story went.

The idea that a surname actually might belong to someone else was unsettling. What did it mean that a precious family name could be so easily swapped out because some ancient, now-forgotten ancestor decided on his own to do a favor for some long-forgotten neighbor? A favor! Why, for goodness sakes, must I uphold someone else's family name? What did it portend for the future that I must stagger under the weight of daily reform to avoid bringing shame or dishonor to a name that by rights was not my own?

Whatever our true ancestral name might have been, I believed that all Japanese Americans shared in common the wish to avoid bringing shame to their family. But Mother carried the idea further. Solemnly, she informed me that while she would hate for anything bad to happen to any of her children, she would hate even more if they were ever to do anything to hurt others. By others, she meant Caucasians. Over and over she repeated the message to her middle child, I being the most likely candidate to go astray and cause harm.

On several occasions, she offered the example of a traffic accident. She would hate for me to die in such an accident, but it would be worse if I were to cause someone else's death. It was a scenario most parents would not choose to contemplate. Or if they did, they would readily choose the reverse outcome as the lesser of two evils. Such a curious idea. Better for one's own child to die than for that child to cause the death of another. As if the greater obligation were to the life of a stranger. As if water were thicker than blood.

Mother's words were not prompted by a lack of parental love. I understood that much. They were prompted by social necessity, by her compulsion "to leave a good impression" and at all costs "to be accepted." Their source lay tangled in rejection and barbed wire, in hostile stares and racial slurs. Being a good citizen was paramount. Better for her son to be a fading line in an accident report than a permanent blot on a police ledger. Still, the terms of the proposition were disturbing. A life cut short was not the debt I or any other Sansei owed America. But it felt like a price my mother was willing to pay.

GAINING ACCEPTANCE WAS ALSO THE FUTURE once envisioned by the indigenous people known as Ainu, the same "Hairy Ainu" Mother once claimed were the only Japanese who were also Caucasian. In the preceding century, when the Japanese pushed north to the island thereafter called Hokkaido, their territorial claim was designed in part to stave off the threat of Russian advance under the imperial rule of the tsar. Seizing the northernmost island and securing it under its own regime, the Meiji government decreed that all its native inhabitants were Japanese.

The Ainu were pressured to abandon their cultural habits, native language, social structures, and religious practices—all the blood customs that made them distinct. Shaving was introduced for men, face tattoos prohibited for women. Many Ainu dove headlong into assimilation, gave it primacy. Convinced that it offered a way to lessen discrimination, they believed it preferable to be a lesser Japanese than a pariah Ainu.

Which is precisely what many of them became—lesser Japanese. There were instances where Ainu were turned into spectacle in much the same way American Indians were put on display in the popular Wild West Shows. They tried their best, the Ainu did, to convert, to become fully Japanese. Nevertheless, others, real Japanese, continued to regard them as alien, even as the Ainu strove to become more and more like them and less and less Ainu, a word that in the indigenous language translated as, simply, "human."

8

WEIRDO

I DEVELOPED A SECRET HABIT. Each morning, I took the rhyming nonsense syllables, rolled them in my mouth like marbles. *Sphinx, minx, tinks, lynx.*

What I said out loud was that my stomach hurt. It hurt. I would have to miss school.

Mother handed me my jacket.

Seriously, it hurt a lot.

It was the middle of the semester, and Bryan and I had transferred to another school. I was a flurry of anxieties, the neurons slamming inside my skull. Laura was lucky to be young. She avoided all this hassle. I did not like strange faces. I did not like third grade. I did not like having no friends. Another new school, so many, this one completing all five fingers of one hand.

Mother handed me my jacket. It was hot out, she agreed. But the wind might pick up later.

The school was called Alta Loma, which translated from Spanish as High Hill. The edge of its playground rose over a slope rather than an actual hill. Maybe the original high hill was brought low when the city started to expand at the turn of the century. Whatever the case, I sensed that the hill of education might be too steep a climb to be worth the effort.

"Hurry, you'll be late," she said.

The move was overdue. Mother had inherited the Japanese abhorrence of imposing on others. To knock on a neighbor's door was an imposition. To borrow a cup of sugar was an imposition. To accept a lift—whether to a market or an emergency room—was an imposition. Seriously, in a medical crisis, hailing an ambulance was fine, but asking a neighbor for a ride to the hospital or expiring on the spot was pretty much a tossup. The family had imposed on Ne-san and Dave for too many weeks.

Sphinx, minx, tinks, lynx.

One day a boy overheard me mumbling the syllables on the school playground. The boy laughed, incredulous.

"What did you say?"

He laughed again.

I ceased saying the nonsense syllables. Or rather, I took care not to utter them out loud in the presence of others.

THE MIDCITY APARTMENT on St. Elmo Drive lay some five miles west of downtown, between Washington Boulevard and the bus line on Venice. If the neighborhood did not achieve the period grandeur of the historic districts like West Adams and Hancock Park, it still hinted at the charm of an earlier, less frenetic time, when urban spaces were expansive and fancy sedans graced the avenues. The two-story building exuded an aura of stability. Decorative wrought-iron railings protected the French balcony windows, which peered out over a cluster of white stucco family residences and other Spanish-Mediterranean-style apartments. Monarch butterflies fluttered gaily through the front yard, alighting on the buttercups.

Mother had secured one of the long, narrow second-floor units, which meant that there was room to take the bulk of the Skokie furniture out of storage. Movers muscled the highboy dresser with the brass pulls, the walnut China cabinet, the dining table with matching chairs up, up to the second floor. European-style furniture was popular among Nisei who could afford it. After the movers departed, Mother spotted a long-beaked hummingbird outside the window, the first I had ever seen. Its busy, desperate wings made me marvel at its ability to stay aloft. It looked like a creature drowning in air.

Barely a half block west, nestled at the corner of St. Elmo Drive and Vineyard Avenue, lay White's Market, a mom-and-pop store bursting with produce and meats and boasting an abundance of sweets and delicacies—Nesbitt sodas, ice cream cookie sandwiches, popsicles, chocolate drumsticks, fifty-fifty bars, half-gallon tubs of sherbet in assorted flavors. Piled high on trays were the Snickers and Milky Ways and Three Musketeers, big ones a dime each. Even refills for Pez dispensers. Every morning, the owner cranked open the metal gates guarding his inventory. The child viewing such an array of riches for the first time understood the feeling of exultation the explorer Howard Carter experienced at the entrance to King Tut's tomb when he espied "Things, amazing things."

If it were not for school, which I disliked in principle, I would have liked this neighborhood with its butterflies and proximity to White's Market. Well, if it were not for school and the presence of other Japanese.

ALTA LOMA was the first truly mixed school I had attended. It stood directly across the street from White's Market. Nora Sterry had had some Japanese kids, including my cousins, and I recalled a handful of Mexican Americans there, but the vast majority was Caucasian. Alta Loma had loads of Japanese and Chinese, Caucasians and Negroes. By the end of the next decade, Negroes, by now called "blacks" or "African Americans," were to establish a community and arts center a couple hundred yards west of the elementary school. It was, and is, called St. Elmo Village, and it became the birthplace of the Black Lives Matter movement. Of course, that came later. In the 1950s, adults persisted in referring to Negroes as "colored folk." Soon, more Japanese and especially more Negroes would enroll at Alta Loma.

In the classrooms, the hakujin children did most of the talking. The Negro children were pretty quiet overall. The Japanese American children were dead silent. What was the world's record for staying silent in a school classroom? There were world's records for the tallest mountain (Mount Everest), for the fastest mile run (Roger Bannister), for the longest river (the Nile). Was there a world's record for keeping your mouth shut in school? Probably not, since answering "here" to roll call undoubtedly disqualified you.

If there were an entire classroom consisting only of Japanese Americans, it would be a silent, obedient classroom, where no one interrupted or volunteered to speak. The kids would submit their homework on time, they would stay up late preparing for tests, they would listen attentively when the teacher spoke. But if the teacher tried to start a social studies discussion, the kids would sit on their hands, their brains like mush. What's your opinion? Thirty-two dark-haired heads staring silently, as into a void. Opinion? Opinions won't be on the test.

Knock-knock. Anybody home?

Nothing would get accomplished. The teacher would scan the classroom in despair, thirty-two inert bodies hewn from insensate wood. Eyes in the back of their heads studying the clock suspended above the rear window, eyes wondering why the red second hand lurched from second to second, while the black minute hand never moved.

This was not true. I exaggerated when I was nervous. There were Japanese Americans who raised their hands and spoke, at least occasionally. Mainly girls but now and then a Japanese boy. Perhaps Bryan, lodged in the back row of his own classroom, bored, pouting in silence, was one of them. He might raise his hand to protest an accepted answer, to dispute an obvious fact, to alter the trajectory of that day's discussion, so that it tailed off in a more interesting direction. Bryan was an original, a helium impulse, a puff of wind as random as an airborne leaf. And like that leaf, he floated away from every effort to fasten him to any branch of fixed learning.

It was not true that Orientals were silent. When they were around each other on the playground or after school, they were noisy, unruly, nutty, just like anyone else. The classrooms in the internment camps were filled with chatter. In the internment camps, teachers reported that after awhile, once the class felt comfortable, they could hardly get the children to shush: they all wanted to talk. But in these classrooms it was different.

At home I talked plenty, talked too much, my voice rising with emphasis as I delivered a well-digested opinion on the current state of education, as I critiqued the performance of the Sunday school teacher, as I delivered a jeremiad on baseball. Everyone in my family read, everyone absorbed news. It was like drinking milk, like breathing air, like checking the temperature before venturing outside. We subscribed to the Japanese community newspaper, the *Rafu Shimpo*, even though we were able to read only the English-language section. We scoured the *Los Angeles Times*, every one of its eight narrow columns, its five separate sections, the stories continued on page eight, on page fourteen, on page twenty-nine. Today's headline was heavy-woolen front-page storm. Yesterday's was mild page three light-sweater stuff.

AT SCHOOL I NEVER SPOKE IN CLASS, never volunteered an answer to a teacher's question. But I was not like the other Japanese American students to whom I did not speak even on the playground or after school. It was funny, somehow, because I could talk readily to my cousins, and I sensed that Sansei kids were more apt to talk to other Sansei than to give them the cold shoulder. But I sensed, too, that if Japanese Americans just congregated with each other, a fuller acceptance of Japanese Americans would never take place.

But that was not the whole reason. The truth was, I was unaccustomed to being around Japanese. It was not that they looked foreign to me. I even liked the fact that in a classroom I did not stand out like a freak. But by now I was used to looking out of place and being the new boy in class. Being the only Japanese in sight was like sleeping on a bed of thorns—it felt uncomfortable but familiar.

One Japanese boy, Makoto, was friendly toward everyone. Small and compact, he even knew judo, according to what others said. He smiled at people, not requiring a reason to do so. I looked away. I turned away as if I did not need anyone to befriend me, despite the fact that friendship was the thing I most desired.

My reaction made no sense. Lots of things I did made no sense. Like keeping my father's army cap tucked in my belt. Makoto Sakamoto would have the last laugh, as it were. Years later, he represented the United States in gymnastics at two Olympic Games. Later in life, he coached other Olympians and was inducted into the United States Gymnastics Hall of Fame. Why was it so hard for me to return a friendly smile from a fellow Japanese?

The one boy I finally broke my silence with was Melvin, a Negro kid, who was not a straight-A student or a popular star athlete like Marc Rice. Melvin replied, "Yeah, you said it," agreeing with me about the day's unbearable heat. Negroes, it seemed, were pretty easy to talk to. Melvin added, "I don't like school." Soon a sun-darkened Japanese kid and a darker-skinned black kid hung out together on the playground. We were not exactly friends, more like schoolyard associates. More like random pencil marks encountering one another's familiar scrawls in the margins of a book neither intended to finish.

Melvin wanted to know why I kept the army cap folded in my belt, the insignia side showing. I explained that it was my father's, worn when he served in the U.S. Fifth Army. My explanation was long-winded, a boast. Father was never a member of the famous all-Nisei 442nd Regimental Combat Team, but he had answered the draft. Melvin was unimpressed. That's dumb, was all he said, gesturing at the neatly folded cap. I had never thought of it that way. After a few days, I left the army cap at home. Tucking it in my belt every day seemed dumb.

MUCH OF LIFE'S TURMOIL I assigned to the girl in the green dress. They were Japanese Americans, the green dress and her sister, and they lived in the downstairs apartment unit. There were two of them, the younger one about my age, jumping rope on the lawn in front of the apartment building. They played hopscotch on the sidewalk. The green dress the younger one wore was made of a satiny fabric, which caught and released sunlight. The dress shone, it shone (I imagined) like an emerald lake at twilight, matchless and confident.

When my mother and I quarreled, we made a lot of commotion. That was what happened when a child had a bad temper and was blessed with a rather loud anger voice. Afterwards, after I got spanked and so on, I felt not anger or resentment but chagrin. Lots of chagrin. I knew how voices carried. Who else had heard mother and son fighting?

Day after day, I tried hard not to notice the girl in the dress that caught sunlight. Ooh, she made me mad. What right did she have to jump rope like that? And hopscotch, it was such an easy game! And that green dress with the shiny fabric and the girl's hair so luminous. Her black patent leather shoes so prideful! She folded her white socks with the scalloped edges just so above her ankles to meet the curve of her calves. Such guile! Kitsune the fox assumes a woman's alluring form. Kitsune can cause family misfortune, can drive an unwary man to distraction.

One day, coming home from school, I saw the girl jumping rope all by herself, her shiny hair jouncing up and down. Her big sister was not there. She was alone. I had never spoken to the girl. She was wearing a dress, I forget what color. I yelled something at the little girl, something loud, insulting, hostile, I forget just what. She looked at me in astonishment, as if a lamppost had suddenly reared out of the ground and spoken. I ran, I scrambled, I mounted the stairs, scurrying safely inside the family apartment. My back against the wall, I breathed heavily, for the moment deeply satisfied. I certainly put that girl in her place. The dress she wore that day was probably green. Shiny and green.

After that, I was careful to avoid the girl. The embarrassment lingered. It was a stain on my Sunday best, another blot on my résumé, a dent in the fender of my self-respect. If she happened to be playing outside the apartment upon my return from school, I had no choice but to turn my head, to scamper inside, daunted as a squeak before a cardboard replica of a cat. Imagine not being allowed to return home in peace after another trying day at the office! What right did she have to wear that shiny green dress? It was confounding.

EQUALLY CONFOUNDING was what happened next in Mrs. Sylvester's classroom. Listen carefully, this is weird. Not Mrs. Sylvester, who was tall, her hair streaked with silver. She looked antique, like a dress made of brocade. She looked like a person who had belly-laughed maybe once or twice in her life, like a person who did not wish to repeat instructions a second time. I was a little bit afraid, but I did not dislike Mrs. Sylvester, whose name reminded me of the cartoon character, Sylvester the Cat, who also was tall, for a cat. I followed directions, did what I was told. Mrs. Sylvester called for hands, but if you didn't raise your hand, you didn't have to get called on. You could stay quiet, quiet as an unoccupied corner of the room.

The noise began on an ordinary afternoon, shortly after lunch, just as we third graders had settled into our seats. It was hard to describe it, the noise. It resembled the high-pitched preliminary hum issued by the civil defense command before the sirens started in earnest and things began to pitch and fall. It wafted eerily through the classroom like an obscure warning signal. A belt in the cosmos needed tightening. An alien spacecraft was set to land.

At first, only Mrs. Sylvester noticed the peculiar hum invading the silence of her well-ordered classroom universe. Her nose turned up, as if detecting the source of the sound depended upon the sensitivity of her olfactory glands.

"What's that noise?"

Everyone stopped. I turned my head, listening intently along with the rest of the kids. At first there was nothing. But then, yes, after a few moments, there it was, high pitched, unabated, now faint, drifting and floating through the room, now more audible, as if someone were fiddling with the volume knob on a short wave radio.

Nnnnhhh.

NNNnnnHHH.

nnnNNHHHhh.

"Who's making that noise?" Mrs. Sylvester demanded.

Abruptly the noise ceased. I joined the others in inspecting the room. Were there rusty pipes complaining through the walls? Maybe a *yōkai*? A ghost? The class prepared to resume the afternoon lesson, but suddenly there it was again, a faint high-pitched hum. I could make out the sound clearly now.

Exasperated, Mrs. Sylvester turned, looked hard at Melvin.

"Melvin, is that you making that noise?"

The noise faded but did not altogether cease. Melvin looked up in surprise, vehemently denied any wrongdoing. I believed him, felt sympathy for him. By this time, Mrs. Sylvester was thoroughly worked up. Her class was nothing if not organized, and she was serious with each lesson. I had not seen my teacher get really mad. I had not seen her get angry before.

"*Who* is making that noise!"

It was no longer a question. In front of me resided a pair of long braids. Thin and skeletal, the braids belonged to Bernadette, whose voice was high pitched, also skeletal, and employed relentlessly to claim attention, which was manna to her soul. Her highest personal aim, which would not be surpassed if she lived to be one hundred years old, was to be Teacher's Pet Forever. Bernadette's knowledge was without parallel, and it made the rest of the class groan. Always the first to raise her hand in answer to a question ("Ooh! Ooh! I know! I know!"), she held the correct opinions on everything.

Bernadette was so combative that whenever another child expressed an idea at odds with her own, she responded with a look so thick with contempt that were it florally translatable it might say, How can a thought so utterly wretched even dare to raise its withered roots under the identical sun that shines so brilliantly upon me? Since I never expressed an opinion out loud, or rather never out loud in class, Bernadette felt confident that I was a no one. Attention was her most precious commodity, like oil to a Texas land baron, and there was no need to waste an ounce of it upon a feeble wick such as me. Indeed, never before had she acknowledged my existence.

Until now.

Her braids serving as antennae, Bernadette suddenly whirled around in her chair and stared at me. I did not like Bernadette's face. Between class discussions, it was as blank as an unplugged television. But it lit with a cruel electrical zeal when the questions began. When the questions started, when her upraised hand was recognized (at last!) by Mrs. Sylvester, Bernadette turned miraculous. The smile sweeping across her face was as triumphant as a landslide burying houses on a hill.

Now there was triumph on her face, although lit with a flicker of surprise, as if she had seen one of the dinosaurs the class recently had molded out of clay suddenly get up and walk. For once, Bernadette did not bother to raise her hand. Ooh, ooh. Her braids swiveled.

"It's this boy, Teacher. It's him!"

It was the voice of rapture, the transcendent tattletale. I stared in wonder at Bernadette's bony finger, which had conspired with the swivel of her neck to identify their target simultaneously. Her braids came to a landing. Everyone's gaze landed. Accusation crushed my skull, my brain soft as jelly. In a nanosecond I understood. In the same nanosecond, the peculiar humming stopped. Bernadette was radiant with triumph. She had solved the Mystery. She had provided the Answer without even raising her hand. It was an apotheosis. What a story she would impress the kids with after school. She would regale her family not just tonight but night after night. Someday her grandchildren would hearken, spellbound, and her legend would grow.

What did I look like at that moment, with my life reduced to an agonized concentrate of humiliation, shame, fear, damnation, and above all shock? It was the hemlock of third-grade unconsciousness, which I had gulped to excess. Mrs. Sylvester's face wore a look of astonishment. Her lips were stapled shut. A clay dinosaur had walked. This odd new boy who never said a word had created a scene!

At last, she admonished me to "stop making that noise." After all, she had to say something. No punishment followed. I was not hustled off to a vice principal just hoping that today's the day he could deliver some hard whacks to a third-grade miscreant. Afterwards, no one talked to me about the incident, except one kid who called me a "weirdo." Melvin said nothing. He did not follow me across the playground and punch me in the face. Melvin was just glad to escape the sharp slap of suspicion.

As for me, I was left to ponder not just the tattered remains of my youth but the unsheltered prospect of what lay darkly ahead. I recalled the morning several months earlier when the disoriented dog worked its way up the long driveway of Aunt Mary and Uncle Dave's house. It was not just an ordinary stray but one profoundly lost and angry. It snarled, paced, made quick nervous snaps as if encountering a phantom lunging at its tail. Beads of white foam hung from its mouth, dripped onto the brick surface of the patio separating the garage from the house. The white foam was the giveaway.

Bryan and I had watched in fascination through the window of the garage, where our sleeping quarters had been fashioned. Our cousin Alan, older and more aware, shouted alarms in the direction of the house. Stay put! Mad dog! Mad dog outside!

What did it mean to be crazy? To be afflicted with madness? It took three bold firemen using long poles with straps attached to the ends and working in unison like a three-headed Heracles to coax and corner the disturbed creature and eventually take it away. Since it did not belong here, or anywhere, it probably got put to sleep.

What brought a dog to the point of salivating madness?

Within a few years, Mother would begin her threats. "Quit fighting me! I will send you to a psychiatrist, just you wait. There is something really wrong with you, you need to see a psychiatrist!" Mother knew nothing about my disgraceful history of stepping in cow poop, of repeating weird syllables on the way to school, of shouting at the girl in the green dress, or of disrupting my classroom with an uncontrollable hum. She would be unable to add these to her storehouse of my wayward actions. Nevertheless, she would build her catalog of reasons, good solid reasons, for payback and revenge.

But for now, our family got ready to move.

9

IGNIS SUM

IN THE NARROW ELL BEHIND the garage of the house on Westside Avenue, the incinerator stood coolly erect, unobserved, motionless as a cement ruin. It had a torso set beneath sloping shoulders and a narrowing, headless neck, which a rust-colored "hat" rested atop. But once a week it collected its wits, gathered energy, came to life. In 1950s Los Angeles, the incinerator occupied a small corner of nearly every residential backyard for dozens of miles in each direction.

For over half a century, homeowners not wishing to pay for pricey and unreliable trash and waste collection services burned their own rubbish. At scheduled hours on trash burning days, smoke roiled the air. Birds perching on rooftops and telephone wires were impartial witnesses to the pandemonium below. For everyone else, fire mesmerized. As it must have mesmerized Prometheus before he stole a fistful of it to bring to man.

Bryan and I were the Vulcans assigned the task of fueling and tending the burn. Flinging open the cast-iron door in the incinerator's belly yielded a satisfying metallic clang. Part of the trick was thrusting and maneuvering the flammable household rubbish so that it all fit in one go—copious amounts of newspapers, magazines, random papers and envelopes, empty boxes and shards of cardboard, clutches of junk mail and even bits of organic waste like carrot ends, bread crusts, mushy celery stalks, murky lettuce. Be sure to separate the cans!

A single match ignited a wad of paper, and the flames leapt and surged in weird spirals and arcs and curlicues. Yesterday burst, popped, disappeared.

The heat intensified as the fire started to rage. Light flammables like comic books contributed to the fast burn. But not books, never real books, which held the fires of learning. Within seconds, a tower of flame leapt upward and the bulk of the waste cratered in the center. Quick, shut the door! Clang! We used the flat of a shovel to slam the door, its edge to secure the latch. We watched the flames dance and pirouette through the slender cracks, their arms reaching for the metal hat.

The house on Westside Avenue was the first our family could call our own since leaving Harms Road. Built circa 1941, it was a modest, two-bedroom ranch style with a detached garage. Its den was converted into a third bedroom, which Bryan and I shared. Set amid houses of similar size and shape, it lay about a half mile east of Crenshaw Boulevard on a street flat as a one-dollar bill.

Mother's first choice was a view lot in Baldwin Hills poised near the crest of one of those leisurely winding avenues with musical names like Don Felipe and Don Mariano. In theory, federal law had put the hammer to the restrictive racial housing covenants, but in 1956 the same realtors who in the ensuing years would eagerly pursue the purchasing power of Orientals shooed them into the flatlands below.

Gaining acceptance remained Mother's childrearing credo, nagging her primary instrument of command. The nagging turned incessant, the anger fueling it explosive. Never did her temper observe scheduled hours of operation. The tiniest infraction ignited it. A chore unfinished, a task not performed instantly, a perceived violation of good order, the wrong word uttered under one's breath. Compliance was evidence of good citizenship. In the internment camps, quarrels occurred on occasion, and sometimes voices were raised in anger. But because the walls separating family from family were so thin, so permeable, people smothered their outbursts, just as they strove to lower their everyday voices. They contained the heat, they practiced self-control until it became second nature. Reported incidents of domestic abuse and violence were exceedingly low.

Every day, every hour, no one in the house on Westside Avenue knew when the next outbreak might occur, Mother and I losing our tempers, the afternoon filling with angry shouts and hot tears.

"I have these chores for you."

"Wait. This is the good part."

I spent a portion of my weekly television allowance on *The Adventures of Spin and Marty*, a featured segment of *The Mickey Mouse Club Show*. Marty Markham was the rich kid who arrived at the Triple R dude ranch in, of all things, a limousine. Stepping into the trail dust near the corral, he sported a suit, a pair of brilliantly polished shoes, and an air of superiority. He was an orphan, this spoiled brat, but based on his attitude and conduct, who cared? If he ever, late at night and alone in bed, grieved over his dead parents or reflected on his state of abandonment, there was no evidence of it. His inheritance, which included his personal butler Perkins, granted him a limitless choice of possessions and endless amounts of freedom—and left him rightly friendless. At his window, only the moon glistened, bright as an insult. The stars abandoned him.

"No. Right now!"

Were I at this moment reading a book or doing extra credit homework, Mother would have exhibited patience. She seldom watched television, didn't see the point. I did. The past did not in any way intrude upon Marty Markham, but the present was a long hike in the desert without a canteen. Only for so long could Marty's display of privileged disdain mask his terror. He did not fit in. On his first day, a swirl of dust dirtied his shoes and suit pants. Marty was a foreign body, an invader, and it was natural that the other boys, who were all normal, rejected him. Spin, the most popular of the boys, overcame his dislike to give Marty a chance.

"Okay, just one minute."

Spin was exemplary. He tried to teach the tenderfoot calf roping, and Marty completely failed, in the process landing in a pile of mud, while casting the blame on his benefactor. What a dope!

"No, this instant!"

Spin did not make fun. Here, try again. Spin was like the perfect older brother. He quickly grasped the tenderfoot's problem. A bad attitude. If he would simply try to do as the others did rather than isolate himself through a veneer of superiority, why, he would become one of the boys, simple as that. Week by week, I traced the slow evolution of change in Marty Markham.

"Okay, okay!"

Spin was on the verge of getting through to Marty.

Click! "Snap to it! *Now!*"

Ah, just ten more seconds! But when Mother said now, she meant *now*! I missed the important part. Darn it. Now I would never know how Spin pulled it off! If only Mother could have waited until the commercial break, I would have done exactly what I was told. Things needn't have escalated. But they did. My retort was the blast of oxygen stoking Mother's fire, and her fire in turn stoked my own. All quiet was broken, the day split in two.

UNTIL I OBSERVED THE CLEANING LADY, I associated anger only with heat, only with fire. *Ignis sum.* I am fire. It made sense. Until I observed this stranger in the house, it never occurred to me that a cold flame might exist. A cold, inexhaustible flame whose burn might be a thousand degrees greater than my own.

The cleaning lady stayed exclusively inside. The backyard was not off limits, but it was not part of the deal. She never raised her voice or shouted in anger. She seethed. If she were a countdown to explosion, her face would have been a timer without a display. Yet everyone around her would have known the seconds were ticking down. The cleaning lady came with ground rules. She would work every Saturday, five hours straight, not one minute more, not one minute less. Her duties would not entail deep cleaning of the laundry area or include crown moldings. Hard-to-reach areas of the living room were out of bounds, but she would clean the baseboards and dust the bookshelves. Was everything clear?

Everything was clear. On Fridays, Mother composed a list of chores. It was her precleaning-day ritual. She issued commands. My duties included scrubbing all the toilet bowls, washing the sink and shower in the small bathroom. Also cleaning slat by slat the Venetian blinds in the converted den. I applied a light cleaning fluid and a pair of towels to the task. Laura dusted and cleaned her room and desk. Bryan vacuumed the house, cleaned under the beds. He mopped the service porch, the kitchen. He was scheduled to make dinner tonight. Laura cleaned the mirrors with Windex, scrubbed the sink in the big bathroom.

It was tiresome, this business of preparing for the cleaning lady's arrival. I wondered why we were wasting valuable time. As usual, I was the first to open my mouth. "Why are we cleaning when what's-her-name is coming tomorrow, I mean the maid?" No one had given me permission to call the lady a maid.

The cleaning lady did not last three months. Her movements exuded cold hostility. Her unseeing stare declared that she would rather punch a window than crack a smile. She said not one word to us children, seldom spoke at all. Her entire demeanor was a silent scowl, a sulk on a stick. When she arrived, we fled to the backyard, out of her line of vision. Through the porch door and windows, we eyed her steady, chain-like movements, room to room, the vacuum cleaner at her side, apparently as provoked by dust particles as the unholy thought of children at play. Linoleum she attacked with bucket and mop, windows with unsparing cleaning towels. If she had had time to hiss out a window, we would have fled like panicked sparrows.

There is a fury that flows like magma miles beneath the earth's crust. Beneath her cold exterior, the lady was like that. I wondered if she regarded our family as wealthy Orientals. She was a Negro, the first I had ever seen enter our own home. In the movies, the maid always looked stout as a shovel.

Negro maids in movies did not show alarm when left alone in a room with a white man. They scurried around solicitously, always smiling and saying things like *yasssuh*. Of course, I did not expect the cleaning lady to evince the same insipid delight as the actors playing servants in movie scripts written by Caucasians. But the thing was, I would never have dared order the real-life cleaning lady around. She was too scary.

Her icy disapproval tracked me into the backyard, where I tried to escape among the croquet balls. The father of the family was called "doctor," and he drove a fat, conspicuous Buick. The cleaning lady, she walked to and from the bus stop. One glance and she knew these children were well clothed, probably idle all day. Maybe the surplus of books attesting to their educational advantage was what ruined everything. There were books everywhere— piled on tables, desks, countertops and aligned on wall shelves and built-ins. Or maybe there was nothing left to ruin. It was the long walk, the wages, the time served. The stinking job.

I heaved a sigh of relief when the cleaning lady quit. She did not give two weeks' notice. One day she quit. The lady of this house was nice enough, very polite. But the cleaning lady had had enough. Good riddance, I thought to myself. "Good riddance," I dared out loud when I was sure she was out of earshot. For once, Mother seemed to agree. She did not hire another scowling cleaning lady. The household tasks, the cleaning assignments, all reverted to their earlier rhythm. I toweled the Venetian blinds. I dusted the bookshelves without complaint. There were no more precleaning jobs to perform before the silent cleaning lady arrived. In the backyard, the croquet balls knocked against one another, their sounds soothing and relaxed.

It was untrue that all internees learned to quash their angers and to cool off. Quiet submission was a rule not always obeyed. At the Tule Lake internment camp, protesting Nisei were accused of setting multiple fires, one of them to the administration building. They were accused of disabling the fire alarm system, of sabotaging the fire hydrants. In August 1965, nearly a thousand buildings all over South Central Los Angeles would be set on fire—like a thousand humongous incinerators out of control and all going at once. The city would watch, stunned, as building after building went up in flames. For nearly a week, the fires would rage. Onlookers would add something new to the municipal lexicon. *Burn, baby, burn!*

GETTING PADDLED REQUIRED ME to pull down my trousers but not my underpants. Paddling constituted the corporal part of my punishment. *Liar, liar, pants on fire!* My buttocks turned pink. Mother experimented with different types of paddles, including one with holes drilled strategically across its face. Supposedly, it was more aerodynamic. Thereafter ensued orders of solitary confinement, which allowed me time to "think about" my misdeeds. Two hours were insufficient. Can I come out? No! Even three hours were rarely enough. Can I come out? No!

At last, my willfulness deemed suitably mortified, I was ready for release. Mother's anger had cooled. She sat me down. Say it. Say it out loud. *I'm sorry.* That part was not difficult, for I had gotten used to apologizing. The next part, the denouement, was more challenging. It was the lesson in civics and the test of historical memory. "What did you do wrong, can you tell me?" What precipitated my latest eruption, and what had I learned as a result?

She watched me as I struggled to recall. After four hours of solitary softened with a Hardy Boys mystery, a John Tunis sports novel, or an anthology of folktales, I drew a blank. The initial squabble was over nothing, the reasons for its escalation so trivial that they did not bear remembering. I scanned the bedroom, the bureau, the shelf of books, looking for a clue. It began eons ago, before Highpockets slugged the home run but after Turtle created the universe, I remembered that much. Mother scolding me over something something and then me answering by saying something in return. Something, something, something.

"I got mad?"

In the evening, Mother would give Father a full summary. She wanted him to scold me, lecture me, contribute to my reform. It went without saying that my television privileges were revoked. When at last they were restored, Marty Markham had mysteriously relapsed, while Spin was forced to start the rehabilitation process all over again.

Laura was a little too young to get yelled at much, but I could have taken a lesson from Bryan, who handled things in his own way. At least I could have learned had we been at all alike. My brother lost his temper maybe once every two years. He weathered every harsh or dismissive word he was subjected to regarding his latest report card. Another C and yet another C! He spent his time alone, leafing through comic books or watching cartoons on television.

What Mother did not realize was that when she chastised the older boy, he turned instantly to stone. The stone did not hear, did not speak, did not defy. The concentrated heat of reform did not penetrate, it left no mark or scar. Truly, the stone was not hurt. It shut its eyes, its ears, its network of nerves. Mother temporarily forced the stone to roll this way, that way, according to her will, and she convinced herself that she had imparted an important lesson. But the stone remained oblivious—as oblivious as Lot's wife after stealing her disobedient, final glance. When all was done, the same Bryan reappeared, stubbornly unaltered, impartial to heat, unaffected by cold, still the same.

On Mother's orders, stacks of comic books were cast into the incinerator's flames, which eagerly consumed the brightly colored bundles, their appetite for dime literacy without bounds. Bryan had wasted all those coins, squandered his weekly allowance. Sergeant Rock and Easy Company succumbed not to German panzers but to fire. Aquaman ran dry. Porky Pig got roasted. My brother did not complain, did not shed a single tear, even as the fire raged unchecked. Nero fiddled while Rome burned.

Bryan learned in Sunday school about another fiery furnace, one that Shadrach, Meshach, and Abednego got cast into. The young Sunday school teacher affirmed that God protected them. But when Bryan, his arms folded in protest, wondered out loud why no one protected the Jews in the Nazi ovens, the teacher became annoyed, warned the boy against speaking out of turn. His question was not part of the lesson plan. The teacher hated it when children were intentionally off subject.

Bryan did not let the Sunday school teacher affect him. Nor his mouthy brother or his sacrificial pyre of comic books. So what? Everything was random. After tending to the incinerator, he reentered the house, ready to settle himself comfortably in front of the television screen, which was filled with Betty Boop, her big, big eyes and her big, mesmerizing head, out of which emerged her teeny-tiny voice. *Boop-boop-ee-doop.*

FOR MY SCIENCE PROJECT, I constructed a volcano. Briefly, I considered building a replica of the backyard incinerator, but the city, its skies thickening infamously into blankets of smog, already had begun to phase them out. Anyway, a volcano was more in keeping with my aesthetic inclinations. Bryan pointed out helpfully that it also was in keeping with my temper.

I cut and twisted chicken wire to create the cone-like shape. The chicken wire refused to cooperate. It retaliated by administering a series of small cuts to my hands. Finally, with Mother's assistance, the shape was secured. Using a spatula, I slapped dental plaster, which Father stored in his office, onto the chicken wire. But the plaster kept falling through the gaps, until Mother showed me how to use strips of newspaper and apply the plaster in thick globs to make it stick.

After it set, I drizzled various colors of paint over the top to simulate lava flows. Mother guided me. Finally, everything dried and hardened. The finished product resembled no identifiable volcano on earth. It was sui generis, a mound of plaster with paint dribbling down its sides. On the day the science projects were due, I set the volcano on a square of plywood. Wow, the thing was heavy. I lugged it all the way to school, stopping to rest on the way.

One by one, Mr. Bruce examined the science projects. That was the man's actual last name—Bruce. He was a science teacher and therefore a logical choice to serve as evaluator. Arriving at the volcano, he glanced at the sheet of lined paper on which I had neatly printed a scientific explanation of magma, which is extremely hot, liquefied rock. If a volcano erupts, the magma becomes lava. Mr. Bruce glanced at the paper, then peered into the volcano from its mouth. Lifted it from its base to see if there were wires connected to a battery or any sort of electrical gizmo.

"Doesn't it do anything?" he asked.

I looked up. "Do anything?" I repeated, my hopes for impressing the science teacher sliding like stale lava down the mountain side.

"Yeah." Mr. Bruce was tall, his face rather pasty but distinguished by a prominent mole. His eyebrows were dark, extraordinarily thick, and they went up and down like nightshades when he talked. "Shoot flames or light up or something?"

One thing I did not do well in a crisis was come up with snappy replies. Say I were caught in an emergency, trapped in a burning bus. Instantly, almost before the bus came to a halt, I would have wriggled through a window to safety. I'd be okay as long as no reporter came up to me afterwards and asked me to comment on the whole incident.

"Um, not really," I replied to Mr. Bruce.

"It oughta." Mr. Bruce's eyebrows rolled up. By the time they rolled down, his entire face darkened into one of those you-shoulda-thought-of-that looks.

I studied my volcano for a long time after Mr. Bruce departed. It was rather pretty. But it did not shoot flames or light up the sky. The woodblock prints of Mount Fuji never show it erupting either. Mount Fuji was not dormant. But it was majestic, uneventful, serene. It did not blow its top. Wasn't that the beauty of it?

My science project received a B.

10

MINISTRIES OF SURVEILLANCE,

A COMIC INTERLUDE

Each classroom contained thirty-two students, the exact number of pieces on a chessboard. Some pieces were expendable, a lesson I first learned at Nora Sterry when I got transferred out of my cousin Larie's classroom after just two weeks, even though I had not misbehaved. The lesson was confirmed at Alta Loma, when I was transferred, again without explanation, from Mrs. Richman's classroom to Mrs. Sylvester's, ultimately to be placed under the tyranny of know-it-all Bernadette.

Thirty-two students, thirty-two chairs. Why was I always the one who had to move? Maybe mine was a face that simply did not belong, a billboard face that screamed, "Transfer Me!" Or perhaps someone in the main office was a master strategist with an all-seeing eye and an unseen hand moving eight-year-olds like me at will. Pawn to e4, to be sacrificed for the greater good.

In the cafeteria, we knew that we were under surveillance. At Alta Loma, the rule was that each child must take a full helping of each menu item and finish everything before being dismissed by teachers assigned cafeteria duties. No child was allowed to stack their tray at the pickup area and leave the cafeteria until their plates had received clearance. The rule would have been tolerable had the food been digestible.

The macaroni and cheese was edible despite its sorry odor. The green beans and beets watery but consumable if you held your breath as you swallowed. But the spinach, oh, the horrid canned spinach! It was not a rich forest green like the spinach inhabiting the fertile fields of a healthy imagination, nor the vibrant green of the dress worn by that Japanese American girl I kept reminding myself to dislike, but a ghastly, washed-out khaki color. The spinach swam, a soggy mess, in a watery base that managed to worsen its vile taste. It swam, no, for swimming implied life, and this, this, was the remains of something brutally tortured and drowned.

Teachers inspected the plates. Dismissed! But when the strategic rearrangement of half-masticated food particles did not meet the inspector general's threshold, it was back to the bench. The child stared at the spinach. The spinach stared balefully back. On a bad day, the entire lunch period passed before the last of the foul stuff was successfully consumed.

THE THREAT OF CANNED SPINACH

The spinach hints of dank colors and khaki moods.
I watch it watching me in its shallow bowl of waiting.
I won't fight it with a teacher patrolling the cafeteria,
his arms folded and alert like two sticks of lit authority.
A single soppy leaf is enough to make me retch.
A gun butt folds my chest in half, my heart left battered
and bent, its signals enfeebled, *mayday, mayday*.
They must load a lot of roughage in a single round.
And it must be good for it to taste so bad and for me
to swallow it daily along with homework and math.
I can't leave my seat for the playground,
where I could lurk beneath some gentler leaves.
I can't go toilet or talk to my neighbors on either side
until I'm done, that's a rule. That's a rule I've learned
at this latest new school, where all I know is how to shut up
like crazy. I watch it watching me, set to explode.
My fork reaches out. Takes another stab at obedience.
This time I miss. Thank God, I'm not dead yet.

By fourth grade, I had entered my sixth elementary school. 39th Street School marked a milestone. For the first time, I completed an entire academic year at the same school, followed by a second year. I made friends, Sansei friends too, having at last grown comfortable being among Japanese Americans. Things were looking up as I entered fifth grade. But learning that I had been assigned to Miss Lefkovitz—the one the kids nicknamed "Miss Lef-ko-bitch"—prompted a respectful inquiry and a puzzling reply.

"Because they love children."

I had asked Mother why people became teachers.

It was nobody's fault that Miss Lefkovitz was a spinster, which was a new and terrible word, a word with spikes. A spinster was a lady who never got married and now it was too late. For Miss Lefkovitz, it was way too late. To pass the time, some children counted the wattles of skin at her neck, where age had taken a solid grip on her throat with no intention of letting go.

A menacing stare was the usual occupant of her face, a look which at least was predictable, like a thermostat stuck at a constant level of cold fury. But when she got mad, a scowl hard as anthracite suddenly appeared, the rouge slathered across her two facial hemispheres became fresh, angry wounds, and Miss Lefkovitz transformed into a crone lifted straight from a fairy tale.

Miss Lefkovitz was forever on the lookout. On the lookout for something to rile her up. Aside from her marital status, everyone knew two things, and only two things, about Miss Lefkovitz. One was that she came from the State of Texas, although she would have been the last to say, "Howdy, y'all." And two was that she did not like boys, did not like them one little bit. They were twigs that needed snapping. Bust them up, feed them to the flames.

Schoolchildren do not understand fury in its range and styles. For them, the alphabet of anger is simple and linear, running a straight line from A to Z. I was able to cease feeling angry at about the letter C, and by the letter E, my burn already was saturated with feelings of foolishness and remorse. But Miss Lefkovitz's anger went on and on, accelerating way beyond the letter M, the letters V and W and X lying in wait. Who knew what might happen were she ever to reach Z.

For several weeks, I managed to exist outside the range of Miss Lefkovitz's notice. Every day, I clasped my hands at my desk in the regulation manner to show that I was obedient and attentive. During recess, I goofed off and shouted noisily now that I knew how to play the games, but inside the classroom I stayed silent and good. I did not reply when Stanley Greenberg whispered at me or when Steve Luskin cracked a joke, although it was hard to keep from laughing since Steve was a funny guy. In time I began to relax, suspecting that my faultless conduct had favorably impressed Miss Lefkovitz. That is, until the day I was proved wrong. And it was all due to my pencil.

My habit was to press hard on the paper when I formed my capitals and my lowercase letters. Penmanship demanded concentration, even when pens were not employed. Each letter must achieve the exact shape and attain the exact height it deserved, and of course in cursive writing, it had to be precisely attached to the preceding letter. The final letter of each completed word must end with an elegant upward lilt. What I failed to notice was how, after I had completed several words in succession, my pencil point wore down. It was the result of effort sustained over time. It was natural. Was erosion to be blamed for the existence of the Grand Canyon?

Lost in concentration, I did not hear the shoes as they clacked across the floor. I became aware of Miss Lefkovitz's presence only when the clacking ceased, when in the noisy silence that ensued I sensed a pair of arms folded in fierce agitation. She was ominous, looming, a terrifying example of impatience married to cunning. With a sound starting somewhere in the back of her larynx but issuing forth like an electrical shock, Miss Lefkovitz's words crackled through the quiet of the classroom.

"Sharpen that pencil!"

I looked up. No, I did not look up, but I glanced upward, drawn to the rouge blazing from Miss Lefkovitz's cheeks. In its customary fifth-grade manner, time stopped, the universe hiccupped. Time did not stop due to the enormity of my transgression, but to allow attention to be more thoroughly focused on me, the miscreant. While I was able to do block letters with straight lines and cursive at the correct angles, what I suddenly saw spread before me on the desk was lettering thick with wasted graphite, lumbering, elephantine, and clumsy, as grotesque as a #1 pencil applied to a #2 task. My pencil point, such as it was, was raised in shame. Miss Lefkovitz now stationed her hand on her hip, which was too narrow a plateau to sustain the full weight of her outrage. Her fury was a claw; invisibly it grasped the miserable user of blunt-tipped pencils by the neck, my scrawny pencil neck.

I rose. Little beast, I scurried to the front of the classroom, where the pencil sharpener was mounted. I felt like the squirrel caught caching a nut, the mouse found nibbling the pilfered cheese. The classroom door was near. I would scamper through it, race up a tree. No, I would sharpen my pencil, all the while listening for my classmates, shrouded in mournful silence. Not even Steve Luskin dared a wisecrack. They were on my side, the kids. They were imagining how awful the feeling if they had been singled out. Furtively, the boys examined their own pencils. For the remainder of the semester, I was terrified of pencil points lacking stiletto tips, disgusted by the inelegant scrawls deposited by fat pencil stubs. I checked and rechecked my pencil points, satisfied only when they were sharp enough to puncture the skin and make it bleed.

Within a week, Miss Lefkovitz discovered a second character flaw. When I practiced my cursive, I tipped my hand to one side, so that the pencil shaft leaned upon the right corner of my hand between my index finger and thumb. The writing position felt natural to me, and the letters came out looking just fine, but meanwhile my pencil assumed an unconventional angle. To

Miss Lefkovitz, the incorrect angle was wholly intolerable, a violation of a mysterious eleventh commandment.

"*This* way!"

The growl starting at the back of her throat was not enough. She wrenched my wrist to the left so that it rested straight on the tabletop and the pencil was positioned perpendicular to my right shoulder. How bony Lefty's fingers were! They reminded me of a rooster's foot. But she was a crafty one. Within days her watchfulness paid off again, as my hand lapsed into the earlier hideous position. *This way!*

Behind her back, kids continued to make fun. They made fun of "Miss" Lefkovitz, unmarried and stale. They made fun of her turkey neck and her age.

"Lefty looks like she's a hundred," offered one kid.

"Naw, more like two hundred," said another.

After school one day, I espied Miss Lefkovitz at her desk. It was late fall, and already she had wrapped herself in her coat, as if eager to leave this cold place of learning, eager to retreat to a fiery coven of fellow witch-teachers.

Across the hall, I observed Miss Eberle and Miss Kajiya, a pair of young and popular teachers. They were chatting. Miss Eberle had recently become Mrs. Unanium, and Miss Kajiya was a student teacher. Their makeup was modern, natural looking. Covered in garish makeup and an old cloth coat, Miss Lefkovitz looked like a remnant from the past, which in a sense she was. What did it mean to be so steely-eyed, unsmiling, and stiff? To look as though you had stumbled into the midcentury, stubborn, rigid, calcified, and alone? To look like you belonged to no one, to no place, to no living thing?

The other teachers were aware of Miss Lefkovitz's reputation. Perhaps their sympathies extended beyond her students' welfare, perhaps they sympathized with her as a tormented relic, a spinster, a bitter Miss Havisham who tolerated girls, while despising boys. For an instant, watching Miss Lefkovitz alone at her desk, wrapped in her overcoat like a desiccated stalk of celery, I felt a twinge of sympathy. She looked so alone. Then the memory of her explosive fury returned.

"She looks two hundred," I muttered under my breath.

HA, HA, I WOULD PAY for my ungenerous thoughts about Miss Lefkovitz later, in B-7 math. Mrs. Wheeler, who otherwise could have passed for an older, sterner sister of Mary Worth, the character in the Sunday comics, was notable for a remarkably unsanitary habit, unimaginable to Mary Worth, of licking her forefinger as she counted through the daily worksheets to be distributed row by row. Lick, riffle, count. Lick, riffle, count.

Every time Mrs. Wheeler prepared to explain the day's assignment, her salivary glands preceded her, starting into motion and continuing nonstop. I knew that when the stack of papers reached me, I would try to touch only the dry edges as I passed the remaining papers over my shoulder. But first I must rise from my seat and hasten to the back of the classroom.

RRRRGGGJJHH. RRRGGJJJHHH. RRGGGKKKKHHHH.

Pencil sharpeners were all attached to a rear wall in these classrooms. There were different-sized openings for different-sized pencils. Once the proper opening was rotated to, it was a simple matter of turning the hand crank. Constantly on the alert for smudgy graphite, I knew better than to work with a dull pencil point.

Except that just as there is a time and season for reaping and sowing, there is also a time and season for sharpening pencils.

"Well! We'll just *wait* while *someone* finishes *interrupting* us." At that moment, Mrs. Wheeler bore no resemblance at all to the Mary Worth family, her look heated but her voice glacial. In the back of the classroom, a boy clutched a half-sharpened good intention.

I knew exactly what Joe Btfsplk felt like. He was the character in the Li'l Abner cartoons with the dark rain cloud perpetually hovering over his head, the one whose very appearance heralded disaster. What did the future hold when a boy, despite his utmost caution, displayed an uncanny knack for stepping into every puddle marked trouble? How many people could leave a bad impression with just an unsharpened pencil—and do it more than once?

"Well, continue," the voice demanded, while the world watched in awe.

Rrgh. rrr. rr.

MR. TROWBRIDGE, the boys vice principal at the junior high, would prove only slightly funnier than an unsharpened pencil. Not because he patrolled the school grounds and hallways like a pair of combat boots on the alert for punks, loiterers, and little jerk-offs to kick in the ass, a duty he performed with alacrity. Actually, he wore shoes, not boots, but he used them to deliver messages in italics. If traffic intersections were to operate on the principle of Mr. Trowbridge's shoes, there would never be instances of congestion.

What made Mr. Trowbridge a wee bit funnier than a disruptive pencil was his square head and his square jaw and his square suit, whose seams always looked ready to split. And above all his hair that sat nerveless atop his head, as if frozen in fear, not a single strand out of place. Motionless and nerveless because it might well have been a toupee. The kids held lengthy debates on the matter. I voted in favor of a toupee.

Less amusing was Mr. Trowbridge's appearance one afternoon on the auditorium stage with a long black whip coiled at his feet. Having shed his suit jacket and rolled up the sleeves of his white shirt, Mr. Trowbridge exhibited thick, muscular forearms resembling slabs of meat hauled from the butcher shop. With handle in hand, he slowly let the whip uncoil. It rose, moving into a leisurely circular spin, as if intent on tormenting the air but only by degrees. Around his waist the whip whirled, gained momentum, gained speed. It rose. Around his chest, then neck high, its motions blurred, too fast for the eye to follow. *CRACK!* It slashed at the air, murdered silence. It bit the sky. *CRACK! CRACK!* The ends of the whip lashed furiously, filling the auditorium with *CRACK!* and *CRACK! CRACK!* and *CRACK! CRACK!* The angels of inattention fell to the stage, stunned, mortally wounded.

The performance was a bizarre highlight, a demonstration of raw power, of rapacious authority. Remonstrance was futile, protest subject to instant annihilation. Never once did the fanged tip dare strike its master. Yet it bit repeatedly through the surrounding air. You best behave, George! Obey, obey, obey. Stray not into trouble, if you know what's good for you. Authority was a whip. It blistered the flesh, it lashed the will in order to preserve and protect and to guide the young. See this line? It marks the future. Toe it. Or you'll see. You'll see what happens to those who don't.

11

BUDDHAHEADS AT HOLIDAY BOWL

EVERYONE IN THE NEIGHBORHOOD had heard the grisly story, but by 1958 the exact site was buried beneath the manicured lawns, cropped hedges, gardens bursting with exotic flowers, and koi ponds gracing the new stretch of houses along Norton and Bronson Avenues. The housing construction had filled the spaces and lots just east of Crenshaw Boulevard between 39th Street and Coliseum, even as Japanese American families had pushed west of Arlington Avenue, at one time the cutoff point for residential sales to minorities.

Small Japanese businesses such as the Enbun Market, a barber shop, and a nursery with trellises and potted plants continued to neighbor the old streetcar route along Jefferson Boulevard. Nisei busily opened new businesses to the west and southwest, lending a Japanese American feel to an area that eventually would come to be labeled Crenshaw Square. New signs and billboards popped up along Crenshaw, and the corporate businesses took root—Boys Market, Sumitomo Bank, Mobil Gas with its flying horse logo. But indisputably the heart of the Japanese community on the west side of the city was the new Holiday Bowl, which went up maybe five or six hundred yards from where the body was found.

In January 1947, Norton Avenue consisted largely of vacant lots and empty fields. A woman taking a morning stroll along the avenue spotted a pale figure she initially mistook for a discarded mannequin. Upon closer inspection, the passerby made a startling discovery. It was not a mannequin but a corpse. The body of a young woman drained of blood and dismembered with surgical precision, its lower half positioned at a diagonal about a foot away from the upper.

Elizabeth Short was just twenty-two when she was murdered. Coming to Hollywood in search of stardom but failing to acquire a single movie credit was not unusual, even back then. Elizabeth Short drifted among different social sets, fraternized with a variety of men, but never found a stable community to come home to. She achieved fame only in death. Once the media set to work, they dubbed her the Black Dahlia.

Judging from her photograph and from available accounts, she was a looker. The same could not be said of Mr. Paul Uyemura, one of four business associates who opened Holiday Bowl at a time when the American Bowling Congress, the official administrator of the rules and regulations governing ten-pin bowling, formally excluded Japanese Americans from membership. A friend informed me that Mr. Uyemura was a veteran of the 442nd. Ah, if that were true, it might explain why he had just one good eye, the other covered with an eye patch, why his jaw was disfigured, and why his lower lip looked violently, permanently swollen. When Mr. Uyemura tended the shoe rental counter, everyone knew better than to stare. After all, he owned the place. Soon, very soon, we kids ceased to notice.

Bowling was America's craze, the latest family pastime, the newest order of capitalist leisure during the Cold War. Across the nation, bowling alleys sprang up, thousands upon thousands by 1958, the year the Professional Bowlers Association was formed. Television shows featured professional bowlers, whose names became as well known to the general public as boxing champions, more famous than professional football players. Don Carter, Dick Weber, Carmen Salvino. Ned Day with his smooth easy delivery. Balding Ray Bluth cradling the ball at his chin.

Holiday Bowl was an immediate success with thirty-six lanes of thunking bowling balls and clattering wooden pins. Jutting high above the street, the neon sign with its mock Oriental letters commanded passersby to BOWL. Day and night, Nisei and Sansei did just that. During and after bowling, the adults ordered a beer or a straight whiskey. Sansei old enough (or tough enough to look old enough) gravitated to the pool tables, where they tugged their shirttails out and took turns shooting eight-ball or nine-ball. Bowlers and nonbowlers scarfed on yakisoba, udon, and chow mein at the coffee shop, whose oversized plate-glass windows were beacons to the salivary glands. Above the windows, an overhang zigged and zagged; it was an architectural feature both playful and energetic.

Nisei bowling leagues sprang up. Leagues for men, leagues for women, leagues for mixed pairs, junior leagues for kids barely able to lug the ball toward the gutter. Kats Uba took us kids to Holiday at least every other week. He joined an adult league, donned his team's shirt, which bore the sponsor's name and logo. His average went up—168 per game one season, 182 in another.

The beauty of bowling is that it is not limited to individual wins or team triumphs. It is a striving for perfection and a metaphor for the second chance. Quickly, we learned that a perfect game consisted of twelve strikes, all the pins toppling over on the first ball thrown in each of twelve consecutive frames. In the 1950s, few bowlers—certainly few amateur bowlers—achieved perfect games during their lifetime.

The second ball in a frame offers the opportunity to knock down any remaining pins. If the bowler completes the spare, the first ball thrown in the following frame completes the score in the previous one. Thus, bowling is the distant hope for achieving perfection and the prospect of correcting a mistake the second time around.

Occasionally a bowler did everything right—hurtling the ball smack dab into the 1-3 pocket—and things still did not work, the bowler getting "tapped." With a resounding *CRACK!* ball met pins, which knocked over other pins according to the logic of proximity and the laws of physics, when inexplicably one pin remained upright, unscattered, untouched, following all the racket and commotion. It was a forlorn sight, a standing ten-pin.

Holiday Bowl meant community not only to the Nisei but also to us third-generation Sansei kids thickly clustered in the Crenshaw area as "Buddhaheads." *Buddhaheads.* The term, even when used by others, was not derisive. Nor did it diminish our sense of self-worth. On the contrary, we Sansei regarded it as a welcome identifier, as inoffensive as the word "hakujin" for white person or "nihonjin" for Japanese. But it was even better because it was slang. We were not Japanese from Japan. Nor were we foreign Americans. I always felt weird, and not just on December 7, when I put together phrases like "we Americans." It was as though I needed a qualifying tag so that the hearers didn't give me puzzled looks. But we Buddhaheads, well, that was different.

Buddhaheads greeted each other, laughing and grinning, at Holiday. I saw my three closest pals—Paul Nakasuji, Gilbert Nishimura, Donald Iwasaki. But lots of other friends too. Alan Nitake, whose father had started a prominent insurance company and who long ago had taught my father to play bridge. Ken Inouye. Ronnie Toyama. Roger Yamanaka, a brave boy with a generous heart, whose father was an executive in the YMCA. A decade later, Roger would join the Marine Corps, and he would die at Khe Sanh.

I would have greeted the girls I had known from 39th Street School too, were I not so shy around them. Not just shy, afraid, afraid of their private confabs and squeals of laughter and preternatural knowledge of what boys were thinking—Betty Jane Ishida, who lived barely a block away; Carol Nishikawa, who lived on infamous Norton Avenue; Beverly Ito, whose father owned Joseph's Men's Store in Little Tokyo; Vivien Uyemura, who was brash and mischievous and loaded with comebacks for guys who got too big for their britches.

When *The Mickey Mouse Club* first came on television, the thought never occurred to me that the ensemble included no Japanese Americans. Buddhaheads did not flaunt oversized mouse ears while shouting their names through a big grin. *Karen! Michael! Tadao!* Television membership was pretend, and anyway I told myself I preferred being on the outside. Maybe it was never enough. Maybe that was why I developed a secret crush on Annette Funicello. The one with raven hair, ebony brows, and midnight eyes. The one who looked different, who nevertheless fit in.

Initially, most bowlers at Holiday were Japanese Americans. But soon many hakujin started bowling there. Why not? It was conveniently located, and it was open to all comers, participation as immediate as the automatic pinsetters, which had replaced the glimpses of pant legs and busy hands at work behind the bowling racks, the newer technology aligning each fresh set of pins in a more perfect union.

But Holiday Bowl also reversed the roles of majority and minority, turning America—or at least the standard terms of belonging—inside out. There, the racial minority engulfed the majority. Holiday Bowl was a strike pitched from the Brooklyn side of the 1-3 pocket. *You may join us.*

You may join us.

And many people did.

Holiday Bowl soon attracted a more and more varied demographic, as if all along its intention had been to serve as an antidote to segregation. I greeted my schoolmate, Steve Luskin, whose power could rival that of any of the aerospace workers bowling a few lines to unwind after night shift. In a few years, as the number of Negroes in the Crenshaw area steadily increased, the bowling alley became even more integrated. Once, I saw husky Bernard Campbell and also popular Ballinger Kemp with his curly hair. After less than a year in junior high, Ballinger would be pulled from the public school and sent clear across town to enroll in an expensive private school in the San Fernando Valley. His mother's plan was to have him attend Harvard, which eventually he would do.

People bowled and ate side by side. The coffee shop's menu expanded. You could get all-American food, including Hawaiian-style dishes, lots of

Japanese and Chinese dishes, and in time grits and short ribs and fried chicken patties with gravy. For many Nisei, integration was less a sought-after social goal than a type of cordial coexistence, which included scarfing food elbow to elbow and jabbering with fellow bowlers black or white.

Sometimes, gamblers and young hoodlums collected. And while you were safe in the bowling alley itself, you didn't want to give guys at the pool tables hard stares. In the parking lot out back, it was advisable to double-check that your car was locked. Sometimes it was better to take the long way around rather than the alleyway, which was a shortcut to Coliseum Street.

By turns deep or superficial, the harmony illustrated by the bowling alley converged with my secret wish to promote a world of friendship and understanding among all people and races. The unexplored component of that wish was that no one who was different—even *essentially* different, as I had come to see myself—need ever feel excluded again. Mr. Paul Uyemura belonged to that world, in fact had been instrumental in creating it. Had she lived, Elizabeth Short would have been welcomed too, and without an initial scrutiny. What shoe size, please?

But then there was Billy Beamon.

It was a comfort to have a community of friends who looked like you, acted like you, felt the same special confidence when you were all together and the same hint of trepidation when one or two of you were alone "out there." But Billy Beamon was like no other. At school, people made fun of him for his effeminate demeanor. It was not just that. Billy was cut from whole cloth. With his high-pitched musical drawl and his rump creating an oddly shaped saddle above his endless stretch of legs, he sounded and looked like no one else in school, like no one else under the sun. He seemed equipped for fast running, or perhaps for riding a tall horse, but he evinced little interest in sports or playground activities. His head looked cylindrical, shaped like a bullet. But Billy Beamon did not fire sharp retorts at those who made fun of him. In junior high, his swishing movements became more pronounced. That is when kids started to call him "homo."

In elementary school, Billy greeted me in the morning. "Hello, Gee-ar-jjh." It was an accent distinctively his own.

And I replied, "Hello, Billy."

Long before we left elementary school, Billy was aware of which children he could greet with impunity. Probably he also sensed which ones, like him, remained imperfect fits in a social web that stretched far beyond the school itself. Billy and I seldom conducted personal conversations because he always seemed to be hurrying off. Things began and ended with the greeting, but the greeting was sincere.

The last time I saw him was at Holiday Bowl, and Billy was again on the move. It was years since I had last seen him around school, and now he wore makeup and a flamboyant scarf. He displayed the same long, loping stride. His swishing movements had greatly eclipsed those that had first declared him a pariah long ago. He was not there to bowl. The rumors were that he lived on the street, turned tricks to survive.

"Hello, Gee-arjjh."

"Hello, Billy."

I was testing bowling balls. Others seemed to find one with exactly the desired weight and grip right away. Not me. Billy moved on, as always. My mind paused, even though my hands kept experimenting with grips. Billy still remembered me, acknowledged me in his sweet, gentle way, as he did when the two of us were children in elementary school, one reveling in the experience of near-belonging, even as the other was spinning ever farther from the pull of social convention, from the limits of social acceptance.

Imagine Billy Beamon in the world of Spin and Marty. It was no more conceivable than a space alien inhabiting the Triple R Ranch. It was a confusion of genres. Billy was not a redeemable misfit like Marty Markham. Billy Beamon was a transgression entirely unaccounted for. He was a spectacle, a street glare even Spin would have turned his eyes away from.

Billy's apartness begged the question: What were the limits of belonging? I enjoyed membership in a community of Buddhaheads without ever having to fill out an application form. I saw no contradiction between that membership and the more expansive principle of fitting in with white America, which Mother had faithfully espoused and which I had continued to subscribe to.

But I had never considered the full range of conditions that allowed one in or kept one out. Elizabeth Short might easily have joined the fun at Holiday Bowl. But could she ever have fit in with the Mouseketeers? Even handsome Ballinger Kemp would have looked out of place at the Triple R Ranch. Marty Markham did not carry the weight of an orphan's actual loss, only the baggage of inconvenience. His was a simple challenge. All he needed was an attitude adjustment, and he would find a home.

For a brief time, Elizabeth Short seemed to have things her way. A pretty face, an alluring smile. But she wound up in an empty lot, her body dismembered, her death turned spectacle. Shunned by most, Billy Beamon danced on a knife's edge. I was like neither of these. At the bowling alley, I enjoyed membership even when I secretly feared that my status was probationary. Even when I felt dangerously close to being the one left out, I knew that I was not. Not utterly. My condition was salvageable. No worse, at worst, than a standing ten-pin. A Gee-arjjh.

PART III

TRAUMA

12

SHOTGUN MARRIAGE

SHORTLY AFTER ENTERING SIXTH GRADE, I was forced into marriage. To be precise, I became, all unwillingly, a husband. Just when I had thought that the bad days were behind me. By the spring of 1958, my scores on a series of standardized tests had convinced the school administration to allow me, as well as several of my classmates, including Gilbert and Paul, to skip ahead a half grade. I no longer chanted strange rhyming sounds like a mystic or other worldly shaman. I had ceased to make weird humming noises in class. I walked, no, I strode to school like a mighty sixth grader, well aware of my prowess in sock ball and kickball. My pencil maintained a sharp point, even without fear of Miss Lefkovitz's skulking.

My problems began soon after the new teacher for the combined B-6 and A-6 class was introduced. Mrs. McConnell was slightly plump but not faded or antique. Her teeth did not protrude in a snarl, and her face did not look like it had chewed all morning on a sour gumball. Like other teachers of the era, Mrs. McConnell wore a dress each day and fashionable pumps. Never did she come to school without her hair groomed and her face made up with eye shadow and lipstick. This was the first teacher I had ever met from Cleveland, Ohio, home of the Cleveland Indians, rivals of the White Sox. Her skin was dark, but the freckles on her face were darker.

Mrs. McConnell knew everything important. She referred to the "international stage." Sputnik and Explorer I. The United States and Russia. Nixon's Goodwill Tour to South America, when he got spat on in Peru, his car pelted with stones in Venezuela. She wanted her class to be up to date on current events. Her class would read about Atlas missiles, about Israel and the Middle East. It went without saying that her students would learn. They also were expected to behave.

"You must act muh-toor," she insisted, addressing the class collectively and placing emphasis on the "t." I had pronounced the word with a "ch," as in a muh-choor apple or a muh-choor pear. Mrs. McConnell's pronunciation was weighty, it carried a higher burden of responsibility.

Mrs. McConnell was not mean like Miss Lefkovitz. She was worse. She was mischievous. She was satirical. She was flirtatious. Out of all the children in the class, she selected me as her reluctant Teacher's Pet. Her sense of humor targeted the entire class, but my small stature, my fuzzy head, and the near-sightedness that forced me from the age of eight to wear glasses ("Four-eyes!") made me a particularly inviting target. The fun was irresistible. Delicious. Like biting into a dumpling.

From almost her first week in the new class, Mrs. McConnell decided that this little gremlin of a boy would be designated her "husband." With a broad smile, she issued the announcement of our "marriage" as if it were an edict posted on the All Saints' Church at Wittenberg. Oh, brother. My mind raced into the future. Torture lay ahead, the delicate ego drawn and quartered. Daily agony. Sure enough, every morning and every afternoon, Mrs. McConnell referenced my unwanted marital status. "How's my husband this morning?" "Let's see, my husband did quite well on this assignment." And so on.

I did not confide in my parents. Marriage was a horrifying concept to a boy too shy to talk directly to any girl. But I managed to compartmentalize. Once the school day was done, school no longer existed, teachers ceased to exist. Only a few bits of homework to scrape together like bits of trash strewn on the ground after the trash barrels were full. Tomorrow was a long way off.

In the morning, anxiety gripped my stomach as I swallowed my Frosted Flakes. Tony the Tiger grinned happily at me. Tony did not attend 39th Street School. He was not Teacher's Pet. Tony knew nothing of the brutalities of marriage.

Exactly what precipitated the crisis was not clear. But it took place at Mrs. McConnell's desk, which was situated at the rear of the classroom. This placement was standard, for it allowed the teachers to catch up on their paperwork while silently observing their students as the latter performed (or failed to perform) their assignments. The students never knew whether they were being observed at any particular moment. Therefore, they (supposedly) policed their own conduct. It was an application of Jeremy Bentham's eighteenth-century panopticon, originally intended for prison populations, although no one referenced this wickedly inventive idea.

When I was summoned to the teacher's desk, I approached warily. Mrs. McConnell was a large woman with a strong, large body. As I approached the desk, I saw the familiar outline of Mrs. McConnell's lipstick and the freckles that frolicked whenever she smiled. Suddenly, hands reached out and grasped me. Two hands, powerful as manacles, connected to two arms from a steel-workers' town. The grip tightened even as her eyes danced with merriment. Any heart must experience a horror the first time it feels insurmountable pressure and the body's sudden arrest.

I struggled simultaneously with my teacher's incalculable strength and the sudden knowledge of my now-public plight, as the other children turned in their seats to watch the drama unfold. Within the fortress of her Brobding-nagian humor, I became not even a Gulliver but a Lilliputian tightly chained. But there was nothing funny about it to me. Squirming, panic-stricken, I momentarily wrenched myself free of one hand, while the eyes of the other children bore down on me like the prison spotlight discovering the escape attempt at the base of the wall.

Her hand managed to catch me before I could effect my escape. How strong she was! Incredulous, weirdly fascinated, the other children watched as their teacher drew me even closer, toward her bosom, then nuzzled the top of my close-cropped head with her lips, nuzzled it, then delivered a kiss. "You're so c-u-u-ute!" she declared. In the next moment, I was able to spring free and break away.

"You queer!" I sobbed, quickly retreating to the far end of the classroom, a rabbit of a child wishing only for a dark endless hole to disappear into forever.

This was the single worst moment of my ten-year-old life. It was all so pub-lic, so savagely public. Humiliation was the tsunami crackling open the plac-id afternoon, engulfing a fragment of human debris, casting it here, sweeping it there, while onlookers watched in wonder and awe.

There was no escape from their gaze. But I regained my seat and now found myself caught in another desperate strait, locked in a life-or-death strug-gle to regain a measure of composure, to control my own sobbing—what a girl I was! The children looked on, too stunned at the outburst to whisper or to laugh. They would talk among themselves later. They would tell their parents about what happened at school. Clearly, which was one of the adverbs I had recently begun to weave into my sentences, the slender thread of my future had been severed once and for all.

The boy assigned the seat next to me was not a teacher's pet. Alan was heavyset, with a large head and a thick torso that proclaimed his toughness and the fact that he would never be any teacher's pet. If you were a rabbit, he was a mangy bear. A Sansei bear with his shirttails hanging out. Sometimes magic happens when you least expect it. Sometimes the shaman appears and lifts the curse. This tough boy, this burly A-6 kid with a head like a bear, turned to me and whispered two words, words totally unexpected and strangely tonic.

Forget her.

The splendid rhetoric of the playground. "Oh, forget you," the boys commonly said, the preferred riposte in the face of verbal challenge or any disagreeable prospect. "Forget *you*," the girls retorted, grinning at the boys when the latter tried to gain their attention through the customary tactics of slander and insult.

And the sobbing subsided.

WORD GOT OUT. Word got out, it couldn't be helped. One day, Mrs. Unanium encountered me after school. By chance, we were alone on the stairs leading down to the first-floor hallway. I was walking down, and she was coming up. Mrs. Unanium had thick blond hair piled atop her head. The year before, I had hoped that she, rather than Miss Lefkovitz, would have been my fifth-grade teacher. Mrs. Unanium told me that she had heard about all the attention I received in Mrs. McConnell's class. I had no reply. But Mrs. Unanium was not teasing, she was checking me for injury. I asked her if I could transfer into her classroom, but she was not teaching sixth grade. I already knew this, and she knew that I knew. She was a nice lady. I wondered if I would ever have a teacher like her.

Even my parents got wind of what had occurred. Other kids blurted things out to their parents, and some of those parents spoke to Florence or to Kats. I never mentioned the incident; I wanted only to bury it. Why was I ever born? Answer me that. Mother and Father never asked me about it, never probed into exactly what had occurred. There was no label for it. Why bring it up since nothing could be done? *Shikata ga nai.* Can't be helped. They did not march into the principal's office or write a complaint to the district superintendent. A direct confrontation with school administrators was scarcely the way Japanese American parents handled things, are you kidding me?

Anyway, what was the big deal? It was not like losing your mother before you turned seven. Losing your mother, what could be worse than that? It was not like going to bed hungry, truly hungry, your only satisfaction lying in the knowledge that not a single grain of rice was wasted at dinner. Mother and Father knew hardship. And Father always gave the same advice. "You gotta roll with the punch. Roll with the punch." Sage advice. My mind filled with horrors. Hundreds of thousands of starving children in China. Millions of Jews gassed. The Black Dahlia, her torso carved in half, the body placed wickedly in the empty lot off Norton Avenue. Roll with the punch. My parents had experienced life. Father knew what he was talking about.

FOR A FEW WEEKS, Mrs. McConnell eased off, sensing perhaps that this time she had gone too far with me. Jokingly, she informed the class that the two of us were now "divorced," and for a week or so, she teased another boy in the class, proclaiming that she had now found "a new husband." But her attention soon reverted to me, the pint-sized kid who continually rose out of his seat and darted a few steps forward, pushing on the ridge of his glasses to make out what was written on the blackboard. Mrs. McConnell resumed her teasing. She just couldn't help it. But I managed to keep a safe distance, never again drawing anywhere close to her desk.

I asked God for help in shifting the attention away. All I wanted was to be just another kid in class. Anonymous. I asked God to take time from his busy schedule. Occasionally God did, and I experienced an entire day without being teased. Other days, when God was attending to more pressing matters, I did not rail against the Almighty, who controlled the seasons, including summer, which spelled liberation. *No more pencils, no more books. No more teachers' dirty looks!*

Under the spell of summer, it was easier to renew my relationship with God, even as I silently confessed my dislike of Sunday school. During the two-week YMCA summer camp, each boy was assigned to a cabin, which was enclosed on three sides, while the fourth was left open like a proscenium arch extending out toward a vast audience of trees. A slope of dirt ran up to the base of the cabin. Assiduously, I gathered white pebbles, as I had seen other boys do. I arranged them in neat, careful order across the dirt, brevity being the soul of wit, or something. When I was done, I was proud of my message, its piety and pleasing humility.

God is first.

Others are second.

I am third.

But all of that was why I could not understand—could not understand—why, why, after all of my efforts to proclaim my reverence and display my humility, and after the summer started and ended and my final A-6 semester began, I was assigned to Mrs. McConnell's class once again.

13

"GOOD EVENING, FRIENDS,
FROM COAST TO COAST"

Mrs. McConnell had an idea. She would add some zest to the mid-year graduation, since the winter ceremony typically lacked excitement, having fewer students and fewer overall attendees. Let the children highlight what they had learned about current events, while taking advantage of the growing popularity of television.

She oversaw the preparation of a large cardboard delivery box, which would serve as the television console. It was stationed at the foot and to the side of the auditorium stage. Several children painted the box a dark mahogany, and along its center, one drew a set of black dials in India ink. The rear of the box was cut away, and the top half facing the audience also was cut out, so that the newscaster, seated on a chair behind a small desk, could face the auditorium audience while reporting various news events. The more reproducible events were to be acted out on stage by both B-6 and A-6 class members.

A clever idea, using this new medium. By now, the majority of homes possessed a television, at least a black-and-white, sometimes a color Zenith. The problem for Mrs. McConnell was that no one volunteered for the role of newscaster. Certainly not me. I maintained a wary distance from my teacher. My deepest wishes in life were to have friends and to stay out of the limelight. Fortunately, her teasing diminished slightly during the course of my final semester. For a time, I even served as sixth-grade class president, a sham title that circulated every few weeks among class members, the president's sole function being to lead the class each morning in the Pledge of Allegiance.

Mrs. McConnell declared that all of the A-6 boys must audition for the role of newscaster. Audition. Such a heartless word. The girls were safe. There was no such thing as a female newsman, neither on television nor anywhere else on planet earth. There was a second required audition, this one for a soloist to provide a musical interlude during the graduation ceremonies. When my turn to sing came, my voice got caught somewhere between a falsetto and a squeaking floorboard. Utter humiliation. As soon as possible, I found my seat, tried to turn invisible, a mote of dust. Mrs. McConnell's eyes sparkled with mirth. She could not help herself. That little boy!

To avoid another fiasco, I prepared seriously for the audition as newscaster. I had not the least desire to be selected for the role, but I wanted to avoid further embarrassment. Over the course of several nights, I assembled news stories on a series of index cards, the way I imagined television newscasters did. Taking Mrs. McConnell's advice, I rehearsed. For once, things went well. Standing in front of the class, I read from my note cards while occasionally glancing at the audience. It was not a difficult task, no more daunting, really, than reading out loud. I completed my news report without a hitch, then took my seat. That was over and done with. What a relief.

Unfortunately, my audition proved too good for my own good. I was elected, unanimously, to play the role of the newscaster at the graduation. Oh, great. The other A-6 boys had not bothered to write notes or to rehearse. They had not taken the audition seriously. I glared at my note cards, wanting to blame something concrete for my unwanted success. Now I knew how a lemming with second thoughts felt after it had leapt from the cliff's edge. My note cards stared back, feigning innocence.

On graduation day, the auditorium seats were filled with parents, relatives, family friends. They leafed noisily through their programs. The lights came up, and the school principal welcomed the audience to the winter graduation of sixth graders of 39th Street Elementary School. I stood at attention next to the cardboard television and joined the audience in pledging our allegiance to the American flag, which stood on one side of the auditorium stage. On the opposite side stood the flag of the State of California. Mrs. McConnell rose to say a few words. Then the show began.

I found my way to the folding chair within the darkened cardboard television console, a small table in front of me holding the script containing the news. At each of Mrs. McConnell's cues, I flipped a switch turning on a hidden floodlight and proceeded to report a segment of news from the last year or so. The floodlight illuminated my face, while also providing sufficient light to allow me to read from the script. The first cue was given, the switch flipped, and—voila! The cardboard box was startled into light and sound. *Good evening, friends, from coast to coast. This is George Uba with the news.*

The graduation production proved to be a hit. Ronald Degnan had won the soloist's competition. Ronald was one of several Negroes in the B-6. Skinny and relatively small, he hitched his pants high on his waist. He was not husky and athletic like Bernard Campbell, and he was not like that girl in the fifth grade, who, on religious grounds, refused to go to the nurse's office on the day she took sick. He seemed like a regular guy. But when he finished his song, a gospel-like melody, the audience erupted in applause. I listened in awe. Never had I heard such a beautiful, powerful voice. Ronald Degnan was a boy opera star. The cheering and applause went on for what seemed like minutes.

The other highlight of the graduation apparently, and remarkably, was the newscaster. Switching on the lamp for each broadcast segment, I started with the same words. "Good evening, friends, from coast to coast. This is George Uba with the news." I mentioned events during Eisenhower's second presidential term and discussed the new Russian premier, Vladimir Khrushchev. I reported on U.S. Marines being ordered into Lebanon to restore order there. (It seemed America was fighting the scourge of communism everywhere.) I did not know what to make of politics, exactly. Ever since the internment, which occurred under a Democratic president, my parents had favored Republicans. Therefore, I was a Republican. My "I like Ike" button was somewhere in my desk drawer at home.

But I reported on other things too, including events that could be acted out, or at least celebrated, on stage. The USS *Nautilus* had crossed directly below the North Pole (wow). The hula hoop craze had swept across America (cue the stage). Alaska had officially become the nation's forty-ninth state (cue the stage). Each time the stage curtain swung open, I switched off my newscaster's floodlight, as other class members proceeded to act out roles relating to the event.

Interspersed with the reenactments, there was choral singing and also a Mexican hat dance number, where I had to climb onstage and join in to make the number of dancers come out evenly. Returning to the television, I reported on civil rights in the South, the Supreme Court having previously ruled that schools in Little Rock, Arkansas, had to be integrated. I was not quite sure of all that the civil rights movement entailed, but I was in favor. I was a proponent (a recent vocabulary word) of civil rights.

At the conclusion of the production, the entire class gathered on stage, drawing enthusiastic applause. Much of the applause seemed directed toward the newscaster in his cardboard television. The evening had been enjoyable after all, and as time passed, I had grown comfortable in my public speaking role. Even if I had not shown the marketable talents of a Ronald Degnan, I had had a starring place in the graduation ceremony. Compliments from the parents of my friends and even from parents I did not know rained down upon me. I exulted. My parents were proud.

Above all, I was free, free to move upward and onward from this point forward. Rid forever of Mrs. McConnell's teasing. Life was glorious. Leaving the auditorium with my parents, I glanced back at the California state flag. Somewhere in its folds prowled a grown bear, a big confident bear, burlier than that boy Alan who was nice to me in a pinch, a bear striding boldly into the future.

To mark my graduation, Mother made one of her special meals. From the sizzle in the frying pan, I knew what awaited. My favorite, Mother's fried chicken, crisp on the outside, savory and moist within. Instead of peas, there were green beans, delightfully salted with bits of fried bacon. We used a *shamoji*, a flat, lacquered Japanese paddle, to serve the white rice. It was late by the time we all gathered around the dining table and Mother said grace. As an extra treat, a homemade cake with lots of frosting sat on the sideboard, and ice cream waited in the freezer. I declared firmly that this was "the best meal I have ever had," even though it was exactly the same meal I had asked for just months before on my eleventh birthday and, for that matter, on my tenth birthday too. As I drifted toward sleep that night, I felt a surge of confidence. From here on out, life would be smooth sailing.

14

NIGHT BEFORE NOON

THREE MOTHERLESS KIDS.

This was the caption Mother assigned the photograph in the album. The three children are hunched together, the two older ones with arms wrapped protectively around the one in the middle, who looks well-fed but too young to grasp the import of losing a mother.

In the photograph, Mary wears a sweater outfit with stripes, Florence a calico-style dress, and Freddie a sweater vest and short pants. The sisters look somber despite Florence's attempt at a smile, as if they appreciate that tomorrow comes masked and threatening. It was 1928, and their mother, Haruko, had been dead for just over one year. Florence had stopped taking voice lessons. The days of following her mother room to room, traipsing around the boarding house, a small laundry basket in hand, all the while singing to make her mother smile, had ceased.

For some time after Haruko died, Issei dropped by, toting baskets of food for the grieving family. The hakujin men exchanged handshakes rather than bows with Joe, but there were no embraces between the adult Issei, no motherly hugs for the children. Issei seldom touched one another to extend sympathy or to express grief. Mourning required space not compression. One woman brought a box of *manju*, the Japanese confection. Mary brewed tea and served the pieces of manju prettily arranged on a tray. After just one bite, Florence knew the manju were stale.

Year after year, she preserved photographs, pressing the decades between the covers of picture albums. For the annual family Christmas photos, the poses never changed, only the sizes of Laura's dresses and of Bryan's and my suits. Mother reminded everyone to say "cheese."

THE BODY IS OVER 90 PERCENT WATER. It is an ocean containing uncountable numbers of small blind facts, which sometimes interfere with each other's operations, sometimes collide, creating a mess. No, it isn't. It's maybe 60 percent water, the body. But like any body of water, it is filled with danger, with treachery.

Mother has cancer.

There was the initial banter with Kats. *You'll have to learn how to boil water.* To us children, she assigned chores in a voice soft and patient. It was her Skokie voice, the one that read the stories and poems and folktales night after night from the volumes of Childcraft.

NOTHING BETTER HAPPEN TO ME, he had said. There it was again. What he had said after Haruko died, what echoed in the children's ears after the market crashed. After the family had left Brawley, Mary helped Papa find the rental in Pasadena, not far from the Colorado Street Bridge. Built in 1912 and celebrated by civil engineers and architects alike, the bridge rests on a set of regal, barrel-shaped arches, which add to the impression that it is sweeping above the surrounding landscape in a grand vertiginous wave. From early on, it had earned the nickname, "Suicide Bridge."

Especially during the Depression, life stranded many a family's future, much against the will of its members, on the ledge of that bridge. If something had happened to Papa, the weight and momentum of that tragedy would have hurled tomorrow off the railing, plunging it into the arroyo far, far below. But Papa was the nail that life's vicissitudes might bend but not break. With age, he gathered rust, but he also retained the tensile strength of his determined youth. He had meant what he said, but he had had every intention to live.

To any child, death can be less abstract than grownups like to think. During homeroom, the principal's voice came over the intercom bearing "very sad news." It was September, the start of my A-7 semester at Audubon Junior High and less than six months before I learned what the word "biopsy" meant. Mr. Kaplan reported that a ninth-grade girl, a girl elected to student office no less, had died over the summer in a tragic automobile accident while vacationing with her family in Italy. I did not know the girl, in fact retained scant memory of the spring elections for student government. I had never imagined travel to Italy, a place on a newsreel, a place of winding mountain passes, of dense traffic circles, of ancient statues and crumbling monuments. A faraway country that a family returned from with colorful stories and vivid memories. Where members of the 442nd landed at Anzio and where "Mussolini," who "was a wienie," once ruled.

For a long time, I reflected on the tragic fate of the girl traveling with her family on vacation in a foreign land. Adults say kids never think about death. That they believe they are immortal. Adults say stupid things. Two years earlier, I spent days pondering the news that Paul Nakasuji's little brother Kenny had died after an illness. I never met Kenny, but Paul's family lived on Olmsted, the next block over from Westside, and anyway Paul was the kindest boy I had ever met, and his parents were nice too. Why did people die young? Why did the unlucky few close their eyes forever, while others were allowed to shout and play on the sun-glistened playground?

BRYAN WAS PUT IN CHARGE OF DINNER. Mother delegated more and more responsibility to him, as the eldest. Following the initial appointment with Dr. Shigekawa in Little Tokyo, and after all the tests and the subsequent meetings with a cancer specialist, Mother understood the upcoming surgery and the treatment options available to a patient with advanced breast cancer, which had spread to her lymph nodes. She was six months shy of turning forty.

Bryan never groused. For most dinners, he followed familiar recipes but sometimes added a dash of surprise. As he experimented with salt and pepper, with cardamom and basil and curry powder, he exhibited a degree of natural culinary talent. He only recoiled at being put in charge.

At fourteen, his best friend was Solitude, his ontological ally, Chaos. At school, Bryan was wayward, often perverse. He liked the role of gadfly disrupting premises, enjoyed staking out odd (yet intriguing) positions. Teachers seldom were inclined to praise him for his originality. Most repaid him with modest grades. Semester by semester, his report cards succeeded in turning Mother livid. She and Father scolded him for not trying harder.

Years later when he attended college, he majored in economics but excelled at bowling. He spent much of his quality time boning up on jazz musicians like Art Tatum and Miles Davis and leafing through the rebellious utterances of poets like Ginsberg and Ferlinghetti and Gregory Corso.

BEFORE SHE WENT IN FOR SURGERY, Mother took us aside one by one. *If anything happens, if I die, I want you to know I love you.*

I sent prayers, volleys of prayers, to God. I asked God to spare Mother and promised to be a better person, more cooperative and cheerful. I was proposing a deal. Quid pro quo. My hands were clasped, they prayed for favors, for positive outcomes, to God, a pair of liquid eyes, a pair of attentive ears, right there beyond the ceiling and outside the roof, watching, listening, alert as an owl. Climbing out of bed, I knelt, my elbows resting upon the bedcovers, my knees pointing at the hard shock of the floor. The attitude and position of the supplicant. At times, the image of medieval self-flagellants supplanted the image of monks at meditation. But I had to stay focused. If not, I must start again. Leave nothing out.

Before I slept, I worried about the dream. It had happened twice. It resembled what I had seen in real life, except for the ending. In the dream, a car sped along a divided highway and flipped, just like the car that actually flipped off the interstate, landing upside down in the grassy ravine that served as the median between the two opposing lines of traffic. We had witnessed the accident, or rather witnessed its immediate aftermath, while traveling on vacation. Father had stopped the family car on the opposite shoulder, where several other vehicles had come to a halt, their drivers intent on rendering aid. Mother warned us children to remain inside as other cars nosed by.

From under the smashed roof of his car, a middle-aged man climbed out, stood up, and proceeded to wave his hands. He was the lone occupant, and miraculously he had survived, apparently unscathed. Father muttered something about speeding motorists, as he climbed back into our car. Soon we drove off.

In the dream, the car launched itself into the air, spiraling headfirst, its body like a fuselage falling toward the grassy median. Who was inside? The middle-aged man waving his hands? The poor girl vacationing in Italy? Who? I had awakened midspin, the sweat crawling across my neck, dampening my pajamas at my chest. The car had entered its flip, this much I was able to recall. Morning prevailed, slamming shut the outcome. And in any case, I did not wish to reenter the dream and see it to its end.

MOTHER SURVIVED SURGERY, cutting the breast, removing lymph nodes. But it was not over. She started the radiation treatments and the meds, the nausea and exhaustion having at her, taking turns. Again and again and yet again she returned to the hospital or the medical offices—this doctor, that doctor, this procedure, that one. When she came home, she had just enough energy to find the bed. Automatically, when we children returned from school, we left loud talk on the driveway, lowered our voices, spoke in whispers, trod silently through the hallway and past Mother's bedroom, where the door remained shut, the room encased in darkness.

What was certain was that the house was wrapped in disease. Quiet prevailed. Not a severe quiet, nor a comfortable one. A mortuary quiet.

Each time Mother prepared for another trip to the hospital, she took us aside.

Laura.

Mother and Father were not about to name their daughter Haruko or to saddle any of their children with hard-to-pronounce Japanese names. Not even our middle names would be Japanese. Laura, the only girl in a house full of boys. Laura, barely older than Mother was when her own mother died.

"If I die," Mother advised each time, there being no need to mince the facts. "If I die," she said this time before reentering the hospital, "I want you to join the Joy Bells."

It was a girl's club sponsored by the church. Laura knew the members. When Sunday school ended, the girls talked earnestly about blouses and skirts. They gabbed about the latest hairstyles and the best-scented hair spray. Laura had little interest in these matters. Big-boned, already half a head taller than her girlfriends, Laura did not walk like most girls, did not talk like most girls. I recruited her to ride shotgun when I pretended to drive the Wells Fargo stagecoach. I drafted her to play tetherball because I always won. I tried to get her to talk sternly to Blackie as part of the dog's obedience training. For her part, Laura tried to adopt our sports argot, our analyses of the White Sox and the Bears, the recent arrival of the Dodgers in Los Angeles.

Up to a point, Laura could play along either at school or church with the girls who stifled their own intelligence, afraid of it, encouraged by others, even by their parents, not to look too smart or to show up the boys. Up to a point. She had no interest in useless small talk or gossip, could never abide girls behaving like mindless piglets at the sight of boys. Her mind grasped the bigger picture, always. Already she knew about the Cuban Revolution and the new astronaut program. Ask her about the Nixon-Khrushchev kitchen debate, go ahead, you'd see. But don't waste her time gushing over pedal pushers and T-straps.

It was not her fault that Laura preferred friends like Dena Hing, who never wasted time in gossip. Still, Mother worried lest her daughter develop a propensity to say exactly what she thought. Outspokenness was not becoming of a girl. She wondered if someone like Dena might prove to be a positive example, a girl who maybe could straddle the fine line between female intelligence and intelligent femininity, even when pestered by boys. But Dena did not belong to the Joy Bells. Dena was Chinese.

Both Mother and Father liked it that their daughter stayed informed. When they told each of us that as adults, "you can be anything you want to be," they really meant it, and they did not exclude Laura. What Mother could not stand was the thought of those boy-crazy Sansei girls who got themselves in trouble as teenagers. The thought was more than repugnant; it was horrifying, intolerable.

That was why pricey, conservative dresses from I. Magnin and Bullocks Wilshire filled my sister's closet, rather than the sporty, flirtatious outfits taken off the racks at Broadway or May Company. That was why, long after an orthopedic surgeon recommended shoes with strong support to deal with Laura's foot problems, Mother insisted that she continue to wear white socks and saddle shoes, even as her friends experimented with stockings and flats.

But therein lay the problem. It was such a male-centered household. If she were gone, how could her daughter learn, in time, to be a lady? That was where the Joy Bells came in. They were good girls, who also knew how to *be* girls. Even I worried out loud about my sister, insisting that Laura's shoes looked clunky.

The pressure to straighten out her children before it was too late was intense, but it was all that kept the terror in check. Guidance and control, control and guidance. This was her charge, her charge as a mother, a Nisei mother. Some community members behaved irresponsibly, hurting the greater cause. This she knew. She heard things, heard plenty. Moms who went bowling three, four, five times a week, who were more interested in checking league averages than their children's report cards. Moms who drank, who were on a first-name basis with the bartenders at Holiday Bowl.

No wonder their kids dressed the way they did, stayed out unsupervised at all hours. Sansei girls barely twelve or thirteen wearing thick makeup and provocative clothes. Secretly, I found them alluring, but Mother was convinced that they were tempting fate and, worse, soiling a hard-earned reputation. Mother reminded us that Japanese Americans had the lowest crime rate of any race in America. I took pride in this assertion but did not ask out loud about her sources.

Mother's condition improved. Her condition worsened. She was in remission. She needed more meds. She definitely looked stronger. No, she was exhausted. The doctors' appointments were frequent, the treatments mysterious and endless. If doctors were gods, they would be the performers spinning porcelain plates on sticks, expertly catching their wobble and respinning the plates an instant before they toppled and fell, toppled and shattered into pieces. Quick! Got it! They would be the ones spinning an entire roomful of plates dizzily on sticks. Yes, they would, if they were gods.

Every night, Mother prayed to the real God, even nights her body felt ravaged, her eyes swelling with grief, her will to live, her will to guide the lives of her children until they reached adulthood the only things suppressing the hurt. Her prayers did not complain about the life that God, hallowed be His name, had passed down to her, but they did contain a rebuke, a tacit one, to parental neglect, the principle of desertion, the stark indifference of death. Only love steeped in bitterness could feel this unrelenting. Only bitterness seared by love could feel so raw.

Misery had given no warning with Mummy, had lain in wait, until out of nowhere, teeth bared, it had leapt. It hadn't its fill.

15

A BOY SCOUT OF JAPANESE AMERICA,
PART I—A MINOR DROWNING INCIDENT

I WAS FLOATING AIMLESSLY in the deep end of the pool. On my back, on my belly, the water held me in feathered arms and a heavy odor of chlorine. I drifted past the eight-foot marker, the six-foot marker, drifted toward the shallow end, relaxed, secure, easily buoyed, scarcely moving my arms and legs. Despite the summer temperatures, the water at altitude remained cold, and by now nearly all of the other boys had climbed out of the pool and wandered off into the quiet remainder of the afternoon. To the west, the sun poked through the openings in the trees, which released a piney scent.

I floated directly into the peculiar sensation I felt whenever I embarked on a camping trip or first stepped into a gymnasium beneath the glare of its lights—the sensation that I was both there and not there at the same time. It was not déjà vu. Nor the period between sleeping and waking. It was the feeling of simultaneously inhabiting and not inhabiting reality. I knew exactly where I was (at the Boy Scout summer camp above Lake Arrowhead) and what I was doing (nothing), but at the same time I slipped outside of myself. Weird. For several moments I closed my eyes. Under the Bodhi Tree, the Buddha must have closed his eyes to better see.

When the powerful weight pressed down and down, gathering strength and intensity, I felt my body surging deeper into a dream. But the dream shattered when my body realized that the descent was real, something above gaining leverage and thrust. I did not have my glasses with me. Underwater the world blurred. The black lines marking the swim lanes wiggled into view.

They drew closer, became savagely distinct. The pressure intensified. I could not rise, could not regain the surface, where the air, which is always blind to human struggle, awaited.

TROOP 636 OF THE LOS ANGELES AREA COUNCIL of the Boy Scouts of America was sponsored by the Senshin Buddhist Church. The church's location on 36th Street, just off of Normandie Avenue, allowed the troop to draw members from a wide geographical arc extending west and southwest from downtown between West Adams Boulevard and Exposition Boulevard and through the whole of the Crenshaw District. At its height, Troop 636 was comprised of eight individual patrols and surpassed sixty members, easily doubling or even tripling the size of most other Scout troops.

All of the troop members were Sansei, although a substantial number were not Buddhist but Protestant. At least one or two were Catholic, another a Seventh Day Adventist, who did not eat meat. Bryan preferred to classify himself as Other. None of it made any real difference to the troop members, since religious observations, just like being reverent, the twelfth of the Scout Laws, consisted primarily of benedictions offered at the start of troop meetings and at the semiannual Courts of Honor. What mattered was that Scouting had deep and widespread roots in Japanese American communities, including in the internment camps, and it exerted a powerful social influence. Its intention was to turn Sansei boys into the right kind of men.

The adult leadership was composed of volunteers. It was composed of Nisei fathers who came from various walks of life but met on a common ground of experience—the shared shock of national revulsion, of racial rejection, relocation, and resettlement. Not that they dwelt on it. Like the energetic V-8s that filled the roadways, they left the past in the unmentioned past, the obstacles of history in the wake of present-day advancement and future success. The image of American boyhood, which combined healthy outdoor activities with lessons in discipline and citizenship, was easy to embrace. Sons should be physically strong, mentally awake, and morally straight.

There should be carryover at school, where the boys should study hard, obtain good grades, attend college, and marry a nice Japanese American girl. For some boys, good citizenship, academic success, and Scout values constituted too narrow a strait to swim through. Adolescents are slippery as eels. Some take dangerous byways or move against the main current. But the fathers, they remained firm, their intentions unwavering. They would see to it that their sons' lives turned out less arduous, less toilsome, and less susceptible to discrimination than the ones they and their own parents had experienced. For these Sansei boys, the word "camp" would refer to summer camp only, a time of spirited fun and practical learning.

Having brainy daughters was fine too, as long as it did not interfere with their marriage prospects. In school, the boys were urged to take classes in trigonometry, calculus, physics, even if their inclinations lay elsewhere and even when girls—and it happened with regularity—outperformed them in science and math.

FOR ME, SWIMMING POOL ENLIGHTENMENT ARRIVED in the form of a prox-imate truth. A pair of hands connected to a pair of arms was pressing down from above. With no opportunity to snatch a quick breath of air before being thrust beneath the surface, I started to panic. Be prepared! No, I was not. My narrow shoulders, sticklike arms, and thin torso made me easy prey. Lungs bursting, I could not last for long.

Bryan was nowhere around. I had always wanted him to be like televi-sion's Wally Cleaver, ever protective, ever on the lookout for the kid brother. There was the time when we were little boys and I accidentally released the helium-filled balloon Mother had bought for me at a local fair. Instantly, its short string took off and the balloon soared beyond reach, lifting high and far into the dusk. I watched in shock, then dismay, and I started to cry. Quickly, Bryan, who was only five or six, soothed me by giving me his own balloon. Being weird did not mean one could not be kind.

This water also felt weird. I could have used a pair of helium-filled bal-loons right then to help me fend off the water's thousand arms and ten thou-sand spiny fingers. Fingers reaching for me like a friend inexplicably trans-formed into a foe. Come. Stay. Take one breath. It was a dare. A summons. I was drowning, how odd. The summers spent at Roy's Swim School—what good were they now? I, who had never wished to be born, wanted nothing more than to live. Then, in a final panic-induced burst of energy, my body squirmed free, and the surface water exploded. Water squirted up my nostrils, and I gasped for breath.

Air! Air! I spun around, my chest heaving, my body in revolt. It was hard to make out faces. The water shot stakes through my eyes. Then I saw the per-petrator. Eugene, a boy in Bryan's Sioux Patrol, the one who had a fistfight with his own dad during a patrol meeting, had been holding me underwater. Eugene, needing an audience, was with a pal. Eugene was laughing. It was as if he had never seen anything so hysterical, and indeed perhaps there was something comically absurd in the picture. What a gag. It was just five damn feet of water!

He was only a year or so older than I, but Eugene knew how to target someone smaller, weaker, how to alleviate the inadequacies he was constantly made to feel behind the shadow of an admired older brother and under the pressures of a demanding father. Picture this minnow of a kid struggling, flopping about, oxygen-deprived, unable to extricate himself. The moment was exhilarating.

"Oh, look, he's gonna cry!"

For once, I really wanted to fight. Maybe it was the adrenaline coursing through my veins. Maybe the fear. I flung my fist in a furious arc, which sent a spray of water into the air. It was impossible to secure solid footing, and the fist missed its target. At first, Eugene laughed again. But his companion did not. Eugene had gone too far this time. Furious, I lunged at the boy a second time, swinging for real, Eugene's friend catching me before I was able to connect. Yeah, it had gotten out of hand. He'd gone too far. I broke free and swung a third time, just grazing the air in front of Eugene's chin. If only my arm were longer, my fist bigger, the water less restricting. Then an adult said, What's going on? Break it up. The fray was broken up.

All three of us climbed out of the water. No one was smiling now. No one was joking. I detested Eugene, who had a habit of openly mocking Bryan because Bryan was different from others. I hated it when my brother shrugged off the snide remarks, already indifferent, deaf, immune, but ready to take poker money from all comers, including Eugene. I detested Eugene. Perhaps he had made me a target in the first place because he had sensed my disdain.

Eugene never attempted to drown me again, not because he feared my fists but because the element of surprise was lost and the fun drained off. The few remaining Scouts were shouting and fooling around, already oblivious to the minor drama that had played out. I wanted to melt into the trees. It was the pine trees that bore witness to my unspoken desire, the lofty, imperturbable pines with their thick scallops of bark. High in the mountains, they released an intoxicating scent.

TO BE CLEAR, I WAS NOT THE VICTIM. The incident embarrassed me a little, but I had been bullied in the past, and I remembered the time I joined with others to bully someone else. That was the year before I joined the Scouts, while I was still in the Gray-Y at the West Adams Christian Church. Verbally tormented, that boy ran all the way home in the dark. Overcome all at once with shame, I followed the lead of the other boys, and we went off, a pack of us, to make things right. We found our way to the house, and we discovered the boy huddled in a corner of his bed, a blanket drawn to his chin. We apologized, sincerely. But the boy never returned to the club.

It would take several years and a bad outcome before I fully grasped how much a victim Eugene was. Eugene was a bad boy, a troublemaker, a renegade. But he also was the victim of circumstance. The circumstance of a father's desperate love, of a father's intense determination to send a wayward in the right direction, to force a son to comply.

An owner and operator of a prominent Japanese American mortuary, Eugene's father was a big man with big hands, which wielded a pocket knife with all the exacting artistry and sensitive restraint the owner of those hands lacked with his son. Out of scraps of wood, the knife whittled intricate neckerchief holders in the form of dolphins and owls and bears. Were he to carve King Neptune, the face would have been that of Eugene's older brother Rodger, a bellwether, a respected leader, an exemplary student, a boy steeped in accomplishment. Friendly and neither mean nor condescending, Rodger was genuinely liked and admired. It read like a biblical parable, two brothers operating under the demands and high expectations of a stern but loving father.

Except that the outcome departed from the original script. Eugene did not remain in the Boy Scouts. He disappeared. In the summer of 1965, there occurred that uprising in the South Central sectors of Los Angeles, six days of violence and protest, which newscasters and reporters quickly labeled the Watts Riot. As the inner city filled with gunshots and was consumed with raging fires, thirty-four people perished. One of them was Eugene.

The rumor circulated that he was looting a store during the height of the chaos when he got shot by a cop. That was the rumor that circulated widely in the Japanese American community. Who could say for sure? Many people distrusted newspaper accounts as much as they did police reports. What was certain was that Eugene did not survive the gunshot wound. At eighteen, he was shot dead.

It was grotesque, the thought that kept recurring. Like a rubber bullet that kept deflecting, but only for so long before it penetrated the skin. I imagined feeling the bullet entering my own body, imagined the blood spurting from the wound and the precise moment when I knew with a certainty fueled with sorrow that it was all over, all over for me and for the hoped-for future that a father had once sought to shape out of a petrified scrap of wood. *I'm a kid, and I'm actually dying.* It would be a weird, uncanny, elusive feeling. Almost like being there and not being there at the same time.

16

A BOY SCOUT OF JAPANESE AMERICA,

PART II—VALOR

Navigating the streets of Boyle Heights in East Los Angeles presented a challenge every Memorial Day. Cars filled both sides of Brooklyn and 1st and clogged the side streets near the entrance to Evergreen Cemetery. But once we got inside, the area reserved for Japanese was easy to spot. A tall, narrow column still juts above the surrounding grave markers. At its pinnacle stands a statue of a Nisei soldier, whose face looks too young for its uniform, like that of someone barely reaching high school, although Sadao Munemori was twenty-two when he died.

Munemori, who was born in Los Angeles and had become an auto mechanic after graduating high school, received the Medal of Honor for valor in combat, fighting with the 442nd Regimental Combat Team in Italy. After single-handedly taking out a pair of German machine gun nests, he died falling on a hand grenade to save his buddies. Just as in the movies, except that in the movies it was always a white guy making the sacrifice and usually a Japanese who had lobbed the grenade.

Munemori's memorial, along with that of three other recipients of the Medal of Honor, fronts a large collection of headstones marked in Japanese kanji and in English. These are the headstones of Issei, like Father's father, in whose memory Mother plotted out the annual family pilgrimage dating back to Father's discharge from the army. For many years prior to the war, Evergreen was the only municipal cemetery not refusing burial space to Japanese. In the previous century, it had been a potter's field for the indigent. Although Mother had never met her father-in-law, the yearly trip to Evergreen was obligatory. As we paused in front of Senpachi Uba's headstone, the moment felt both awkward and solemn. Mother said, "Well, we should probably say a prayer," and for half a minute or so, silently, we did.

Beneath the long brave shadow cast by Sadao Munemori, imagery of Japanese Americans in uniform was inspiring. I remembered the photograph featuring Father and Uncle Toshio, two brothers nearly of different generations, but both serving in the military. There was no doubting Father's courage, but it was difficult to imagine him hurtling his body forward in a zigzag sprint toward a machine gun nest. More likely, he would have assessed the situation and begun inching forward on his belly. Maybe if Uncle Toshio had been old enough to serve during the war, something would have pissed him off, and he would have set off in a one-man charge against the German entrenchment.

My own uniform belonged unmistakably to a boy. In the early years, I had relished wearing it and marching in formation, left-right, left-right, column left, column right. In the early years, I had enjoyed displaying the paraphernalia for every Court of Honor, the cap angled just so, the troop-identifying kerchief looped around the neck, the uniform adorned with troop insignia and with patches commemorating different camping experiences and signifying individual rank. There had been a time when I had watched with envy as the older boys paraded in white spats above their spit-shined shoes, a sash boasting rows of merit badges draped across their chests.

Not now. Camping had taught me practical skills—using a compass, identifying plants, tying a variety of knots, starting a fire with flint and steel—but I had tired of Scouting, did not like to wear the uniform. Girls seemed unimpressed by it. My sights were set on college. I had been accepted to USC and UCLA, and I could choose which one to attend. Maybe USC, where I could follow in Father's footsteps and become a dentist.

Upon returning home from my last Court of Honor, I hung my uniform on a pair of hangers and spread my merit badge sash across my bed. I had to admit to myself that the colorful round merit badges looked impressive: Swimming, Nature, First Aid, and so on. I particularly liked the one for Athletics, which consisted of a wing. What if there had been a Bully Prevention merit badge? I pictured myself moving among five-year-olds, separating the bully from his victims, consoling those victims, offering wise counsel to the bully, who eagerly awaited his reform. Do a good turn daily.

But if the requirement for that merit badge had required hard blows, kicking and wrestling on the ground, if it required a fistfight with some teenager who liked to mix it up, the merit badge would not have been easy to obtain. Grownups were fond of saying bullies are just cowards. All you have to do is stand up to them. That was not always true. There were some bullies who liked fighting, who excelled at inflicting pain. Of course, Sadao Munemori would have earned his Bully Prevention merit badge *presto*, just like that.

From the uniform, I unfastened the new medal, with its stern eagle head and red, white, and blue ribbon. I inspected the medal closely. It was a serious medal, weighty and handsome. If it could speak, no doubt it would offer words as brave as its own smart appearance. Alongside it, I placed the Eagle patch, which could be sewn permanently onto the breast pocket of the uniform. But it wouldn't be. For within a few weeks, I would quit Scouting.

Already, membership in both Boy Scout Troop 636 and Explorer Post 636 had begun to decline, the new decade signaling an inexorable shift in interests among Sansei youth. Attitudes had changed. Hostilities previously suppressed occasionally spilled into the open. Before a competition at an area Camporee, I had overheard a troop member say derisively, "I wanna beat those Gray Boys." I had never heard the term, but immediately I grasped its racial inflection, knew that it referred to Caucasian boys from a suburban Scout troop. I had heard the term "white boys" used in a derogatory manner and "white people" used in a neutral way.

I had lots of hakujin friends at school, and I prided myself on eschewing racial epithets. At the same time, I recognized the potency of words intended to denigrate, even when I did not know exactly where they came from or what they meant. Why would a Caucasian be "gray"? Did it have to do with the Civil War? Epithets directed at Japanese I had heard all my life. Epithets going the other way I had heard less frequently. But I knew that their usage was a legacy of Which camp were your folks in? Where were you born since it could not have been in Los Angeles? It was a legacy of housing covenants and of white flight to the suburbs, of opinion polls urging the repatriation of all Japanese by a margin of ten to one.

Over the past year, a new set of adult leaders had sought to restore interest in the Scout troop and the Explorer post. They had exerted pressure on us older boys to hasten our advancement in rank. Having lots of Eagle Scouts was a potential selling point. Peeved at the evident lack of enthusiasm for their directive, one adult leader had issued an ultimatum. Finish up or clear out. My decision had been to do both.

Now I returned the Eagle Scout medal to its plastic box and secured it in my bureau. There had been a time when it all mattered so much, just as I once had dreamed of serving gallantly in a medal-bedecked uniform of the United States Fifth Army. That was before finding out that my eyesight was so poor, it qualified me as 4-F.

Later I would open the bureau drawer and from time to time inspect the medal. It was a neat medal. The merit badge sash I folded and put away. Eventually, it vanished, along with the uniform and cap, the belt with its Scout emblem, the dress spats for the Courts of Honor, and the Eagle Scout patch. For a long time, I kept track of the medal lodged in the corner of the bureau, until years and years later, it too, tired of its confinement, took wing and flew away.

A year or so earlier, I did gain one distinction. I was elected to join the Order of the Arrow, an honor bestowed upon Scouts demonstrating leadership qualities and camping skills. In truth, I could think of nothing I had done to distinguish myself for my camping ability, although by now I had attended more than two dozen camping trips, summer camps, and district-wide Camporees. My one special talent was being able to raise an axe high into the air and bring it down sharply on the head of a match lodged upright into a log—thereby lighting the match. The talent won points at the Camporees, but it was hardly a practical skill.

Before I was elected to the Order of the Arrow, I had joined Explorer Post 636. One Scout from each troop or Explorer post in the greater Los Angeles Area Council was elected per year. Initiation in the Order of the Arrow required surviving the Ordeal, which consisted of subsisting for one night alone in the mountains with just a drop cloth, a sleeping bag, a knife, and a canteen of water—plus enduring twenty-four hours of silence and reflection. Thereafter, at future ceremonies, including Courts of Honor, the inductee was allowed to wear the Order of the Arrow sash, across whose white background was emblazoned a brilliant crimson arrow.

Days before setting out with other Scouts from across the Los Angeles Area Council to brave the Ordeal, I learned that my pal, Mike Nakayama, might have tampered with the election. Compact and fearless but always with a ready grin, Mike often hung out at his grandma's house across the street from me. An erstwhile member of the Sioux Patrol, Mike was a spoonful of mischief, who also knew how to handle himself. He was a trickster, a shenanigan waiting to occur, and I, without knowing it, became his latest accomplice.

Taking me aside, he confided, "I stuffed the ballot box!" The air rushed from the blimp of my ego. Mike's grin broke into full laughter. He had pulled one off again! Of course, he may have been joking, he liked to joke around. I did not know. But I was not about to snitch. After all, who would be the one left looking stupid, a *bakatare*? I went home feeling glum.

Nothing calamitous occurred during the Ordeal. No boy got stranded on a ledge or abandoned in a ravine. No boy, finding himself lost and forgotten, was forced to examine moss on a tree to discover which way was true north. No one tripped over a slippery rock, breaking a leg and requiring a makeshift splint and a stretcher. Everyone survived. There were a few mosquito bites. During the night alone, I quickly fell asleep beneath the big pines and the starry sky.

Observing the hours of silence during the Ordeal was easy. More difficult were the orders to carve an arrow out of a piece of wood, which required a certain amount of dexterity with a knife. We initiates were also provided with materials to glue sets of artificial feathers onto a black cardboard shield. No one explained exactly why we were pretending to be Indians except that everyone knew that camping in the woods, shooting arrows, and donning Eagle feathers were things Indians were supposed to do. A real Indian would have scoffed at my arrow, useless either for hunting or battle. During the long period of silence, I reflected on my friend Mike, the one who tested boundaries, who confidently broke rules. Secretly, I envied him, wondered what it would be like to have his nerve.

NERVE WAS WHAT MIKE NAKAYAMA needed plenty of when, just a few years later, as the Vietnam War ramped up, he was ushered into the United States Marine Corps. Mike told the story of how, during basic training, the drill instructor singled him out in front of the other members of his platoon.

C'mere recruit. The drill instructor pulled Mike to the front. *This is what a Gook looks like!*

What the hell? Are you shittin' me?

Nerve was what Mike showed plenty of in Vietnam. Despite his growing cynicism about the military, about the war, he became a bona fide war hero. On battlefields, he faced ordeals, real ones, suffered battle wounds, life threatening. His unit worked as a team, and he received medals for gallantry. Fortunately, he did not become another lamented battlefield casualty, remembered afterwards with a flag-draped coffin or, like Sadao Munemori, with a stone statue permanently standing guard over an acre or two of graves.

Something in Mike—certainly something far beyond the training he experienced in the Scouts—helped him to survive and endure with true valor the brutality and terrors of actual combat. When he returned to the States, he had changed. The mischief had evaporated. Mike Nakayama became a community activist, a respected voice in the anti-war movement.

17

A GLIMMER OF LIGHT

Normalcy returned to the household by degrees. It was not a fulfill-
ment like the swallows reappearing at the Mission at San Juan Capist-
rano, which the television newscasts faithfully recorded in panorama and in
close-ups. More like jaybirds bickering at first light. *It's mine! No, it's mine! I
was here first! No, I was!*

We children managed our squabbles, but seldom did we share. Quickly
we learned that we were on our own for breakfast and lunch. No one said,
"I'm frying eggs, do you want some?" We waited our turns at the frying pan.
Laura, at least, prepared sandwiches for Father's lunch. After two or three
months, he asked her if she might apply some mustard to the sandwich. In
the evenings, we ate the dinners Bryan prepared. We ate in silence, not because we were mad about something but because we had nothing in particular to say. Father cautioned Bryan about gulping his food and milk. Slow down!

Bryan went to the bedroom and retrieved Mother's dinner tray. *Thank
you, that was delicious.* I was assigned KP. Mother had retained acronyms
from our time at Fort Leonard Wood, and "kitchen patrol" meant washing
and drying dishes, just as SNAFU meant "Situation Normal, All Fouled Up."
I had already guessed that her version of the term was sanitized.

Spring drifted into summer, summer into fall, fall into winter, the seasons indistinct, each a slow thickening, a smothering, like a gradual settling
of the earth's tectonic plates. Mother rejected all of my requests to join friends

on a school team or to attend a club meeting or to remain after school hours at the junior high "for just one thing." How could she rest, let alone recover, if her children were out and about after school, risking injury or, worse, behaving like rowdy Sansei yogore and getting into trouble? No, even ailing, a good Nisei mother knew where her children were at all times. All after-school activities were declared off limits.

On Mother's nightstand were a lamp, a notepad and pen, pill bottles, a cup resting on a doily, and a copper-colored cowbell about four inches high, rhomboid shaped. The cowbell made a tinny sound. Come at once. Mother needed something. Following her first surgery, she displayed her scar. The words "modified radical mastectomy" became part of our everyday vocabulary. She showed where this portion of her chest had been plowed flat.

On television it was different. On *Father Knows Best*, Margaret Anderson was always busy at the stove, an apron tied to her waist, at the very moment—*Ecce Homo!*—Jim Anderson returned from work, hailing her cheerfully day after day. On *Leave it to Beaver*, June Cleaver wore a tailored dress and high heels all morning and night. June was tall and pretty, wore eye shadow and lipstick, not one strand of her hair out of place.

Television moms endured a lot of criticism. But Margaret Anderson was the family's sine qua non, the only one ever seen actually at work. Hers was the imperturbable demeanor that declared that the family would prevail no matter what heap of trouble the son Bud had landed in this time. And June Cleaver never patronized or belittled her sons. She never made fun of Wally's wise-guy pal Eddie Haskell, an easy target, sarcastic and insecure. Critics thought June was dense. But the truth is, she withheld judgment. Neither Margaret Anderson nor June Cleaver ever lost her temper. Best of all, television moms never got sick.

Mother resisted the fate that the biopsy and the troubling X-rays ordained. I was under the impression that she underwent both radiation treatments and chemotherapy almost simultaneously. But I may have been mistaken, for chemotherapy was still in its nascent stages in the treatment of breast cancer. Radiation therapy was what she received at Fort Leonard Wood to treat the calcium deposits on her lung. It was the radiation therapy that had left her allergic to fish, her favorite food. Laura said it had been a pneumonectomy involving the removal of the lower left lobe of the lung. Or did she say it involved a bronchiectasis? From an early age, Laura could absorb the medical information and sort it out. She recounted most facts clearly, I lost them in a haze. The doctors marveled that things were going as well as they were. Mother asked them how she was holding up. They praised her perseverance.

Hope hobbled on, disaster dazed, a survivor leaning on crutches. Mother would not surrender, although she made no attempt to hide pain or to mince suffering through saccharine reassurances. We children must not be misled. She was not cured by any means, she would have us know.

Mostly, she slept. Deep within a pillbox of nightgown, sheets, blanket, and bedcover, she withdrew, slept, commingled with ghosts. Drawn curtains contributed to the gloom. Without makeup, Mother looked completely different from the pretty lady I remembered from Skokie, the one who would slip into a black dinner dress and wear lipstick and earrings and a necklace of luxurious pearls, her youth illumined by the luster of her hair and scented with a touch of perfume. Not this one. This one barely stirred, blanket and bedcover as still as stone.

Through the break in the curtains came a glimmer of late-afternoon light, the room otherwise buried in shadows. She was one of those shadows, weightless beneath the bedcovers, until the shadow acquired form, until her presence was declared in the shallow sounds of her breathing.

How was your day?

Fine.

Help me turn over.

Okay.

Help me up. I want to use the bathroom.

Okay.

Hold the water glass a moment. I must take my medicine.

Okay.

You can go.

Okay.

This is the scar from the mastectomy.

I've seen it.

You kids don't know how much I love you.

I know.

You can go.

Okay.

Give me a massage, would you.

Okay.

On my back. Right there. Thank you. And there.

Can I go?

Yes. Tell Bryan I want to see him.

Okay.

When I departed, I shed the gloom along with the sliver of light. And then I recalled what the light reminded me of. My habit, when I was about four or five, was to slip out of bed and into the hallway late at night, clutching my green-and-white-checkered napping blanket, which I proceeded to spread neatly on the floor outside Mother and Father's bedroom, the edges set parallel with the baseboard. Beneath the mild touch of the light at the far end of the hall, I fell asleep, knowing that long before sunrise, a pair of tender hands discovering me there would collect me like a raisin, store me safely in bed.

I washed my hands, gave them a good hard scrub. I disliked giving the massage, fingers touching flesh. I finished my chores. Bryan entered the kitchen, started to prepare dinner. I started my homework. Damn, there's that bell.

PART IV

————————

LIKE CHILDREN BICKERING

18

WORDS AT WAR

We CHILDREN COULD NEVER PINPOINT the exact moment Mother rejoined the household's routine. For weeks at a time, she remained in bed. Sometimes she slipped out for an hour or two. Sometimes not. But one morning she rematerialized, and after a while, she became a daily presence.

At first, her movements were tentative. A sojourner returning from Aokigahara, the dense forest on the flank of Mount Fuji, might have moved in this way. Aokigahara harbors ghosts of the dead. It is the place where compasses reportedly go mad and where in ancient times the people performed *ubasute*, the practice of abandoning the elderly, those no longer of practical use and another mouth to feed, to die. It's not really true—it's just a legend.

When Mother came back, she was not alone, impatience and anger accompanying her like a pair of spirit watchdogs. Not one day, not one half of a day, went by without Mother finding something to find fault with, something to criticize and correct in her children, to hurriedly fix. Her children complied silently except for me. I had turned thirteen, then fourteen, my temper managed at school but barely contained at home. Mother released the dogs, and soon, to the consternation of the rest of the family, she was snapping at me and I was quickly responding in kind.

We made a pair, mother and son, a pair of children screaming and yelling, our fury unchecked. Mother had the good sense to shut the windows one by one so the neighbors could not hear the two of us at war. I hurried after her, throwing the windows open again. We took turns, slamming the windows shut, slamming them open, the bad words and the family secrets blistering the air, the neighbors left reeling in shock.

When not enveloped in fury, I recalled the old days when I tried so hard to behave. The old days like the old cartoons, where a devilish elf perched on one shoulder, a good angel on the other, the two of them locked in a Manichean struggle. Sometimes the bad angel posed as the figure of Retribution. Back and forth it patrolled, vigilant, tempestuous, alert as a trigger. Its moral position was complex, often dubious, but its outrage was not to be denied. It whispered in my ear. *That's not fair! Don't take it! Strike back!*

The good angel came equipped with a halo around its head, but the good angel lacked vigor. It whispered, *Count to ten before you get mad.* So stupid, it just made me count fast. The good angel made no effort to understand me or to soothe me at the spot where my anxieties collected. I wanted the good angel to clobber the bad angel. I wanted it to knock the bad angel upside his head and to force the being that existed on the plane between the narrow shoulders to start behaving right. Over and over, the bad angel prevailed. *Don't let her get away with this. She never lets up on you, never, never, never, never. Don't let anyone get away with anything.*

"You have a bad attitude, that's your problem!" Mother shouted. "You're selfish!" "You're ungrateful!" In between, she issued dire warnings. "I'm going to send you to a psychiatrist! You need a psychiatrist!"

Paddling was out. Now, Mother delivered sharp, stinging slaps to my face. Slaps were instantaneous. They were personal. They left me feeling violated and enraged. I never struck her in return. Never. But I stared back, my jaw thrust out, as if inviting the next one and the next to my face. "Go ahead," I screamed. "It doesn't hurt!"

She screamed in return. "You are no longer a member of this family!"

Who fucking cares?

Still, I would nervously await Father's return that evening from his office, knowing that Mother would have had time to arm herself with a full recap of my wrongdoing. Fortunately, Father never rushed at me, furious and indignant, the way some dads did, their closed fists ready to deliver the final sour notes to another day of disharmony. Instead, he gave me a look more exasperated than angry, no doubt wondering how in heaven's name he ended up with a son like this one.

Thank goodness for the silent treatment. Thank goodness for the three or four days of relative peace and definitive quiet, the time during which Mother communicated with me only via notes scrawled on scraps of paper.

Long ones—*Did you remember to take out the trash?* Short ones—*thank you.* I grew comfortable under the terms of the silent treatment, but I felt mortified at my behavior, mortified that I had displayed my teenage turmoil so publicly to neighbors, who must have exclaimed to each other over their happy dinners, "My, what an awful child, what a bad temper, what a below-average personality."

After a few days, Mother tired of the effort to communicate solely through writing or with Bryan or Laura serving as intermediaries. My brother and sister moved cautiously during this interval. They had committed no wrongs, but a minefield did not care who was walking across its surface. Bryan retained the ability to drift and float into space; Laura stayed attached to the earth, able to regulate her steps. Still, Mother's "as for *you*" was the early warning signal that neither of the other two would escape her wrath altogether.

A summons to Mother's bedroom meant that she was ready to receive my apology. It was a rather formal moment, punctuated with a forgiving embrace signaling an armistice rather than a lasting peace, but I was no longer required to itemize each of my transgressions. Afterwards, Mother informed me (this was important to her) that she was allowing me back into the family.

There was never a two-way exchange of apologies. Mother was not at fault. Always I was the one in the wrong. She had nothing to apologize for. A commander in chief does not apologize for maintaining order in the ranks.

"I've sacrificed so much for you." This was one of her more baffling statements, sometimes uttered as a lament following my apology, more frequently uttered as a complaint. Mother did not work outside the home. Or even inside. Her work consisted of delegating tasks. I could think of no long, hoped-for wish Mother had been denied due to her sacrifices for her children. She had not traveled around the globe as her Ne-san eventually would do, but in truth she did not like long flights and exhausting itineraries. She was committed to no hobbies other than working crossword puzzles and playing solitaire. In the past, Mother and Father had dressed up for dinner with friends like Mr. and Mrs. Shiozaki or Mr. and Mrs. Hayakawa, but interacting socially was demanding, and Mother much preferred to stay at home.

Much easier to grasp was her charge that I was "ungrateful." She understood gratitude as more than an expression of feeling but as a quality of existence. Her father sacrificed his university background, his status in the Imperial Valley, even his dignity to ensure the survival of his children. Her mother, dying, was thinking what was best for her children. But even were the Issei not immigrants toiling under the sun, their children owed them gratitude. Just because. Gratitude to the parents superseded all else. A child's immediate acquiescence was the first sign and measure of gratitude. Did Mother ever in her life say one harsh thing in reply to her own father? Did she ever refuse to do as her mother bade? The idea was absurd. Every night, Mother prayed her gratitude openly.

But this son was ungrateful. About that, there was no dispute. Father put in long hours at work, took us children to church and to our activities, paid the bills and provided for all the family needs. He deserved regular expressions of gratitude and a cooperative middle child but seldom received either. I expressed my thanks to Mother after a delicious birthday meal or because she allowed us to select a favorite amusement park to go to but never *just because.*

In truth, I could match Mother word for wounding word, but I did not realize it. The power of my words was wholly unexpected. It was akin to Dorothy's discovery that all along she possessed the ability to click her heels and return safely from Oz—only in reverse. Fed up with servitude, fed up with feeling like a lackey ordered to clean latrines while the leader reclined in the bedchamber, I lashed out. No, I did not really lash out, I issued a complaint, extended a mild accusation, displayed a childish pout. But it was enough. Was it ever.

"You're just lazy," I said one day, balking at my latest list of chores.

Lazy.

How to explain what happened next? My words were met with an explosion of energy no less wondrous than frenzied. Instantly, Mother transformed into a housekeeping whirlwind, like a character in a cartoon—but a character seething with rage. Still in her nightwear, she lugged the vacuum cleaner to the living room, her lips set in a fierce line. Ooh, she would speak to no one right now, don't even try.

She struggled to move the hassock, the heavy arm chair. She attacked the carpet, attacked the corners of the room as if they were guilty of harboring a felon. Alarmed, I tried to help. She waved me off. It was not a moment she had anticipated but a moment for which she was prepared. She waved me off. *No, no, you stand there and watch!* Her lips were locked in a tight, uncompromising fury. *You watch!*

I watched. She yanked the vacuum into the dining room, where its protesting music made an odd accompaniment to the carnival-like stenciling on the walls. The four Queen Anne chairs were thrust to the side, the arm chairs at the head and foot of the table also drawn back. Mother made quick work of the room.

She proceeded into the kitchen. First the broom, the dustpan. By then her arms and brow bore beads of sweat. The mop was flung across the linoleum floor. Ajax and steel wool smote the kitchen sink, until it yielded each minuscule particulate. By the time they were finished, there was no trace of grime, no hint of yellow insurrection. Both halves of the sink were left white, all white and perfectly passive, like sheep with their eyes gouged out.

There. I had supplied the opportunity, which she had seized, to let me know the depth of her fury. How dare you! *Oh, no, no!* She glared fiercely at this child against whose false accusation she would martyr the last few drops of her existence. Refusing my reparations in the form of assistance was not enough. I must pay dearly. On my own I tried scrubbing the bathroom sink with the Ajax, but she elbowed me away. She would not permit it. No, no, no. She would not accept my help. You watch. You watch. Lazy? Who's lazy?

It was an exquisite eruption of energy, which an unsympathetic observer might have labeled spite. To disprove my accusation, she would work herself to death. So there! Finally, Mother retreated to her bedroom. Long ago, when she first fell ill, I had adopted the habit of listening quietly at her bedroom door to check to see if I could detect any movement or breathing. Not today. Today I dared not approach the door. The long arm of the vacuum cleaner leaned accusingly against a wall, the cylindrical body looking weary and spent, like a metallic corpse. The house cowered in cleanliness.

It would be years before I would suspect the reason why Mother flew into such a rage that day. Her father was still alive then, still strong and not one to curb his thoughts. Even into his old age, he would retain a wiry musculature from his labor-intensive seasons in America. His was the strength of the plywood board nailed across the window, the sturdy bulwark against the fury of the storm. This man had been direct to the point of bluntness. I had no way of confirming my suspicion, but it occurred to me that my grandfather must have called Mother lazy (*namakemono* in Japanese, which even sounds accusatory), a descriptor leveled too by her Ne-san when Florence did not work with sufficient energy around the house ("Shake a leg, don't be lazy").

Fortunately, Mother never again lapsed into such a death-daring cleaning frenzy. But she stayed mad. One day, seething, she said for the first but not the last time, "I hope you have a son exactly like you!" It was an ominous pronouncement, a curse that turned upside down the parental wish for their children to be bearers of the next blessed generation.

For a boy desperately afraid to talk to girls, a boy who had not had a girl express an interest in him, Mother's words were less hurtful than intended. They contained an encouraging concession. Despite everything wrong with me, I might someday marry and have children! Such a sweet possibility! If a girl I liked agreed to marry me, that outcome was just dandy. And if a pair of girls were so inclined? The unlikely dilemma both pleased and disturbed me, especially at night before I fell asleep.

Under morning's bright glare, I analyzed the implications of having a son exactly like myself. The boy would be as thin-skinned as an egg. He would be resentful. Ungrateful. He would get good grades but not reach the top of his class. Not like my friends Frances Endo or Mike Watanabe. He would be okay at sports but not exceptional. He would be receptive to constructive criticism but frequently fail to profit from it. In public, he would wear an armor of confidence, which would allow him to be outspoken and occasionally cocky. After each outburst of temper, he would be overcome with remorse and a sense of foolishness. In seventh grade, he would go out of his way to introduce Caucasian friends to Japanese friends in an effort to "bring the races together," afterwards marveling at how negligible his impact had been.

The imaginary son would not be naturally mean. He would never experience a father's hand lifted against him. And anyway, no matter how ferociously his grandmother wanted at a given moment to retaliate against her rebellious son, she did not really wish to have a grandson who acted like a little prick.

Feeling almost giddy about my future, I took a nickel from my pocket. It was there for a reason. I flipped the nickel in the air. Heads, I would marry and have children. Tails, I wouldn't.

I caught the nickel in my right hand and smacked it down on the back of my left.

Okay, two out of three.

19

HAROLD AND LAURA CAREW

W E ENDURED THE TIRESOME TRIP to the cottage in the town of Sierra Madre just twice a year, but it started immediately upon our arrival in California. The Buick sniffed through congestion along the Harbor Freeway, dashed through tunnels, then banked onto the Pasadena Freeway, known as the Arroyo Seco Parkway before the war. A testament to an earlier age, this stretch of road demanded a slower pace, its lanes undulating in graceful curves intended to mimic the ocean shoreline, some twenty miles away. The freeway was not hard to negotiate, just slow going: drivers needed to stay alert, maintain their lane, observe the speed limit, slow for traffic merging suddenly from stop signs.

In the early days it was the bucolic route favored by wealthy Pasadenans with splendid motor cars. But soon it became a busy road for ordinary folks commuting to and from downtown and for Sunday drivers trying to access the foothills to the northeast. It skirts the northern tip of Chinatown, glides through Monterey Hills, slices Highland Park, and meanders along the Arroyo Seco bordering South Pasadena before spilling out, gentle as rainwater from a bucket, onto the roadway south of Colorado Boulevard.

Cradling the Thomas Guide, Mother provided a constant stream of information as we headed north, then east. There's Pasadena Junior College. I went there for a while, she said. We know, we children replied. Past Allen and Hill and through East Pasadena with its motor courts. Eventually, we crossed a more rustic two-lane road, with slow-moving pickup trucks grinding along like metal cows. When an orange grove appeared in the distance, we knew that we were drawing near at last. A dust devil swirled, hung in the air as if suspended by ennui, before it descended.

The trip was a wool blanket worn by three kids, cramped and restless in the car's sticky interior, wiping sweat beads off the collars of our Sunday best. Mother had already warned us against bickering. But the warning was un-needed. We children quarreled a lot, but we knew how to behave in public, especially in the presence of hakujin. Father was a short-sleeve shirt, a pair of arms browning in the sun, and a head of hair cropped well above the collar line. Mother dressed simply in a light blouse and a skirt soft as the voice speaking toward Father's ear. She hummed as the radio played.

A MILE OR SO PAST THE ORCHARD LAY THE HOUSE where the widow Laura Carew resided, her husband having passed away after a brief illness while the war was still raging. In his day Harold Carew, who remained alive in Bryan's middle name, was a respected journalist who served for years as book page editor of the *Pasadena Star-News*. In 1930, he produced the three-volume *History of Pasadena and the San Gabriel Valley*. Photographs render him conventional for his era—serious, refined, a man who dressed well, hobnobbed with prominent civic leaders, the great privileged oak trees under whose inviting shade business acumen was collected and dispensed. The elites relied on Harold Carew's literary reviews, recognized him as a touchstone of high culture.

But he was not one of them. He was an intellectual, a poet, a social progressive who believed in building bridges between different sets of people. When the war broke out, he repudiated the hatred directed toward Japanese Americans, decried the newspapers' foul use of racial epithets. Rotten Japs, indeed. He openly opposed the talk of incarceration. Mother spoke of him with a respect bordering on reverence. Katsumi had never met anyone quite like him.

How different the man was from Katsumi's own father. Standing before his father's casket at the funeral so long ago, the son had wondered who exactly was this man who toiled like a galley slave, the sweat gathering across his shoulders and back, skin cracking, hair smelling, who in dying had become indistinguishable from the labors he performed? Katsumi could not recall a single instance of his father taking him aside and offering him "fatherly advice," the way it was done in the movies. His father scolded him once or twice when his son was still a boy but otherwise neither criticized nor praised him. Once was when the teacher held Katsumi back in the first grade. How incompetent that teacher was! Later, when he had skipped ahead two full years, his father never offered a compliment. Had he done so, his son might have chewed on it for a while, whether or not it left a taste.

One of the few lasting memories he had retained of his father always nagged at him. It was the memory of his parents walking along 1st Street in downtown Los Angeles, his mother, whose own father was town mayor of Imabari in Ehime Prefecture, deliberately maintaining a three-pace distance behind her husband, an acceptable practice in various regions of Japan.

His father moved without concern, without bothering to check on his wife or to maintain a walking pace that would at least be comfortable for her. It was clear that he had no expectation or desire to walk alongside his wife or to acknowledge his marital status. Man, worker, child-maker, breadwinner, all of that counted. A husband, on the other hand, was—nothing. Katsumi remembered. He had no intention to be unkind, but he remembered wondering, who was this guy? Why did he allow his wife to trail behind him like a dog?

At twenty-one, Florence Funakoshi also could not help but compare Mr. Harold Carew to Papa, whose work-stiffened face attested to his decades of manual labor in a foreign land. During all this time, her father had learned barely a handful of English words. What for? You cannot fill your belly on words. You may as well try to eat a smile. But Mr. Carew had allowed Florence to glimpse worlds operating far beyond her own, tantalizing possibilities layered with elegance and sophistication, rooted in unchallengeable belonging.

It was Mr. Carew who had served as Florence's cultural mentor and in a sense her muse. It was Mr. Carew, not her own father, she had turned to following the dentist's unexpected marriage proposal. Before replying, Florence conducted Katsumi to a Bible study meeting, where both Mr. and Mrs. Carew met and spoke with him. Little did the twenty-five-year-old dentist suspect that the meeting was an audition. Afterwards, Mr. Carew had pronounced Katsumi a fine young man. Mrs. Carew concurred. Hold onto this man, she had advised Florence.

The relationship with the elderly widow was different. Florence could not compare Mrs. Carew to the mother she barely had time to know, the memory of whom grew dimmer and more elusive with each passing decade. Besides, the Carews were childless, and Mrs. Carew was not by nature motherly. What she recognized in the young Florence Funakoshi, who following high school had found part-time work as a hairdresser, was a sparrow with clipped wings.

Mrs. Carew never chaperoned the girl on junkets to the high-end shops on Pasadena's Lake Avenue. She did not invite her to sit in a special box seat during the annual Rose Parade. But she fit in. Or could have done had she chosen. Could have embraced the jeweled life Florence had observed from a distance through newspaper accounts containing photographs of fashionable women with acid tongues, group shots of civic leaders whose portraits got willed to museums, full-page spreads on debutante balls with sixteen-year-old girls formally coming out into society.

Florence had never actually seen a photograph of Mrs. Carew taken at one of the fancy balls the rich people attended. She never saw Mrs. Carew at the racetrack or accompanying her husband when he attended a charity event sponsored by the exclusive Valley Hunt Club. But she knew that if Mrs. Laura Carew ever did attend one of those events, if she ever did, people did not cast curious looks in her direction. Goodness, what are you doing here? She was no oddity. Not back then.

AT ONE TIME, the house on Mariposa might have resembled a modest parsonage. It nestled behind a larger house that fronted the street and was accessed by a narrow walkway bordered on one side by fruit trees. Time had taken its toll. The roof needed cleaning, the pine needles having accumulated above the crumbling eaves and at the foot of the rain gutter. Outside the front door, the bougainvillea was untended and overgrown.

Inside was unbearably stuffy, the odors having settled. The room smelled of years of human occupancy and of unwashed dog. In the first couple of years, there were two of them, two massive German Shepherd mixes with intelligent eyes and eager, busy tongues. There were two dogs, and then one. I gave the survivor a light pat on its head. Lightly patted its head, knowing that my hand would retain the stink of unwashed dog kept too long in the close quarters of parlor and living room. A modest kitchen with a screen door led to the outside. A hole seemingly chiseled out of a wall led to a bedroom. Pat, pat, pat. After a while, my hand no longer reached out to the furry smell. The poor creature lost interest and wandered back to lie down at the foot of its master.

Mrs. Carew looked like another century. At a glance, she reminded me of the lady pictured on the box of See's chocolates, which Mother presented as a gift. Her hair was white and appeared untended, although not as untended as her dog. Her dress was a print, faded and shapeless, and punctuated with a Peter Pan collar. Maybe, decades ago, the print was shiny and new and the dress had been in fashion. She resembled the actresses playing the old matron roles in black-and-white movies of the 1930s.

She always greeted "Florence" and "Katsumi" with hugs. As instructed, we children greeted the lady with the words, "Hello, Mrs. Carew," and the lady returned our greetings with a smile. That one was Bryan Harold. So this one must be George. Of course, the girl was her namesake, although Laura was not accorded special attention. How splendid Florence looked, with her three well-behaved children, her reliable husband. They'd brought a box of chocolates. So sorry she had nothing to offer them. Some water, perhaps?

I sipped from the glass. Mother smiled gaily. The water was tepid. Worse, the glass retained a peculiar smell. It was not a stink, exactly, but a peculiar odor of something washed out yet left over. Neither of my parents drank alcohol, not even a sip of beer or wine, so I had no olfactory point of reference to help me track down the nature of the smell. Mother and Mrs. Carew chatted.

Father said very little. He had forgotten to remove his sunglasses, so he looked like a bank robber about to make a dash for the getaway car. His weight shifted from one side of his chair to the other. My eyes wandered, although I kept a lookout lest the dog return, intent on a second round of friendship. There were bookshelves loaded with books in leather bindings. Up close, the books smelled musty like too many human hands, like too many unwashed years.

While Mother chatted, there was nothing for the rest of us to do but stay locked in our chairs, while our eyes pried through the parlor and the cluttered living room, past the knickknacks and other items collecting dust on the rollaway desk. There was nothing to do but allow the imagination to clamber through the windows and pluck the peaches from one of the fruit trees, the ripe ones, savory and delicious, their peach fuzz soft against the hands. Nothing to do but bite into that sweetness, chew contentedly, taste the prospect of escape.

MAYBE IT WAS BECAUSE THE COTTAGE was run down and its life seemed so stale that Mother's reaction came as a shock on the afternoon of the telephone call. Mother's share of the conversation was brief, but otherwise her voice sounded normal. Everything changed once the call ended and the phone was settled in its cradle.

"Mrs. Carew died."

Oh. My first thought was, oh, too bad. I returned to my homework, which was spread out on the table across from Mother. I felt a twinge of pity. But also a degree of relief. There would be no more long drives to Sierra Madre.

I did not have time to entertain another feeling, for without warning something burst. Grief poured through the breach, overwhelmed whatever emotional catch reservoir grownups like Mother depended on to stop its surge. It was uncanny. I was accustomed to tears being bullets. I was accustomed to tears taking aim at something, at someone. Not this. Mother flung her arms across the table, dropped her head, sobbed uncontrollably.

In the movies, the adults extend tender support to the grief-stricken. Someone leans over, provides a consoling arm while murmuring, "I'm sorry." But I remained silent, words of comfort like fragments of fishbone stayed lodged in my throat. "If there is anything I can do," the sophisticates say, their voices flowing with unctuous concern. I did not know what to do or what to say. I was an eleven-year-old doing homework, which I returned to, having done nothing to comfort my grieving mother, and gradually, entirely on its own, her sobbing ceased.

I have a confession to make. It turned out I was wrong, utterly wrong, about Mrs. Carew, although I did not find out until much later. I said that she was not by nature motherly, but I was mistaken. More than half a century after her death, I came upon a handwritten three-page letter, which Mrs. Carew had composed in reply to a letter from my mother. Mrs. Carew's entire letter was focused on me. Me! Who at that point she had never seen or met and who lived half a continent away.

It was dated September 1952. I was in kindergarten in Illinois and facing a problem. Over the years I had forgotten, or perhaps I should say suppressed the memory of, what had occurred at my first school. Mrs. Carew's letter to my mother began, "It is a horrible tragedy to dear George—I have never known any adults to be as CRUEL to each other as can children, so they are calling him dirty names—." Mrs. Carew wondered whether the teacher was sufficiently "sympathetic" and asked about the feasibility of my attending a private school for the remainder of the year.

My mother's letter to Mrs. Carew must have been rather detailed, perhaps alluding additionally to my personal failings, for Mrs. Carew's letter went on to say, "I think I would avoid the word 'responsibility' to George—it seems to antagonize him. I would try not to disturb him with responsibility but positively build up his self-confidence. Take time to arrange things for him to do which includes some responsibility—invite (never command) him to do them—if he fails, ignore the failure, if he succeeds at all, build up his ego. There is much time for him to grow into it, if as I suspect, his temperament resents it. Poets, actors, writers, creative artists are like that—and who knows that George may not become one of these!"

There was, and is, a fourth and final page to Mrs. Carew's letter, a kind of addendum. It says, "read last" and is addressed "To George—Bless his dear hurt heart!" It starts by reminding me that my home is like a warm bird's nest, and it encourages me to be brave, like Daddy, in leaving home each day, knowing that at the end of the day I can return bigger and better. It affirms that I should not bicker with "the children who aren't polite and kind" but instead "understand and forgive, because in their homes they don't have as much love as yours." I have no doubt my mother read this last page to me aloud. But I was five, and I do not remember it.

20

ROTTEN

Prophecies should come with warning labels. use responsibly. Even words not requiring a prescription should be marked caution. Then again, sometimes prophecies are the sole medications for wounds, the salve that for an instant quells the hurt.

"I'll die soon, George Uba, and it will be all your fault!"

It was as if Mother were delivering the Momotarō prophecy in reverse. In the Japanese folklore, Momotarō is the boy who emerges famously from a peach—a miracle of new life and a remedy for childlessness. The elderly parents are overjoyed. Momotarō grows into a fine young man and a redoubtable warrior who protects his parents and saves them and his village from the demons, the *oni*.

I recalled the first time I spotted the peach tree outside Mrs. Carew's house. At the base of the tree, a peach had fallen. Ants, serious and intent, swarmed across its bruised and rotting skin, its stone lying partially exposed, crusty with age, like a face worn away through solitude and discontent. The ants were relentless, but Bryan warned that if they gnawed all the way through, they would encounter trouble. Inside the peach pit was a toxin. Even an ant, which could lift fifty times its own weight, would die if it reached through and bit. How different was the folktale, wherein the peach pit contained the hero-to-be Momotarō on the verge of being unwrinkled into existence. How do you unwrinkle contradictions?

Mother's prophecy was dire. It was concussive. And it was brilliant. The inclusion of my first and last name was genius. Not only did it personalize the blame, but it enhanced the rhythm. I alone, as if down to the last digit of my serial number, would bear responsibility for my mother's untimely death. If this were the fate that awaited her, I would have preferred to be identified as just one of numerous causative factors. But no. Mother's death was imminent, and the onus fell entirely on me. I was the onus, the demon oni, not the hero who slays the oni ravaging the village but the ravager who slays.

"All your fault."

The words were hurled at my face like spit.

An ordinary bad son was a wayward, the prodigal who had left home, while his devoted parents awaited his older but wiser return. Hullo, I'm back! What's there to eat?

Blessed be the adjectives. *Kusatta.* Rotten. The rotten fruit, the rotten meat the flies were drawn to, the rotten cabbage discarded smellily in the trash. That which was thoroughly rotted could not be salvaged. *Saitei.* The worst, the lowest. Flesh gone bad.

It was less than two years since Mother's first cancer surgery. Day by day, she fought the cancer and the cancer treatments. Day by day, she fought me, her son. Once uttered, her words bore repeating. Month after month. Time should have diluted their power, but it did not.

ALONE, I WONDERED WHEN IT ALL BEGAN, when my life first veered left instead of right. I remembered at a very early age encountering Santa Claus beneath the cheery lights at Marshall Field. Surrounded by festive wreaths and holly, a tall, brightly lit Christmas tree nearby with gaily wrapped packages scattered around its base, the children waited in turn to sit next to Santa in his oversized chair, which resembled a throne.

Ahead lay the question I dreaded. "Have you been a good boy this year?"

In the black-and-white photo Mother purchased, impersonator Santa lacked the girth, not to mention the crimson colors, of the real Santa, although his fake beard cascaded invitingly like white-water rapids beneath his chin. A tiny elf could have had fun sliding down that beard. Photo Santa looked reserved rather than jolly, but I remembered the man in the red suit waiting patiently as the line of children inched forward, until each in turn took their seat and declared their Christmas wish. In the photo, which Mother eventually framed and hung on the wall at home, I wear an overcoat, a matching cap, my eyes resembling little black buttons.

As for Santa's question, *the* question—I did not know how to answer it without telling a fib. Mother stood nearby, just outside the velvet-draped ropes where the adults were allowed to observe. I considered saying no. No, I have not been a good boy. I fought with Bryan. I picked on Laura. I had temper tantrums, kicking the hallway wall with my feet and leaving scuff marks. At least Mother would not have to look at me like the little Pinocchio liar I felt that I was otherwise about to become. No. Then Mother could smile and think, at least the boy is truthful.

But I could not bring myself to confess out loud, in public, in front of all the other children united in a year's worth of good behavior. Why must I retrace the long trail of missteps and misconduct that had delivered me to this moment of exposure? What was the purpose of this interrogation? I looked up, and that was when the photographer snapped the picture. I looked up, and without answering, I cast a shy smile, hoping that Santa would think that this Oriental child did not speak English.

Through the years, the truth about the bad son would circulate, but largely within the confines of Mother's family or among select Japanese American friends and relatives. It would circulate so that others grasped both the severity of the son's wrongdoings and the depth of his mother's travails. I should not even have cared, but I did. In Los Angeles, the neighbors on each side knew about my bad temper, but at least I did not make a headline in a newspaper, did not become a feature on a television newscast like the pint-sized shoplifter forced by his parents to wear handcuffs outside the grocery store or the shirtless waif made to stand at attention in his front yard while holding up a cardboard sign identifying him as a chocolate thief.

Whatever my myriad transgressions, I never was subjected to such humiliation, never subpoenaed before the Board of Public Opinion. No one was more dedicated to controlling the output of news than Mother. The problem for me arose when I caught adults staring at me when they thought I was unaware. It was not their fault. They were merely trying to reconcile the intel they had received with the bashful thank-yous that kept coming their way, like handwritten notes trying too hard to leave a good impression.

THE ACTUAL MOMENT OF SURRENDER brought a curious rush of relief. It was in the middle of another quarrel, and this time I shouted back, "Okay, go ahead! Send me to a psychiatrist!"

Even though I had abandoned weird habits, I knew that I was not like other children, who were normal and healthy, like shiny peaches ripening on a tree. As Mother frequently exclaimed, "There's something wrong with you!" It was now years since she had begun threatening to send me to a psychiatrist. Bryan laughed when he first heard this—he couldn't help it. A shrink! Japanese Americans did not go to psychiatrists. The thought was more shameful and alarming than a Nisei couple obtaining a divorce.

But secretly, and for a long time, I had begun to wonder if a psychiatrist might help me curb my anger, even if the rot, the rot deep inside, persisted. For so many years, stupidly, I had believed that those who were completely mad, completely insane, were freed from suffering. Maybe, all along, I was wrong. Maybe it was better to seek a cure. Yes, it was shameful to go to a psychiatrist, and I hated the thought of bringing public shame to my family, to my relatives, who were innocent bystanders, and to Japanese Americans in general. I (and probably they) would be marked for life. Still, even an alley cat falling to the bottom of a rain barrel sometimes needed a boost before it could scratch its way out.

That is when the odd thing happened, which is to say, nothing happened. I braced myself, prepared to submit, even started to believe that I would benefit from professional help, despite the fact that from now on the normal kids would probably steer clear of me. For some reason, Mother failed to locate the right psychiatrist to straighten me out. Weeks passed, a month, another month. I was prepared to go, almost eager. Mother and I continued to argue, to fight.

But as time passed, the threats to send me to a psychiatrist dwindled. Eventually they ceased. When Mother was infuriated, she continued to slap me across my face, followed up with the days of silent treatment. It was cheaper, possibly more satisfying, certainly less shameful than having a cuckoo son see a psychiatrist. After the initial slap, the two of us glared at each like implacable foes across an invisible Maginot Line. She slapped me over and over. One. Two. Three. All. Your. Fault.

PART V

DEPTH PERCEPTIONS

21

POWERS OF THE FOURTH ESTATE

Mother's adult life was bracketed by two successful journalists. Harold Carew was one, and Bill Hosokawa, editor of the *Heart Mountain Sentinel*, the camp newspaper, was the other. Mother was employed at the newspaper, assigned mainly to minor duties. Bill allowed her to report on crime and on fires. But in the camp there was a dearth of both. So-and-so's scarf got stolen, but it turned out it was merely misplaced. Mother did not earn a byline.

Following the war, Hosokawa became an editor of the *Denver Post*. He shared Mother's faith in loyalty confirmed through acts of compliance. Fittingly, it was his newspaper that featured a front-page photograph of my grandmother, Misao Uba, who in 1952, following passage of the McCarran-Walter Act, which abolished the "alien ineligible for citizenship" provision of earlier nationality laws while retaining a quota and immigration preference system, became the first Issei to become a naturalized American citizen in the State of Colorado. A staunch defender of the Japanese American Citizens League, whose wartime leaders urged cooperation with rather than resistance to the government's internment edict, Hosokawa later authored several books, including *Nisei: The Quiet Americans*.

The book received praise, but it also was attacked by an emerging generation of scholars and social activists for its alleged submissiveness and quietism and its failure to adequately credit those Nisei who were vocal in their opposition to internment from the start and to the loyalty questionnaire that followed afterwards. Mother detested the No-No Boys who comprised membership in the Heart Mountain Fair Play Committee, Frank Emi in particular, who years later would become one of her own hardheaded son's heroes for his defiance and willingness to be jailed for the sake of his convictions. Back then, things were different. Most Nisei were vocal in criticizing No-No Boys, and some were energetic in rejecting them. Mother had met Frank Emi and regarded him as a troublemaker.

But she remained Bill Hosokawa's steadfast friend and ally, exchanging annual family Christmas letters and photographs with the Hosokawa family. Through most of her life, Mother remained an inveterate letter writer, and she received praise over the years from relatives and from friends in the Skokie neighborhood with whom she stayed in touch through her detailed, sprightly holiday letters.

She also received praise one day at a 39th Street School PTA meeting. By the time she reached home, she was eager to share her story. Earlier, she had let on that she had worked on the newspaper in the internment camp with a man who was now the editor of the leading newspaper in the entire Rocky Mountain region. Suitably impressed and prepared to assume that Mother possessed keen powers of observation and reporting skills, the PTA president called upon her to address the entire assembly, which contained many hakujin ladies who wanted to learn about the camp experience.

The request was more than Mother expected. Nevertheless, overcoming her nervousness, she performed what she recognized as an act of civic duty. She proceeded to describe the rows of tar-paper barracks with the thin partition walls between each apartment. She mentioned the communal showers and the long lines for the mess hall. She described the dust seeping through the floorboards and the freezing winter blasts of wind. As a Japanese American, she elected to understate her personal level of discomfort, and she made no undignified mention of the financial losses sustained by her family and others.

During the ensuing question-and-answer period, one woman had remarked sympathetically that Mother must have hated living under such squalid conditions and wanted desperately to get out. Seeing her opportunity and seizing it, Mother had replied, triumphantly, "Yes, but first we had to win the war!"

How proud she looked when she reached this part of her account. How grandly she must have spoken at the PTA. How impressed her audience must have felt in the presence of such patriotism. First, we Americans had to win the war.

MOTHER CONTINUED HER POPULAR CHRISTMAS LETTERS. At one point the magazine ads for the Famous Writers School had their say. Why not give it a try? Her own father, widowed, had turned to her once, long ago, and said something that cut deeply, so deeply that later in life she would turn the memory over and over, like a person feeling for a sore in the mouth, each time hoping that it would be gone but knowing that it was there to stay.

She was a teenager. He had come home from work, his face and hands browned from the sun. Removing his work shoes at the door, he regarded his daughter, who was browsing through a magazine. When the thought came to him, he cracked it open like he would a nut.

"Mary has the beauty, and Freddie is a boy. What have you got going for you?"

He was not a thoughtless man, just a busy one, a foreign-looking immigrant preoccupied with survival. He was a father musing out loud. A widower long accustomed to plying the beads of necessity. Hurtful? If anything, his words were meant to inspire.

To be sure, Florence was never unpretty. But young Nisei fellows did not go around saying of her, "That's some dish!" Since the moment she married, all of her efforts had gone into being a wife and then a mother. Not just any wife and mother, a Nisei wife and mother saddled with particular obligations and social challenges. A faithful wife, a relentless mother. The best kind. The only kind.

Was it possible that all along she had possessed a hidden talent that merely needed to be uncovered?

The cost for the correspondence school was a little steep, and she had to sign a contract. But the school sent books and binders to help each student make progress toward becoming a published author, and it boasted a staff of professional writers.

Her first writing effort was a four-page, first-person account of her experience in the Heart Mountain Relocation Center. It was less a description of her daily life in an internment camp than a summons to patriotism and a ringing justification for submitting to the government's wartime will. She spent hours editing and retyping her work, employing her forefingers in the hunt-and-peck technique. She wanted it to leave an impact, just as she once had done at the PTA meeting. Within weeks, she received her manuscript by return mail. Evidently, it had been carefully examined and here and there commented on in red pencil.

In the reader's summary, one sentence stood out. It said, "I assume that you are being sardonic." She consulted her Webster's. That one word was the nail puncturing all her publishing hopes. She never submitted another manuscript to the Famous Writers School. Leaving the program quietly, she did not request a refund.

I COULD APPRECIATE MOTHER'S SECRET desire to be published. Entering ninth grade, I eagerly signed up for the school's journalism class. Mr. Krause introduced those of us new to journalism to the lexicon: layout, masthead, inverted pyramid, banner headline, and so on. The class was responsible for writing and producing the junior high newspaper. Mr. Krause wore the same black suit to class each day but removed the jacket and rolled up the sleeves of his white shirt, ready for work. He looked midthirties, long-armed, lanky, his frame suited to his narrow nose and hawklike face. His outward appearance reminded us of Ichabod Crane, who got chased through the woods of Sleepy Hollow. But unlike Washington Irving's venal and conniving schoolmaster, Mr. Krause was an earnest, dedicated teacher.

Students who previously had taken the journalism class were the editors. They assigned duties, directed reporters, pondered layouts, devised headlines, announced important decisions. Unlike other classes, where students remained stuck in their chairs for the greater part of an hour, we moved from here to there, noisily chatted and conferred, and literally spread our work over the desks, sometimes working frantically to meet a deadline. The paper was produced in cooperation with the print shop. Galleys were checked and double-checked for typos, for misprints, for factual errors.

Each fresh edition was folded and stacked in news racks, where students of every grade picked them up. It was thrilling to watch kids throughout the school reading the four-page newspaper and sharing its contents. I wrote reports on sports events like the B-8 versus A-8 softball game and several other campus activities, all less important stuff.

We learned. We learned a lot. For most of us, journalism was our favorite class, Mr. Krause our favorite teacher. Which was why his announcement near the end of the semester hit hard, came as a shock. He stood as usual before the class, peering at us through his black horn-rims, his look penetrating and inscrutable. No one was prepared for his announcement.

He would not be returning to school. Not next semester, not ever. He had made a life-changing decision, he informed us, addressing us as if we were adults, a decision he had pondered for a long time. He would leave teaching and in a few weeks enter a monastery. He intended to spend the rest of his life in a monastery.

A monastery? Almost at once, I pictured men in dark robes and cowls, climbing gravely up steep mountain paths. These men ate meagerly from clay dinner plates, spent hour upon hour in silent meditation and prayer. Rope belts cinched their waists. The tassels from the belts barely stirred, as the breeze sifted through the monastery's lofty heights. Gone forever were the unruly shouts and random noises of kids. In time, all the soiled things of the world were cleansed from consciousness. But gone too were the rewards that were his due from teaching and inspiring his grateful students. As though they had never existed.

A week or so later, having received our yearbooks, our entire class formed a line. The really popular teachers were aware of their popularity, and, accustomed to the ritual of signing yearbooks, Mr. Krause brought his own ink pen (not a ballpoint). I waited patiently near the back of the line. I was not one of those students always at Mr. Krause's desk, pestering him with questions, sharing a joke, or soliciting an opinion. I was too shy to approach any teacher in that way. Yet this was the best teacher I had known, a teacher serious but not stern, disciplined but not tyrannical, watchful but not cold.

With his student editors, Mr. Krause wrote long commentaries filled with advice and encouragement. His ink pen had an exceedingly sharp point, and his handwriting looked faintly spindly yet precise and well-defined, rather like Mr. Krause himself. When my turn came, Mr. Krause took my yearbook and hesitated. It was only the briefest moment of hesitation, but I could not help notice. My heart sank. What did it mean? Then he proceeded to write.

Returning to their seats, some of the kids opened their yearbooks with the eagerness felt on Christmas morning. What gift of praise had their teacher bestowed upon them? I waited. If I opened the yearbook immediately, perhaps I would get smacked in the face, would blush with shame. What if it said, "Best of luck. Mr. Krause"? Or worse, "Strive to improve as a scholar and person." Or "I'm sure you'll mature over time." Everyone would be able to read my face.

So I waited. I waited until the bell rang for the next class period, waited for that period to end, which was the last period of the day. When that bell rang, the students scrambled into the hallways, found their individual lockers, gathered their Pee-Chees and the books needed for that evening's homework.

I plunged my head into my locker. It was too dark. Maneuvering the yearbook halfway out and into the hallway light, I found the page and instantly recognized Mr. Krause's handwriting. The message was brief yet spread across a corner of the page like a haiku.

> How seldom did I hear your voice.
> Still water
> runs deep.

Of course! The words hit me at once! I should have spoken in class. That was one thing I needed to work on. I must learn to speak in class. I must overcome the bouts of laryngitis that continued to afflict me in classes where I was expected to speak out loud. Wearing turquoise-colored socks once a week to catch the eye of a girl would never be enough if I could not manage to speak in class. How seldom had Mr. Krause heard my voice.

But to run deep as well. To be more than a surface of contamination. To be deep, maybe fathoms deep. A teacher to whom I hardly ever spoke, a teacher I admired and who was departing for a monastery, saw something that filled me with gladness. How strange that the ones who knew you best sometimes knew you least, and the one who hardly knew you at all detected your innermost desire to be.

But it was baffling too. How was it that a person who enjoyed widespread respect and popularity, as Mr. Krause did, should want to give it all up? Mr. Krause was much admired, and he belonged. He had achieved the very thing I believed all my efforts should be directed toward. But it was not enough. Mr. Krause never returned to school. I never learned what happened to him. I remembered only his narrow face, his pointy nose, the words scratched into my yearbook.

Please, God, let me live was Jimmy Stewart's plea near the end of Frank Capra's film *It's a Wonderful Life*. George Bailey, the character played by Stewart, is initially driven to the brink of suicide by a financial crisis. *Please, God, let Mother live, and help me not to be such a rotten person* was the other George's rather wordier plea. If a naughty child—no, say it, a rotten boy— were sentenced to life in a monastery, he likely would start his morning devotionals with such a prayer, taking care, lest the heavenly Editor in Chief prove a stickler on grammar, not to split the infinitive.

22

WUNNERFUL LIFE

FAMILY ALBUM

To the one that solved the riddle, thanks.
This is me at seven in the wool shorts and jacket.
My mother is so pretty and does not look mad
at anyone. Bryan boasts the odd bow tie,
the first of countless accessories
calculated to set him apart
and keep him there. Laura sits unnoticed
in the grip of someone's arm,
because she is my sister and a girl.
My shorts are navy and they itch.
Maybe that's why my eyes blink when the flash pops.
Or maybe there's something I don't care to see.

And the one, the one with the large hands,
with his mouth shut,
must be come hell or high water my dad.

FATHER DID NOT READ POETRY. Unless jingles and rhymes counted. One of
the adages he was fond of repeating went, "Sticks and stones may break my
bones, but words can never hurt me!" Words could not hurt him. Included were
the hate words, the *Jap* words, which could never make him bruise or bleed.

Held to their utilitarian function, words produced memorizable truths or indisputable facts. I got the part about the sticks and stones.

What exactly was the relationship between platitudes and silence, the still water that ran deep? Were platitudes a kind of flotation device that buoyed the spirit when all around lurked threats of annihilation, the hope of rescue nowhere in sight? Fathoms deep, irony and ambiguity feathered soundlessly through the dark. Having long ago lost functioning eyes, they pursed their lips and tried to speak. In the depths, where nothing listened, they tried to speak.

My first spatial memory was of Father's dental office on Chicago's South Side. In the waiting room, Bryan and I clambered aboard the chairs, which boasted deep, soft interiors and curvy chrome arms, a style Mother identified as art deco. For some reason, I associated their curved lines with the sailboats floating gaily on Lake Michigan. Father allowed us to take turns stretching out in the deep fold of the dental chair, which was like sliding onto an upholstered tongue. Father used the foot pedal to pump us up, pump us down.

I recalled the mobile cabinet set on casters, its mustard-colored drawers containing row upon row of pointy instruments, which I was careful not to disturb. Thin as a metal crepe, each drawer glided smoothly into its cabinet slot on sets of ball bearings, one drawer mounted atop another, each making a pleasing sound. A nearby countertop with a black marble surface held an autoclave and a pair of shallow basins, which emitted an unpleasant blend of antiseptic odors and metal.

At the newsstand, Father fumbled in his pocket for change, as if it were of utmost importance to feel the size and texture of each coin. The first words I associated Father with were "two bits," which meant one quarter. It sounded funny. Bryan and I must have added up to two bits. The newspaper contained many words, on Sundays it grew thick with them, but after a while the words became a mere jingling of loose change in my ears, the sudden glint of fat quarters and shiny dimes.

EVEN COMPARED TO MOST OTHER NISEI MEN, Father was quiet. Quiet but not silent. Not stern. Over the years, he must have released large quantities of dopamine, for he laughed heartily at a good, clean joke, even though he could not deliver an effective punch line himself (*Let's see, how did that go?*). At the Boy Scout summer camps, Michael Shigezane's wisecracks and deadpan humor sent Father into bursts of unrestrained laughter, which induced all the boys to laugh harder since here was this adult, see, with a sense of humor. What a crack-up.

At home Father was a devotee of *The Lawrence Welk Show*, which was wholesome family entertainment with sprightly music featuring the Lennon Sisters harmonizing or Myron Floren on the accordion. Welk spoke English with a thick Germanic accent, but it was his parents who were the immigrants, settling in North Dakota and raising the son who one day would prosper as a musician, bandleader, television host, and real estate entrepreneur. Father laughed appreciatively when we kids mimicked Welk's trademark approval of Bobby and Cissy performing a polka or tap dance. One time I went to a bookstore to purchase a copy of Welk's autobiography *Wunnerful, Wunnerful* as a birthday gift. They were sold out.

Occasionally, Father displayed a satirical sense of humor. On a Sunday afternoon, the members of the Spartans Gray-Y gathered at Los Angeles' Rancho Park to show off and test their model airplanes, each one constructed of delicate balsa wood and equipped with an oversized rubber band that ran through the fuselage and engaged a propeller at the nose. Each model airplane kit was different, but they all came with a set of directions, dozens of fragile pieces, and a small tube of glue.

My model was a forest of repair, requiring painstaking reassembly (with Mother's help) after taking a hard plunge on the asphalt and skidding into the curb during a test flight. My friend Jon Mayeda had constructed a very handsome model. Father noticed. He said to me, "Why doesn't your plane look like *that* one?" Very funny. Jon and his dad were too polite to laugh. After my crippled plane flew nearly straight up, turned on its nose, and came straight down, it received a green ribbon for Best Crash.

Growing up, Father did not have model airplanes to build and crash. Or toys of any sort, really. Years later, he recalled nights the children went to bed hungry. At dinner, when Mama would exclaim, "Oh, good, just enough rice," the children would remain silent, acquiescent, unwilling to disabuse Mama of her happy illusion, even as their stomachs churned. Times were tough all over. No one handed you life on a silver platter.

Anyway, Father did not care about toys. He liked sports and competition, and until late in life, he continued to open the newspaper first to the sports section. In the 1930s, he played on the top Nisei basketball team in Los Angeles, the team his brother Mahito played on and his brother Hideo soon became the star of. In college, Father sparred with members of the college boxing club, and the coach, in need of a fast welterweight, urged him, albeit unsuccessfully, to join. After his father's death, he focused his primary attention on the pursuit of his future professional career, and having earlier skipped ahead the two years of school, he received his dental degree from USC at the age of twenty-one.

Father hadn't time for college boxing, but he remembered how it was done, the jab and the left hook combination or jab and right cross. Circle to the left, to the left, away from the opponent's power. One time, after losing his temper with his mouthy teenaged son, he squared off with me. *What, you want to fight?* Suddenly, Father assumed a boxing stance. Despite his glasses, he resembled a professional boxer, his fists raised, ready to parry and strike, his weight balanced on the balls of his feet, ready to circle to the right or to the left. A wave of fear swept over me. Quickly, I backed down.

For some reason, Father and I bonded over professional boxing, whose championship bouts were reported live on the radio in the 1950s. Back then, boxing was something boys and men talked about, they just did. One June evening, I listened to the live broadcast of the heavyweight championship bout between Floyd Patterson and Ingemar Johansson. I was attending a Boy Scout troop meeting, and a group of boys gathered around my transistor radio, rooting hard for Patterson, a true gentleman, soft-spoken and well-mannered, famous for his fast hands and peek-a-boo defense.

But it was the brash, party-going Swede who sent the heavy favorite crashing to the canvas not just one, two, or three, but an astonishing seven times in the third round. Patterson gamely struggled to his feet after each knockdown. But after the seventh one, the referee stopped the fight, declaring Johansson, famous for his dangerous "toonder and lightning" left hook, winner and new Heavyweight Champion of the World. The unthinkable had happened. When Father arrived to drive a bunch of us home from the troop meeting, I gave my radio a glance, as if granting it the opportunity to issue a retraction. Peek-a-boo, just kidding?

"Patterson lost. I can't believe Patterson lost."

"Yes."

"Were you for Patterson?"

"Of course." A brief pause followed. "I'm always for the American."

Well, yes. But didn't Father also want the American to win *because* Patterson was a Negro and his retaining the championship belt lifted and inspired Negro Americans? I would readily have agreed had a sociologist of that day informed me that some triumphs generate cultural capital—like Joe Louis knocking out Max Schmeling, like Jackie Robinson successfully stealing home plate.

A Floyd Patterson knockout of Johansson would have meant more than a win. And a loss, a devastating one at that, was more than just another loss. It should have been recognized the way astronomers spot a destructive asteroid streaking through the solar system, headed toward earth. Like the one that covered the planet in dust, wiping out the dinosaurs.

"I'm always for the American," Father repeated.

Indeed. Years after he left the army post in Missouri, he could recall the hakujin dentist, a man he worked alongside of at the clinic, who upon learning about the internment, wondered out loud how his Japanese American colleague could submit so willingly to the military draft after what the government had done to its own citizens. "I don't get it, Kats. Aren't you bitter as hell?" the man had said.

Nope, was the reply. After all, here was a man who later in his life would stoutly declare to protestors (like his own son during the Vietnam War), "My country, right or wrong" and "America, love it or leave it."

And yet this was the same man who had written Mr. Carew from camp regarding a question simmering among Nisei men like himself, on whether they should demand from the federal government a guarantee of their future American citizenship before they expressed their willingness to serve in the United States armed forces. So Father had not answered yes-yes in haste, after all. There had been a hesitation, a period of deliberation. A veteran of the American Expeditionary Forces in World War I, Mr. Carew had typed a four-page, single-spaced reply. It expressed strong sympathy for the Nisei plight but also urged Katsumi to agree to possible military service—without appending any demand.

Over the years, Father collected trophies and cups for bowling and golf, received numerous awards and citations for duplicate bridge. Quickly, he amassed more than triple the number of tournament points required to qualify as a Life Master, while privately lamenting the quality of play of some of his bridge partners. In one tournament, he competed head-to-head against the internationally recognized bridge expert Charles Goren. Armed with a good hand, Father and his partner bid correctly, played well, and won.

On weekends, Father took Bryan and me to watch professional sports at the Los Angeles Memorial Coliseum. Through the summer of 1959, we watched the Dodgers launch home runs over the Coliseum's short left field porch, which the sportswriters casually dubbed the Chinese Curtain, and later we attended games at Chavez Ravine, where longtime residents (primarily Mexican Americans) had been evicted, their homes demolished, to make room for the new baseball stadium.

Father never griped. He also never shouted or cheered out loud at sports events. Not if Deacon Jones made a game-saving tackle for the Rams, not if Hodges lined a ninth-inning home run or Koufax hurled a shutout for the Dodgers. It was not that he kept his reactions bottled up; it was just that words of encouragement, of celebration, or of dismay had no effect on the outcome. In games like golf and bridge, the chatter was minimal. Even in bowling, he let the ball crashing against the pins make all the relevant noise.

Always he acted the part of a good community citizen. He supported the Y, became an adult volunteer with the Scout troop, served occasionally as an usher at church, until eventually the family's attendance became irregular. For many years, he maintained an active membership in the Japanese American Westside Optimist Club, where he was elected to the offices of club secretary and vice president.

I took pride in Father's accomplishments, took pride in his position in the community. But I noticed that when other Nisei men urged Father to run for president of the Optimists or to serve as Scoutmaster for Troop 636, he always declined, although he continued to carpool boys to and from campsites high in the San Bernardino Mountains and to and from Friday night troop meetings. For our summer camps, he took several days off work and devoted himself to the task of adult supervision. Often, even late at night, we boys were rowdy, sweaty, and loud. But Father never yelled at us to pipe down like other dads were prone to do.

Maybe he had already considered the consequences of becoming a club president or a Scoutmaster. Had anticipated the long-winded introductions, the interminable speeches at awards and scholarship ceremonies, the discussions of new initiatives at club meetings, at executive sessions—enough already! All those opinions he would have had to sift through, all those words he would have had to dispense. At least in his own office he controlled such expenditures quickly and efficiently. Say, ah!

TOO BAD WHEN A SON GRATES ON THE FATHER, when the father angers the son. When we argued, I bristled with sarcasm. "Oh, you're never wrong, are you!" When kids didn't have a speedy comeback for a putdown, the other kids would say, ooh, what a burn!

Father did have a comeback. "Not with *you*, I'm not," he retorted angrily. I stared petulantly at the floor. Ooh, what a burn.

Father had always found Bryan and me perplexing. If only we were as easy to figure out as a club finesse, as decipherable as the heart lead from dummy. All his life, Bryan rejected participation in competitive sports, disliked clubs and organizations, although he was rather good at poker and decent at bridge. At a certain point, he refused to take communion at church, and on occasion he proclaimed that he was an anarchist.

I was worse. I had the chip on my shoulder. I was the one who mouthed off, full of opinions and complaints, just a bundle of nerves and retorts. Sounding off, brimming with confidence, the atmosphere corrosive with half-digested commentary—the kid who knew so much, oh sure! Meanwhile, who took the bait every time Florence was in a mood, allowed the fight to erupt, and got his privileges revoked?

It must have been hard, indeed, to reconcile this opinionated teenager with the nervous, lonely child he and Mother had worried about at the start of my school years. Separated from all of us during basic training and again during Officer Candidate School, Father had written the lengthy, frequently passionate letters to her (he missed her so!) in which he also asked after me, the troubled son. In one letter, he wrote, "Does George seem to dislike school? I hope not. I realize that we must build up his self-confidence and I'm going to give him more attention as soon as we're together again." Gosh, how could a kid change so much in less than a decade?

Only Laura made any real sense. The youngest child was controlled, diligent, above all rational. She did not make a sour face when Father warned that *accidents happen to careless people.* Instead, she absorbed truths, planned ahead, avoided mistakes. Even with her mother, she was sensible, her tactics sound. Authority figures were fallible. She knew from experience, perhaps reconfirmed at school and at church, how the wrong word uttered under one's breath could bring the clap of thunder and a deluge of consequences. She obeyed her mother's commands, dutifully and without hesitation. She listened, stayed smart. When a mother's temper flared, Laura knew that the child was the one who had to stay under control.

The important thing was to provide Laura with an ally. When the storm raged, she would need a protective eave to shelter under. Or maybe not. Maybe just a voice of reason to confirm what she already suspected to be true. Laura always waited until Father got home from work. In private, she confided in him time and again, sharing what Mother had said or done. Like the time Laura was prohibited from leaving the house or seeing any friends for three whole months because Mother discovered her playing with some coins found in an old, unused purse. She was a kid fiddling with coins, just counting and stacking them. But Mother, inexplicably losing her temper, had no interest in explanations and was determined to make the punishment severe. Despite her consternation, Laura waited until she could talk in private. You are right, Father was able to confirm to her that evening. Mom is wrong. When she gets like this, she is not rational. *You are right.* Laura felt reassured. She was not going mad.

FATHER'S STROKE OCCURRED LESS THAN TWO MONTHS after his sixty-fourth birthday, with the Christmas lights already brightening the avenues and plans finalized for the Marina del Rey Boat Parade. The stroke may have been abetted by aplastic anemia. Who would have thought Mother might possibly out-live him! Over the intervening years, she had regained sufficient strength and vitality to do volunteer work, even as her participation in a Nisei social life continued to dwindle and shrink. Long, long after the first cancer surgery, one doctor answered her query, admitting that he had given her only a 5 per-cent chance of survival.

Before they moved to the townhouse in Marina del Rey, Mother and Fa-ther sold the house on Westside Avenue and moved into a commodious two-story residence in the Blair Hills section of Culver City. Blair Hills was an affluent white enclave well removed from the urban areas about to be torn apart in the summer of 1965, during the fearsome unrest that extended well beyond Watts. Importantly, the public school system in Culver City ranked among the finest in the state.

The move paid off later on when Laura graduated with a double major in psychology and sociology from UCLA with high honors and a Phi Beta Kappa key. Culver City High had prepared her well. About her undergradu-ate work at UCLA, she answered an inquiry with simple candor: "It wasn't hard." After Father moved his office to Westchester, his old medical building on Santa Barbara Avenue remained, but the street itself was rechristened Martin Luther King Jr. Boulevard following Dr. King's assassination.

In time, the demographics in Culver City changed, and the house in Blair Hills started to feel too big. Mother and Father moved again, this time pur-chasing the townhouse in Marina del Rey. Laura completed her doctorate in psychology at the University of Colorado and accepted a postdoctoral posi-tion at Vanderbilt University, while Bryan, who found employment with the government's General Services Administration following a two-year stint in the army (assigned, much to the family's relief, to Korea rather than Vietnam) and a brief bout with graduate school, eventually moved from humid Wash-ington, DC, to Idaho.

I married. Father appreciated his daughter-in-law. Like him, Janice was quiet and uncomplaining. Oh, how he loved his granddaughter Tracy and grandson Eric, both kids smart and adorable. Actually broke down, accord-ing to Mother, when the first grandson, the newborn Michael, died after eight days in the neonatal ICU, a victim of a condition the doctors identified as asplenia syndrome. Father weeping. A sight neither unimaginable nor eas-ily imagined. Just like the sight of Father struggling to make sense of a son's poems.

When it came, the stroke was severe. The dental practice was sold for a fraction of its worth; there would be no return to work. The stroke robbed him of speech, of memory, of coherence. He had shaved every day of his adult life until now. Now his face became a field impossible to tend. Stubble grew, then a beard, which got trimmed, just barely. Unable to synchronize his mouth with his intentions, Father sometimes stammered, "Laura," when he meant to say, "Florence."

He was relegated to forced silence, to quizzical looks as he studied the dinner plate, the stuff on the dinner spoon, which Mother had precut into manageable squares. He needed help in the shower. He forgot how to laugh. During all his life, he had never asked God for much. Retaining the ability to floss his teeth or to understand a joke would have been nice. He could not recall Lawrence Welk.

Mother tended to him every day. She took him to the hospital for consults and for blood transfusions, which he still required. Every morning, every evening brought trials. She slept in Laura's bedroom, it was easier that way. She worried about the future, fretted over Laura, who was experiencing chronic health problems of her own. Dutifully, Mother cared for Father year after year—longer than the time spent in the barracks at Heart Mountain or the shoebox at Fort Leonard Wood. I stopped by in the evenings. I had graduated from USC and from the University of Michigan, and now I was finishing my doctorate in English at UCLA. I stopped by the townhouse regularly on weekday evenings. I would drive another twenty-five miles before I got home.

In vain were my attempts to restore Father's speech, but they were worth the effort. The man seated across from me at the kitchen table was willing to try. Before we began, I reassured Mother that I'd already had dinner, hiding my annoyance at her look of relief. It was not her fault. Mother was worried about herself, about Laura, worried about making ends meet when it was all over. There was no debt. But the man who shelled out college tuition for all three of his children and never once, not once, complained or asked for so much as a thank-you in return, had left his wife in a quagmire of doubt.

Meanwhile, she remained steadfast, loyal. To have weathered so much in her life and now to be caretaker for her husband, dying—who in heaven's name could understand what she had been through? Certainly not this son sitting across from a brain-damaged man struggling to recover a remnant of speech.

TEACHING THE STROKE VICTIM

I try to teach you to speak.
You in your pajamas wrongly buttoned,
your face dirty with beard, listen. The tongue

is your oar, its rowing constant,
the labials poof or hum, depending.
And the dentals, well, you must remember
those infamous pliers from school.
The last time I let you fix my teeth,
you drilled without enough local, the repair
being so minor and I being your son.
Now we talk. Your sounds are rudderless,
they grope for an invisible shore of sense.
The chest wheezes with frustration
at the violent intimacy of language and being.
Now we ease our way back to beginnings.

Today I open my book, and the word is *patience*,
a soft word, a lost art. That time
at the kitchen table when I lost mine
and you started to sob never quite
leaves me. In the years after your death,
I hear you sounding out the easy vowels.
I think of sons who make their fathers cry.

The morning of the first snow brings a light dusting across the treetops. All day the snow flurries, and all night it collects in drifts. By the following morning all the yards have benefited from a good bedtime story, for they each lie fast asleep under a thick white blanket. By twilight, the street melts into threads of slush banked by snowdrifts on each side. Up and down Harms Road, the porch lights waken. Dinner drags on. Mother helps me with my overcoat buttons, my mittens and boots, and last my costume. Bryan does not need help.

We pile onto a child's sled. Father dons an overcoat and a scarf, which protects his neck and just covers his mouth and cheeks. He wears a hat and gloves. The cold whips against our faces. His gloves take hold of the rope, and without having to utter a word, he pulls the pirate and the ghost up the road, through the slush. We are going treat-or-treating, all the way to the Plettner's house. Pull faster!

23

IN TRANSIT

White Flight

It wasn't supposed to go like this—my second and third years of junior high and my first year of high school, with so many kids moving out of district. I saw the start of things in the eighth grade, observed a pronounced acceleration over the next two years. Hitherto, I had not heard the term "white flight." It had not occurred to me that Caucasians should need or want to flee.

Throughout my first year at Audubon Junior High, I imagined the different races mixing in harmony. Caucasians were clearly superior in numbers, a condition I still found normal. This was the school where minorities, including Japanese Americans, Chinese Americans, Korean Americans, and Negroes, could meet on familiar and friendly terms with the white majority. At a school named after the famed watercolorist John James Audubon, the kids, metaphorically speaking, were all birds of a feather.

Except that I thought, weirdly, that it was paramount that the white children should feel comfortable first, then I could worry about myself and others afterwards. I made an effort to introduce new friends like Bruce Stanton and Wayne Bloom and Bob Weaver to my Buddhahead friends. Bruce was slightly pudgy, Wayne was handsome but shy, and Bob was an egghead with freckles and glasses, whose father served the country as an aviator during the Berlin Airlift.

Perhaps I would have been better advised to concentrate on how Audubon the painter achieved his effect of making his avian specimens look as though they were captured in motion or about to take flight. By the time I completed my final year at the junior high school, the shift in its racial balance had become quite evident, particularly in the lower grades, with the school no longer resembling the one I had entered as a seventh grade "scrub," only three years earlier.

A substantial number of my white classmates transferred to other schools immediately following the winter graduation ceremonies, and over the following summer the exodus grew. I was not privy to all the reasons why classmates left. All I knew was that they vanished. Bruce and Wayne and Bob Weaver were scarcely the only kids who moved on.

Nor were Caucasians the only ones with the urge to leave. By the time I completed my first two semesters at Dorsey High School, Mother wanted to move too. There was no term for Asian flight, but the rumblings from home grew in strength and intensity semester by semester, even as Mother continued her struggle to recover from cancer. More Negroes entered the school district. Mother and son had something new to quarrel over.

Mother still associated being the sole minority family in a white neighborhood with fitting in and making a good impression—and now with safety. Nothing was more important than protecting her children. Scattered throughout Los Angeles and Orange Counties, some Japanese American families did reside in all-white neighborhoods. Some lived there due to work considerations, some purposely chose to live in areas far away from where other minorities, including Japanese, congregated. Easily, Mother could have moved away from the house on Westside Avenue, abandoning it with no regrets.

I declared bitterly that I would not budge from the house. If they moved, I swore that I was gone. Meaning that I would run away for real this time. My friends were at this school, dammit!

Mother had her reply. When she got worked up, she exclaimed, "Friends don't matter!" But friends did matter. They mattered a lot. Even Mother knew this. What she meant was, you can make other friends. You can make white friends.

Mother was genuinely pleased whenever she encountered my buddies Bobby Nelson or George Schnitzer. She would have been delighted to have Mike Aloia or Steve Kemp, Marc Schenker or George Alevizos or Richard Rubenstein, come to the house. All of them still attended Dorsey. It was just that when she was agitated, there was no reasoning with her. Once, when Father overheard Mother utter these words about friends not mattering, he said, "Oh, c'mon, Florence." Ooh, she got mad at Father that time.

Changing Rhythms

At the assembly for tenth graders held in the school auditorium, Mike Clifford was introduced as a former student of Dorsey High. Lanky and handsome, the type of all-American looking boy that surely roller-skated and rode bicycles through the Crenshaw and Leimert Park and View Park Districts when Mother and Father first went house hunting in Los Angeles, Mike reprised his hit single "Close to Cathy," which he had sung live on national television on *The Ed Sullivan Show.*

All of my previous conditioning prepared me to relate, however vicariously (and in fact only vicariously), to Mike and Cathy, even though Mike was a complete stranger and Cathy present only in absentia. At home, I had attempted on numerous occasions to cultivate the soft, dreamy look and sound of a musical Lothario. In the shower, I turned the water on high while crooning "Put Your Head on My Shoulder" and "Venus in Blue Jeans" into the faucets marked HOT and COLD.

That day, Mike's performance for the tenth graders met with polite applause. That was what I noticed. Afterwards, there was no clamor, no surge onto the stage, fans and autograph seekers vying for recognition, for a handshake, a touch. Most of the kids simply got up from their seats and filed out of the auditorium, trudging back to geometry or English. For Mike Clifford, former student at Dorsey High, things must have looked different to him that fall afternoon when he performed his hit single in an auditorium thickly populated not just with white kids but with Buddhaheads and Negroes, some of the latter cool and suave in dark trench coats and shades.

It was different too when the other young guy, also an erstwhile student of the high school, returned. His appearance was unscheduled. Accompanied by a drummer and a side guitar, he performed an impromptu jam session outdoors on the Circle Lawn. Even in junior high, when his music career was taking off and he constantly cut class, he was famous for bounding onto the auditorium stage, his movements as irrepressible as the music he hammered out on the keyboard.

Increasingly, he was being summoned to studio recording sessions, invited to places featured in travel brochures. But when he returned to school, he was at home. Everyone knew him or knew someone who knew him. He played a wild jazzy piece, then something R&B, jouncing on his portable piano stool, his black hair not yet long, not Jheri-curled, but electric with excitement.

The kids, especially the bloods, gathered on the Circle Lawn. Bloods was a generic descriptor, not a gang identifier, but it was cooler than saying "Negroes." They leapt to their feet, clapped their hands, moved their bodies in time with the rhythm. They moved, they shook, they boogied. Without missing a beat, the musicians waved to old pals, waved to new pals as if they were old pals. The movements of the keyboard artist were frenetic, as if from the cradle onward, his life had been overbooked. The music played. The pulse of the school jumped several syncopated beats.

Professional destinies sometimes lie near, sometimes an ocean away. Within a year, the keyboardist's talents were courted internationally. A group largely unknown outside of Liverpool, England, became famous. Late in their association, they considered making Billy Preston the fifth Beatle. Over the years, Billy Preston performed with big names everywhere, including Eric Clapton, including a band that had just launched its inaugural tour, a group calling itself the Rolling Stones.

Dorsey was like that. It was racially mixed, progressive, wide open, changing, with pockets of tapped and untapped potential. There was the tale of a former student who became an original member of the Beach Boys. There was the older man who belted out tunes in the locker room while he dispensed towels in the boys' shower. You oughta turn professional, Ron, the boys said. Ron Townsend did exactly that, joining with Marilyn McCoo, who had graduated from Dorsey a few years earlier, and becoming one of the five members of the popular rock group the 5th Dimension. Imagine, from towel cage to album covers!

I liked my school. It was alive and unexpected. I liked it more than my parents knew, and not just because of the girls. I liked it particularly when the racial distribution leveled out, became almost even—one-third white, one-third black, and one-third Oriental. Somehow the school had changed me. I had ceased to believe it essential to be enveloped in a white majority. In fact, an even distribution seemed just about right. My worry now was that the racial balance was precarious, that it could not be maintained, and that the school's harmony was partly an illusion, as the white population continued to decline.

"Ue o Muite Arukō"

The song kept running through my head, its rhythm not precisely upbeat but nevertheless uplifting, a good song for any season. It was recorded in Japan in 1961 and was sung in Japanese, but its American release was withheld for more than a year and only then occurred after a music promoter renamed the song, intent on capitalizing on a Japanese word recognizable to a Western audience.

"Sukiyaki" was the first recording from Japan ever to climb into the Top 40 in the United States, eventually reaching No. 1 on the charts. I wished that I understood the lyrics. All I knew for sure was that it was a song named after a food and that its lyrics had nothing to do with the Japanese dish of thinly sliced beef and bland tofu, of vegetables, mushrooms, and glass noodles, which Mother sometimes prepared for Father. The ingredients existed side by side, complementing each other without being evenly blended. That sukiyaki tasted best with a raw, beaten egg.

The song's real title was "Ue o Muite Arukō," which translated roughly into "looking up as one walks." It was an appropriate title for me, now that I had reached such age that my temper had acquired legs. Mother forbade me, absolutely forbade me, to leave the house. I slammed the door on my way out. Bryan and Laura must have wondered, as they moved discretely out of range, didn't they ever get tired of yelling at each other, those two? Mother did not believe that I would run away permanently—*that* kid could not survive on the street for one day—but she secretly feared that in a rage I would fling myself in front of something dense and metallic, maybe a truck or a bus.

I looked both ways at the intersections. I walked up and down streets and around and across neighborhoods. It was best late at night, after a rain. Were I high above the city, I could follow a trail made of stars. I covered blocks, miles, going east on 39th Street, north on 6th Avenue, west on Exposition. I looped back along Crenshaw Boulevard, headed south past Holiday Bowl, before repeating the route.

Along the way, I was not assaulted or robbed or startled by a group of punks in a car slowing down to hassle me. I did not swerve into the street blinded by rage and swift headlights. Instead, what started as an escape quickly turned into a brisk walk, the walk into a meditative stroll. Along the way, the music played steadily in my brain, Lethe to the mangled teenaged soul.

The song was not exactly a love song and not a dance tune. I tried to recall the Japanese lyrics. I sounded out a few syllables and hummed the rest. The song had something to do with walking along and looking up, looking up toward the sky or past the clouds, and not dwelling on what had happened in the past. I mistook the title word "arukō" for the expression "I recall." No matter. After singing and humming awhile, I felt upbeat, all the turmoil swept away like harmless detritus following a storm, the surface I walked on firm and dry.

Somewhere out there the future beckoned. I would try to make friends with it, wherever it led. My personal transformation, badly needed, as I did not need to be told, waited for me around the next corner, waited for me to get a move on. I did not hate my mother, far from it. For all the guilt and anxiety I had felt over my lifetime, for all the crushing bouts of alienation and loneliness, I admitted to myself that Mother was the one person constant in her insistence—notwithstanding her tendency to exaggerate ("You scored near the genius mark on your IQ test!")—that I possessed special abilities and potential.

Little did I suspect that the Japanese songwriter composed the lyrics to his song while laboring under a thick cloud of disappointment. The words came to him as he walked home following a student rally, which had been called to protest the ratification of a security pact ensuring the continued presence of American military forces in Japan. The rally failed to achieve its objective, which was to halt the ratification and put an entire end to occupation.

A future marked by student protest rallies! A novel idea. A future marked by vocal denunciators, by swift and violent upheaval, when even the lyrics of the inner city changed, the term "bloods" replaced by "blacks" and eventually "African Americans," the word "Orientals," with its colonial, Eurocentric associations scrapped once and for all, replaced by "Asians" and "Asian Americans." Even the phrase "internment camps" replaced by the harder edges of "incarceration camps" or "concentration camps." I had known life only as a *preoccupation* with being a secondary kind of American—dutiful, compliant, conventional, and frequently invisible. Someday I would learn that it was my own mind that had been occupied—ideologically so. For now I walked my angers off, turned in circles, sang a song whose words were foreign and whose underlying protest it would take me years to grasp.

24

RITES OF REFUSAL

As badly as I wanted to be like everybody else—that's how badly my brother refused to copy anyone. In high school, Bryan would not participate in service organizations, after-school clubs, school council, or athletic teams. Some kids joined eagerly, seeking that badge of recognition and belonging, while others let themselves gradually be seduced. Bryan did neither. He never campaigned to attend parties or school dances or even Friday night sock hops. He neither drank nor smoked on the sly. Even movies, which Mother had forbidden Bryan and me to attend ever since Hollywood started stuffing its cinematic fare with scantily clad, cleavage-baring stars, held less attraction for him than they did for others. His disinterest in the activities gripping the lives of most teenagers reassured Mother that he was not like those out-of-control yogore boys apt to get themselves or others into trouble.

But it worried her too. Mother sensed that her son's social development was a bit, well, delayed. By now, Bryan had lost his adolescent pudginess, what had allowed him long ago to play the role of Alvin of the Chipmunks so effectively in a lip-synch performance put on by the Boy Scouts. In fact, this more grown-up version of Alvin had turned rather handsome, and one or two girls at the high school had noticed. They sent clear signals his way, but Bryan was slow to respond. It was not that he disliked girls, but he disliked dancing, disliked parties with all their gabbing, joking, banter, and relentless flirting. Especially the flirting. The storm of convention descended, the need to belong blew hard, whipping rapidly into a gale—and still Bryan stood firm, solitary, unmoving as stone.

Monitoring, restricting, and curtailing social activities were parental necessities, no doubt. But at the same time, Mother wanted each of her children somehow to turn out all right, to be normal in the end. It was understandable. When we were old enough, she would open the gates to a social life. Let us enter, cautiously at first, and eventually we would inhabit the space as responsible Japanese American adults. But by the time Bryan approached his final year of high school, he still had made no effort to step through those gates. I, on the other hand, could scarcely wait to burst through.

WHEN MOTHER ALLOWED ME to attend Betty Jane Ishida's graduation party, which all the Sansei ninth graders of the winter class of Audubon Junior High were invited to, I was both pleased and relieved. Now I would not have to use any of the face-saving excuses I had devised to account for my no-show. Mother knew that it would be a private party with a mix of boys and girls. And there would be slow dancing. Did she realize that there would be slow dancing?

After I completed my first semester of high school, I received permission to attend the chaperoned dances at the Crenshaw Athletic Center on Vernon Avenue, provided that I signed up for summer school and maintained my grades. Maybe the oral test Mother had administered ("Do you know what an erection is?" "How about the rhythm method?") was also a factor, having yielded satisfactory results regarding either my level of knowledge or my level of ignorance. Permission to attend dances at the CAC was granted on a "trial basis." Life itself operated on a trial basis.

Sharon Higashi was the reason I was eager to attend the dances. I had told no one about my fantasy life, particularly Sharon, who had plenty of guys interested in her. I felt inspired and emboldened by what I thought was the daring romance of the characters Winston and Julia in Orwell's novel *Nineteen Eighty-Four*, which I had been assigned to read for summer school. But when I attended my first CAC dance, I was afraid to act the role of Winston to Sharon Higashi's Julia. I could not bring myself to ask Sharon onto the dance floor, even though she was not stuck up. How would I even approach her? It was not my mother's fault I chickened out.

Sharon's friend Punkin was not as pretty and not as friendly. She exercised her right to make an unpleasant face when I invited her to dance, as if fearing that being in my proximity might prove contagious. Funny how facing rejection by Punkin seemed more bearable than summoning the courage to ask Sharon to dance. But dancing was not as much fun as I had thought.

For most of the evening, I lurked near the record player, bashful, self-conscious, fearful of being the last boy to be approached during the Ladies Choice.

Every school day seemed to divide in two. Half of it was filled with embarrassment, doing and saying exactly the wrong thing at the wrong time, while drawing unwanted attention to myself. The other half was filled with love, or at least its enticing prospect. Mother granted me permission to date, although permission was expressed in a puzzling way. When Mother heard about an upcoming school dance, she asked, "Are you dragging?"

Huh? Dragging, I quickly surmised, was a word boys used before the war when they were obliged to bring a date to a dance. Like dragging a ball and chain. It's a man's world. Men get to call the shots.

But in defense of women, not all of them spent hours pining away by their telephones, longing for a boy, any boy, to finally call. I learned this lesson the hard way after calling one girl, then a second, a third. Dragging was not as easy as it sounded. They were too polite to clobber me with a big fat no. Instead, they said, "*Who* is this?" After school, I managed to talk face-to-face with another girl I knew, but my voice quavered. Quickly, anticipation was down on all fours, sniffing for a biscuit of hope.

It would have looked rather comical as a cartoon, a boy completing a class in public speaking but speechless in front of anyone wearing lipstick and a bra. It was funny in a tortuous way to imagine legions of girls whispering and laughing at my clumsy efforts. Sit! Stay! Don't follow me! My best hope was that my dating inquiries had injured their self-respect, and they would keep the whole travesty to themselves. There were reasons why I never received invitations to the private parties held by the popular girls' clubs at school, just as there were reasons why those clubs felt the need to exist in the first place.

But no one failed forever. Did they? Mother insisted that I marry a Japanese American first, a hakujin second, those being the only two dating choices as well. On Saturday nights, I sat in my bedroom, alone and brooding in front of my rows and rows of books. That was what girls were relegated to doing on weekends, wasn't it, reading books? At least those who didn't have sleepovers to go to or parties to attend?

I had tons of books to pore over. *Huckleberry Finn, Madame Bovary,* and *A Tale of Two Cities. Brave New World, Animal Farm,* and *Invisible Man.* A pal at school offered me some advice. You think too much, he said, meaning that I took reading too seriously. I was ready with a slick reply: A man's gotta fight oppression and tyranny in order to be a man.

If only I were as bold as my prepared speeches. Then no one could have kept me confined to a home library. I'd have been long gone any night of the week. Maybe I would not be getting loaded or getting busted. Maybe I wouldn't be out and about, looking for trouble. But I'd be hanging out with steely nerve, ready for this and ready for that. I'd be a wildcat on the prowl. You don't like it, *tough*.

Anyway, I had not always been on the receiving end of plural negatives. I too had dared to say no. There was the time one of my teachers tried to pressure me to participate in the school production of *The King and I*. Mr. Lomeli, who also served as the junior high's drama coach, kept after me, pestering me for weeks. He did not want me for the lead. He needed me to play the role of one of the King of Siam's children ("It's easy, just sit there at the king's feet, and on cue, exit stage left"). I shook my head, politely shook my head.

Mr. Lomeli kept after me, and finally I agreed to participate—as a stagehand. Paul Nakasuji and I handled the heavy stage curtains through the evening performance, repeatedly pulling the ropes attached to pulleys. It was work demanding timing and strength. The production a huge success, the performers took multiple curtain calls, as the stagehands hidden in the wings pulled and pulled as one. Like smooth operators, like real men.

Then there was the big blowout. It came after Mother made that curious, disagreeable suggestion as my graduation date from junior high drew near. She urged me to return to 39th Street School and say hello to Mrs. McConnell, the teacher who, you know, had her fun teasing me. Supposedly, this reunion would signify that all was forgiven, that I had successfully moved on, the past over and done with.

Within the family, Mother found it difficult to overcome her residual hurts, difficult to forgive, impossible to forget. But toward institutional forces she bore no grudge. I was by nature more relenting. But to go back to Mrs. McConnell and pretend that I got the joke and that all was well?

Hell, no.

I flew into a rage. Mrs. McConnell may not have intended harm. It was all so cute, wasn't it? All so funny. Just teasing. In those days, definitions were different. Actions went unchecked. No one thought they merited mention, let alone formal punishment. Censure and intervention? Those words were foreign. Just go back, go back for a minute or two and say hello?

Hell, no.

CRADLING ORWELL'S BOOK IN MY LAP, I tried to recall why I had found Winston Smith and Julia such absorbing characters to begin with. Initially, I had been attracted to them because they had dared to find love. But what I remembered now was how they challenged the mind-control system, despite being under its constant surveillance. The deeper attraction, while it lasted, lay in their will to be different and their refusal to comply. I recognized those traits, they even existed within me, but I had consistently repressed them because I had placed so much faith in fitting in. How ironic that my own big brother, whom I had scorned for being weird, was the one who all his life had challenged the thought police.

Refusal spelled liberation for Bryan, who stood apart from the crowd. Who would not allow anyone to keep him from being anything other than himself. Likewise for the No-No Boys, who declared no on the basis of legal and ethical principle, even as they remained subject to the military draft and to federal prosecution if they refused their physicals. And for today's wayward yogore, who could inspire fear and loathing but also a grudging respect because they too refused to comply.

Understanding refusal in its various registers was a valuable lesson, even when one did not adopt the practice in every instance. By the by, I broke into the dating circuit when Susie Yamamoto called. Susie called me on the telephone and asked me if I would take her to the Sadie Hawkins Day dance at school. It was an invitation I quickly accepted.

25

YOGORE NATION

*Y*OGORE.
The word had a ring to it. A street ring. Like *badass*. Like *tough shit*. Like *up yours*.

In Los Angeles by the mid-1950s and early 1960s, yogore were regarded as drug users and street punks, kids full of swagger and attitude. They rejected quietism, obedience, conformity, the accepted path. They spat on good citizenship, seceded from one nation under God. *Study hard, get good grades, stay out of trouble, go to college, marry a nice Japanese American. Jeez!* They were fed up with the comparisons, fed up equally with the warnings and the pep talks. They refused to stand in the corner, refused to copy letters in a book or numbers on a blackboard. They'd rather wrestle life violently to the ground, and if it resisted, knock it senseless. *Take your straight-A report card and step aside, punk, I'm walking here.*

Yogore.

Etymologically, the noun derives from the Japanese verb, *yogoreru*, to get dirty, soiled. Even in prewar Japanese America, yogore existed—aleatory cats into numbers, grease monkeys into fast cars, movers and shakers into jazz or parties or booze, or just marginalized rebels. Some sported "drapes," the pachuco-style uniforms of young, edgy Mexican Americans. But among Nisei, the term "yogore" gained its broadest currency and was used most disparagingly for those Sansei youth of the postwar generation who strayed from acceptable appearance and conduct, thereby soiling the reputation of Japanese, including those who knew firsthand what it felt like to be despised during war and expelled from their homes.

The postwar blueprint made no allowance for deviation. *The bent nail gets hammered down.* So goes the Japanese proverb, which even Sansei learned. During the postwar years, yogore were the bent nail that hammered back. They embodied resistance. They were brash, full of bravado, panache, noncompliance. They identified with warriors, were ready with hard stares and knuckle sandwiches. *Let's get it on*, they liked to say. Most hated school with its confinements and myriad stupid rules, hated mimicking middle-class white people. Their gut reaction was a left hook to the status quo, an uppercut to conformity.

Yogore hung out with yogore, some seeking tough dudes from other minorities to hang out with and to fight with or against, depending—black guys on the West Side and Mexicans on the East Side, guys who embodied presence, not its deferral. Why must it be the burden of all Sansei to grab hold of the rope of education and cling, monkey-like, until it hoists you to middle-class security? All those Sansei kids taking classes with the white kids in chemistry and physics, trigonometry and calculus, in preparation for professional careers in medicine, dentistry, engineering, accounting, business, and law, and after that, after all that, for a wife and family and a safe home in the suburbs—*screw that noise!*

WITH MY PUNY FISTS, I did not relate to yogore as street fighters. But I connected with their alienation, envied their boldness, silently applauded the protest inherent in their style. Yogore were the retort made visible. The signature look started with the white tee, the khaki trousers hitched high above the waist, their creases sharp as a blade. The hair well oiled, swept straight back, the comb marks visible. The hair longer, the look more urban, more downtown than James Dean's. Sometimes a hoodlum stingy-brim hat like the ones the black dudes sported.

Hitch that belt with one hand, swing the loose fist in a wide, dangerous arc, in front, behind, in front—ready to batter down the wind. They strode, they strode chest out, chin up, like they were leaving fraught yesterday in the dust, like they were ready to punch tomorrow in its ugly face. Yogore were the soiled elements of the community, but it was no accident that when they carried their style just right, they not only commanded respect from their peers but also looked, in the parlance of the day, "clean."

Gary Goto glided across Jefferson Boulevard, smooth as a facial scar. Some yogore were tall and suave, like razor-thin Earl Iwamoto, son of the professional wrestler, Mr. Moto, one of Father's patients. Gold-toothed Dave

Suga hung out with pals at the pool hall at Holiday Bowl, his silk shirttails draped nearly down to his knees. One eye twitched as he lined up the eight ball. Sometimes yogore bunched together in slick-looking cars gleaming with Turtle Wax. When you caught them staring out the window, you knew they were not cowering. They were coiled.

Even I took to sweeping my hair back a bit further and a bit further, using a gob of stinky hair stuff from a jar labeled Murray's, which some black guys used to keep their hair stiff and straight. But my hair lacked swagger. Usually it looked slightly lopsided atop my head, as if it had not fully recovered from a disorderly dream.

YOGORE GIRLS WERE REBELS TOO. Less like nice girls steeped in rectitude and good grades. Less obedient, less compliant, not at all invisible. Mascara and tight skirts were the rage everywhere, but yogore girls accentuated sexuality, their skirts tighter, their bras pointier, their lipstick more inviting. Their eyelashes crawled out from their eyes, spidery with allure. Some cultivated bored looks. Some were naturally pretty. But even the less pretty ones looked sexy. In the school hallways, even guys too shy to do anything about it whispered, "Oh, what a fox! Man, what a babe!"

The yogore girls and the yogore guys looked good together. Together, they remapped the body image of young Sansei. They were too hip for thick glasses and slide rules. Some yogore girls sought out boyfriends from other races—not everything having to be either white or Japanese. They were in the vanguard in the multiplication of desire. They *were* desire, plus the middle finger in your face. Cool as conspirators but also fed up, they were capable—listen, fool!—of anything.

Some yogore lacked self-esteem. Too many bad grades, too much crap to contend with at home. I didn't always like what yogore did. I recognized that building self-esteem by intimidating others was not a good thing. But often it was more complicated, yogore were more complicated, not the mere opposites of successful Sansei youth. Yogore rejected the low profile, which was the safe profile for Japanese America. You want to watch my every move? Okay, check it out. Here it is, in your face. That was part of it, the stare back, the hard penetrating look or the I-don't-care-what-you-think shrug. The principle of surveillance stood on its head.

NOT ALL YOGORE FACED A BAD END. Some turned their lives around and achieved respectability and conventional success, their secession from the norm protracted but ultimately impermanent. More than a few straightened out years later. They cleaned up their act. Some never popped uppers and downers, got drunk, sniffed glue, but simply liked the attitude and the look. Some excelled at sports. Some even hit the books.

The contradiction between the soiled appearance and the purified outcome is a familiar one in Japanese culture. Every Sansei boy that I knew of was inspired by the story *Chūshingura*, in which forty-seven samurai carry out a clandestine plot to avenge their leader, Lord Asano, who has been forced to commit seppuku, ritual suicide, following an unsuccessful attempt on the life of an arrogant official operating under the jurisdiction of the shōgunate. Biding their time, the now masterless samurai wait for months, for years, for the precise moment to strike, in the meantime slipping into pedestrian trades and menial occupations or even feigning lives of dissipation.

Masterless samurai were known as *rōnin*. From my earliest days, I had taken pride in the fact that a samurai lay somewhere in my family's ancestry. If this were the feudal era, lots of yogore would have aligned instinctively, perhaps actually, with samurai and maybe in particular with rōnin, "wave men" who moved this way and that way, having been cast adrift following the death or overthrow of their feudal lord. Lacking the support and anchorage of a clan, many rōnin struggled to get by, in the process gaining reputations as thugs or vagrants, some slipping into lives of actual dissipation, others finding employment as mercenaries or becoming bandits, highwaymen, or enforcers for gangs.

In the story of *Chūshingura*, the rōnin bide their time. When at last the opportune moment is at hand, they regroup and proceed to attack with merciless zeal, avenging their lord's lost honor by slaying the government official cowering behind his guards. Privately, the shōgun admires the display of courage, loyalty, and steadfast determination, but in rule-laden Japan such a breach of order cannot be tolerated. In the aftermath of the incident, the samurai are ordered to perform seppuku, which one by one they willingly, courageously do, their glory now preserved, their legend unassailable. What they have done is to escape surveillance until publicly, even ostentatiously, drawing attention to themselves as warriors following an unorthodox route to achieve their end. One difference was that Sansei yogore preferred to start with warrior-like ostentation because they already had been labeled of no account.

Literally all Sansei in the community knew yogore. It was impossible not to. The kids who flaunted their refusals. The ones who pledged allegiance to their own and no others, the ones determined to grow up on their own terms, sometimes for the better, and sometimes, oh, for sure, for the worse.

26

A MAYONNAISE SANDWICH

In the Boy Scouts, Eugene was a yogore. My friend Gary Kuriyama, small but fearless, pretty nice actually but not a guy to try to bully, cultivated the semi-yogore look. Jeffrey Kinoshita, one of Father's carpool regulars, was the tall, quiet boy always occupying a corner of the rear seat by the window, his eyes hooded, a black trench coat covering his Scout uniform like an added layer of night. We others did not try to reform Jeff. Instead, we admired his tough solitude, the fact that he looked dangerous and cool. He disliked most of the adult leaders, Father being one of the few exceptions. *Thanks*, Jeff murmured, when Father dropped him off last at his house on Welland Avenue, one block east of our own house on Westside.

If Father had thoughts about boys like Jeff, he kept them to himself, as if concealed in their own trench coat. But years later, he shared something troubling he had heard from a Nisei friend, a local businessman, who claimed that recently he had gotten into an ugly dispute with Jeffrey Kinoshita. Not a big deal were it not that the businessman said that Jeffrey had threatened to kill both him and his family.

Father related the story to me, his look expressing his struggle to reconcile his image of the quiet teenager in the trench coat with a dangerous adult capable of such violence. Jeff committed no such murderous act, but things spiraled downhill all the same. Within a short time, I heard that he had been arrested on a charge of armed robbery. Later he got sentenced to a prison term at San Quentin Penitentiary. Neither I nor my father had ever heard of a Sansei being sent to San Quentin. Sometime later, Jeff was released, but his recovery was cut short when he died of a drug overdose.

TRUTH TOLD, I LIVED NEXT DOOR TO A YOGORE. But at the start, Russell Kambe was just a seventh grader mentoring me in the ways of manhood. The heavy grunts and the clanging of metal against metal and metal against cement signaled that Russell was working out with the barbells and dumbbells in the Kambe garage next door. He tightened weights on each end of the barbell and did presses or performed the clean-and-jerk. With a deep flex of his knees, his tailbone settled toward earth, his arms reached out, his cheeks sucking in all the available oxygen.

He was a pocket-sized Zeus. Before he attempted a lift, he pitched sharp, shallow whoofs into the air. Russell was in Bryan's grade at school, but Bryan showed little interest in learning the niceties of performing dead lifts. Watch your back, Russell warned Bryan's substitute, me. With the twenty-pound dumbbells, he proceeded to do curls in multiples of ten. Russell was compact, no more than a bantamweight, but when he flexed his biceps or threw out his chest, his muscles jumped out visibly, as if eager to perform their own reps. Also impressive was his cotton T-shirt, grimy like Brando's in *A Streetcar Named Desire* and reeking of sweat.

Russell was the first boy I knew who scoffed openly at *The Mickey Mouse Club*. He grimaced whenever he caught me humming show tunes. He could not fathom singers like Andy Williams, composers like Percy Faith, comics like Red Skelton. He shared no interest in solving mysteries with boy detectives Frank and Joe Hardy, especially if it required sitting in a chair reading a book for hours on end. He could not care less about Spin and Marty. Likely, he would have knocked Spin's block off.

Watch this, Russell said, maneuvering his body near a small square of cardboard used to soak up oil spots. He launched into a series of one-armed push-ups. One set was performed using his right hand, the other using his left. They were miracles of contortion, balance, and strength. "That is boss," I conceded, giving credit where credit was due.

The year before, Russell had been the one who showed me how to scale fences and ferret along stucco walls, lurking behind bushes and trees and spying into backyards, while pretending to be commandoes. He had taught me how to play "splits," a game requiring a knife. The idea was to fling the knife and make the blade stick in the ground within about twelve inches of the opponent's foot. Each successful thrust meant the other guy had to cast their leg out further and further until they no longer could do it, and they lost the game. Or—they got nailed in the foot, and the thrower lost. Russell had quickly sensed that I didn't enjoy the game that much. But he wasn't sure why, it was just a pocketknife.

"Let's trade blows," he suggested. After a final set of curls, he had detected my waning interest in watching muscles grow. We took turns. I struck him on the meaty part of his shoulder. He did the same to me. With each set, the blows grew more forceful. "C'mon, hit harder!" Russell was encouraging. "Look, I'll use my left hand." His left hand blows were test launches rather than the full measure of Nike missiles. Still, they landed.

"Ow, that one hurt! Stop!"

Russell stopped.

Such situations warranted reconsideration. Victories gained too easily offered little in the way of satisfaction. "Okay, let's do knuckles," he said. I fared slightly better at this popular game, which involved launching the middle finger off of the edge of the thumb and scraping the opponent's knuckle to make it bleed. Each flick required speed and accuracy. After several minutes, my knuckles bled. It wasn't fair. Over time, Russell's knuckles had grown too hard, just like his chin, just like his chest and arms, just like his willpower. To my credit, I continued for a spell in my efforts to inflict pain by using my fingers like jackhammers. But ultimately to no avail.

Seeking refreshment, Russell opened the spare freezer conveniently kept in the garage. The freezer was long and deep, but our close inspection turned up only frozen meats, lots and lots of frozen meats. No popsicles, no ice cream, nothing good to snack on.

"Hey, you got something to eat at your place?"

We climbed over the stucco wall separating the backyards, gave Blackie pats on her head, and found our way into the kitchen. I drew out a loaf of Wonder Bread from the bread bin. Peering into the refrigerator, Russell located the jar of mayonnaise. I handed him a knife, and he proceeded to lather the mayonnaise onto the white bread. Mother entered the kitchen. She liked Russell, we all did. When she saw that the sandwich he was preparing had no meat, she quickly pulled open the meat drawer and offered him some bologna and ham.

"Oh, no thank you. This is fine!"

Mother stared at the meager fare. Russell enryōed, too polite to impose, too polite to accept anything more, anything beyond the two slices of bread enclosing a layer of mayonnaise. Mother started to draw the slices of meat from their packaging.

"No, really, this is fine."

Mother stared. "But you've got nothing inside."

"This is good. I like it this way."

To prove his point, he took a big bite from his mayonnaise sandwich.

WITHIN A YEAR OR SO, Russell got into scuffles, thereby making practical use of his weight training. He started to ditch school, and later on he messed with drugs. Although he never wore his hair long and slicked back, Russell at some point morphed into a yogore. The fights multiplied. He liked fist fighting. Some people at school thought that he had a chip on his shoulder. That he was a troublemaker or bully, looking for other boys to intimidate and beat up. They were wrong. Some guys are built rugged, are born tough. Russell had a natural affinity for cracking jaws, just like Bryan's taste for comic books and mine for fifty-fifty bars on hot summer days.

But he was no bully. Was strutting not the natural gait of a bantam cock? Was a wise guy's jaw not the natural landing point for an irrepressible fist? He was always ready to get it on with bigger boys, the ones who thought they were hard and tried to stare him down.

"What 'choo looking at, punk?"

"Nuthin'. What you looking at, fool?" Russell fought black guys, white guys, Oriental guys. He did not care. He did not discriminate by race.

All the other kids ran like lemmings to the edge of the cliff whenever a fistfight broke out. "Fight! Fight!" they shouted, their voices a rising crescendo of fascination, alarm, and glee. If the spectacle lacked the decorum surrounding a duel between samurai, it nevertheless captured something of the excitement, anticipation, and dread. Usually, Russell emerged victorious. He was willing to absorb a few punches in order to deliver a hard left to the body, a shot to the jaw. It was a conversation with fists. Say your piece. Here's my answer. Make your point. Here's my reply. Now I'm gonna deliver several sentences in a row.

For a time he hung out with Tony Yano. The two of them could be heard lifting and clanging weights in Russell's garage. I was cautious around Tony, a stocky guy who did not say much and seldom laughed. His body lacked the angularity and his legs the length that made certain yogore look enviably cool. Tony did not wear his hair long and swept back. But he excelled at street fighting, no-holds-barred kick-you-in-your-balls street action.

One afternoon my piano teacher mentioned that Tony had been thrown in jail for allegedly beating another boy with a Coca-Cola bottle during a street fight. The legendary Japanese duelist Miyamoto Musashi, who slew his first opponent at age thirteen, fought unfairly too, as when he killed Sasaki Kojirō, a legendary swordsman, by striking him with an oversized *bōkken* that

Musashi had carved from his boat's oar after intentionally arriving three disrespectful hours late for their duel. Musashi was the rōnin who famously declared, "I am no lord's vassal." Russell and Tony were like that: they were "wave men" moving this way and that way, but no lord's vassal.

One time I saw Tony and some buddies—Russell was not there—gang-chase another boy down an alley after school let out. It was a kid named Sandy, a talented jazz pianist. What's going on? Sandy looked frantic, Tony and his friends in fierce pursuit, eager to take care of business. They carried no visible weapons, but they did not need any. Someone had messed up, someone was going to pay. It was horrifying to think what might happen to Sandy if he were caught. There was no pay phone nearby to call the cops. Sandy was on his own. The boys raced down the alley. I hoped that Sandy's legs and feet were as fleet as his fingers and hands.

By the late 1960s and early 1970s, more and more handguns and rifles would find their way onto the streets. It would be different from the days when there were knives, yes, but relatively few guns, and most fights were settled with fists. But when the guns appeared, along with the increasing flow of drugs, things took a turn for the worse. When Tony Yano was killed, it happened just yards outside the Yellow Brotherhood House, which had served as a rehab center and shelter for guys kicking drug habits or otherwise cleaning up their acts. Its members had engaged in extensive community outreach to keep kids barely reaching junior high school off drugs and out of trouble. Apparently, heated words got exchanged before the rifle shot went off.

THE LADY WHO CAME UNANNOUNCED to the Kambe home introduced herself as Mrs. Green. Afterwards, Russell's stepmom told Mother the story. By now, Russell's truancies and institutional malefactions had worsened, and Mrs. Green's son Paul had become Russell's best friend. Everyone knew that Russell and Paul hung out, that they did everything together. But Paul was not a tough guy like Russell or Tony Yano. Mrs. Green worried. She pleaded with Russell's stepmom to keep Russell away from Paul. She was afraid of the bad influence on her son. She feared that Russell would induce Paul to do things, to get into serious trouble with the police.

If a Japanese American boy were a bad apple, the police scratched their heads, drove to the house and talked to the parents, who would be sure to straighten things out. How seldom did they bust Japanese Americans! But Mrs. Green knew full well that the cops didn't look at Negro boys in the same way. If they got into trouble, watch out. So please, please, could you keep your boy away from mine? I'm asking this as a favor.

When Mother repeated the story to me, for once it was not a life lesson, not a warning to heed her advice or to avoid Russell's path. Mother told me the story because she still liked Russell, who was tough without being mean, hard without being cruel. There was no doubt that Russell was a yogore. But yogore were all different. Mother always remembered him as the next-door boy content to snack on a mayonnaise sandwich, politely declining her offers to stuff the sandwich with bologna or ham. He was the boy who hopped over the backyard fence and quietly played with Blackie until someone noticed he was there and invited him inside.

Years later, at a local college, I met a pleasant coed. By then, I truly had taken a separate path and had lost contact with so many I knew as a boy. But I asked the girl about her last name. Susan Kambe had grown up on the northeast side of Los Angeles. We immediately felt a connection; it turned out that she was Russell's cousin. Russell had not died from a gunshot. Nor had he perished in a fight. Susan confided that he had served time at the Chino Men's Colony, but that he was doing better now, much better—he was off drugs and was trying to turn his life around.

Hearing this news was gratifying. When I asked her to tell Russell that I wished him well, I knew that she would relay my message. That was the end of things, almost.

A few years later, an obituary in the *Rafu Shimpo* caught my attention. I reread it, even though I knew the act of rereading would not change the outcome. By this time, Susan and I had gone separate ways and I had heard no more about her or her cousin. The newspaper mentioned a tragic automobile accident. It identified the victim as Susan Kambe, twenty-six.

A postscript arrived several years after that, and I learned of Russell Kambe's fate. He took ill, perhaps an aftereffect of the prolonged drug usage or perhaps due to the way bad luck likes to follow misfortune. Russell succumbed to the illness. Were his cousin alive, she would have experienced a rush of sorrow, the kind of powerful emotional surge reserved for those you were hoping to see gifted at last with another chance. For me there was a slow spread of memory. That was not how the story was supposed to end. Russell hops the fence separating the houses, pets Blackie, woofs down another crazy mayonnaise sandwich. Susan Kambe, the sweet, lovely soul, had died. And now Russell, at forty, had too.

Miyamoto Musashi lived into old age, never having lost a single one of his more than sixty duels. In his retirement, the famous rōnin took up writing. As for Russell's friend Paul Green, I never learned what happened to him. If Russell were around, he would have been sure to wish Paul a long life.

27

HIGHER GRAVITIES

How stupid it seems. In retrospect, infantile, except that no infant would have been guilty of it. For years, I had clung to my fantasy, I had dangled it before my eyes like a tantalizing, poisonous mushroom—the oh-so-secret belief that I would die young. It was not a wish. I did not wish to die by the age of sixteen. Wishing you had never been born was not the same as wishing to die. But an early death was fate, what I privately, dramatically, called my doom. It would be all over then, all my worries gone. That was the darkest secret, the one I had kept all to myself.

I had comforted myself in advance with the requiem, the solemn faces, the refashioned memories. No more daily blunders, no secret tallies of failure, no unbridgeable gulf between intention and result. I had ghostwritten the speeches. I had gloried in the spectacle of death, which was a tattered fuselage, a Best Crash commemorated by a file of mourners and a wreath.

Except that in the months leading up to and succeeding that grim age marker, nothing catastrophic occurred. Not to me. Only all around me. Around me so much was taking place that bore witnessing, so much deep suffering and wider shock requiring a full lifetime to learn from, to reflect on, to remember.

The photograph appeared in the newspapers and was reprinted in *Life* magazine. The man was a Buddhist monk, well-known in Vietnam. On a June morning, he seated himself in the lotus position in the middle of a busy roadway. He doused himself with petrol. His was an act of political protest against the persecution of Buddhists by the minority Catholic-led government of President Ngô Đình Diệm.

Most Americans, including me, knew little about Vietnam except that it formerly was called French Indo-China and that Madame Nhu, the president's sister-in-law, was called the Dragon Lady. The American government had begun sending military advisors to halt the spread of communism. I went along, at first, with what my government told me.

Thích Quảng Đức lit a match and applied it to the petrol covering his body. Flames leapt into the air, but according to witnesses the robed figure did not scream in agony. Maintaining his sitting position, he did not utter a sound. Around him, passersby and other, younger monks gathered. They looked on, transfixed, horrified. The next day the world was greeted with the searing, unforgettable image of the man on fire. The world looked on in wonder and disbelief.

In September a church in Birmingham, Alabama, exploded in flames. It was the city where five months earlier the civil rights leader Rev. Martin Luther King Jr. composed his "Letter from Birmingham Jail." The explosion followed less than three weeks after he delivered his "I Have a Dream" oration on the steps of the Lincoln Memorial in Washington, DC. Hearing Rev. King's words on national television and observing the large numbers of white people also in attendance that day, I had felt inspired and hopeful. No one of sound mind, I thought, could possibly disagree with his message of racial harmony.

Four African American girls died in the firebombed church. Birmingham was a city already ravaged by the violent suppression of civil rights protests. Three of the girls were fourteen and one was eleven, their bodies left unrecognizable by the blast and subsequent fire. One girl was decapitated. Reporters called the act "cowardly." The word was puzzling. Of course, planting a bomb might be cowardly, but did murder become "brave" as long as it was committed in full view of others?

Within hours, two African American boys were shot dead, one by police. The other was a thirteen-year-old named Virgil Ware, gunned down in a nearby suburb, while riding on the handlebars of a bike being pedaled by his brother. The newspapers reported that the white youth who shot Virgil was just sixteen. He was a sixteen-year-old Eagle Scout. Convicted of manslaughter, the boy was sentenced to seven months in county jail. The sentence was suspended.

In December came the flood. Like the fires, it was not imaginary, it was real, and it occurred close to home. The Baldwin Hills Dam required a fissure barely a few centimeters wide to unleash calamity. In the flatlands below, many residents did not even realize that a water reservoir held in check by a dam constructed of compacted earth overlooked luxury homes, pricey automobiles, and expansive, winding streets. Belatedly, city engineers would realize that repressurization activities in the nearby oil fields along La Cienega Boulevard and ground subsidence in the immediate locale were invisible factors behind the dam's failure.

The dam burst just after 3:00 P.M. on Saturday. Floodwaters cascaded down Cloverdale Avenue and the nearby streets to the south and west of Dorsey High School. The waters surged furiously, gained velocity, as if released from a point of higher gravity. Some homes were quickly shattered or enveloped in mud and debris, while others were spared as the waters rushed and churned down the roadways, the paths of least resistance. Having swept down the hillsides, the waters quickly engulfed entire streets, swallowed bus stops and landmarks, shorted the power grid, and sent vehicles hurtling like rafts on a river. The Village Green apartment complex was inundated. At the intersection of what had been La Cienega Boulevard and Rodeo Road, a car and driver vanished into a watery hole.

Before the dam disaster, there was the cool October evening when the bus containing my friend Gilbert and me and the other members of the B and C basketball squads returning from our away games at Manual Arts High School pulled up to the entrance of the Dorsey High School gymnasium, where dozens of people milled about.

Ordinarily, the crowds dispersed quickly following the junior varsity and varsity basketball games. Not this day. Coaches and teachers kept telling people to disperse, but no one left. One of the coaches came to the door of the bus. He hustled us directly into the locker room with strict instructions. Go to your lockers, change out of your uniforms, don't bother to shower. Get dressed, go home.

Word quickly reached the locker room. It was Calvin Elliot, the football star, who had graduated the previous June. The ruckus occurred after the varsity basketball game. He was the peacemaker, the one trying to break it up. Now they were waiting for the ambulance. They had waited twenty minutes.

I changed quickly into street clothes. Leaving the locker room, Gilbert and I passed the door that opened onto the coaches' office. I said, look. I had spotted a towel. The towel covered the abdomen of the figure lying on the ground, the former football star, Calvin Elliot, who had been stabbed.

Rumors abounded. Maybe a member of the Gladiators was responsible? Someone claimed that the guy was out to get Ray Nelson. Ray? My seventh-grade track mate from the Homeroom 202 relay team? Calvin Elliott was the one who stepped in, tried to defuse the situation. Be cool, now. Then out of nowhere the knife. He got stabbed. Man, he was just trying to break it up. Where's that damn ambulance?

Calvin Elliot clung to life, as rumors circulated through the school in the days after. It was a deep wound to the abdomen. It was only a shallow wound. Vital organs were missed. Vital organs were hit. His family was with him, and his friends visited the hospital. I had never met Calvin Elliott, only watched him shag punts on the football field as the other team stormed down on him. He was muscled but not especially big. Lying under the white towel in the locker room that day, the blood pooling, he seemed to shrink. One thing was certain—the unaccountable wait for the ambulance. Calvin had been a team captain, a leader on the football squad. Day after day, I had repeated to myself that it was only a flesh wound and that Calvin Elliott would survive. Until he did not.

My birthday passed. Then, on a Friday in November, Coach Bravo, one of the varsity football coaches, stuck his crew cut through the cafeteria door. The rest of him followed. Coach Bravo was one of the PE teachers shepherding us through the locker room the previous month on the day Calvin Elliott got stabbed. His interruption of study hall that fall afternoon was unexpected. His body looked husky behind his windbreaker. Coach Bravo looked grim. Without preamble, he addressed us.

"The president has been shot."

How impossible to describe the ensuing shock. It was like saying the moon had just fallen out of its orbit. It was the freefall in the nightmare that didn't stop when the eyes opened. The nightmare that your mind insisted was a dream because the reality was unbearable.

"He may not make it."

Silence. The deep-as-outer-space kind. I could not move, could not glance at the other kids, everyone unable to muster thought. The world slipped its foundation, everyone united in disbelief. President Kennedy lay in the hospital in Dallas.

Until one kid who sat in the row in front of me could not contain himself. He liked to fool around, one of those characters who squandered their time in study hall. What's-his-name could not endure the silence and alarm, could not fathom the paralytic dismay that gripped his classmates, the inexplicable weight of solemnity. Without planning or forethought, he released a burst of laughter.

It was a cackle, not intended as a wise-guy noise, but something spontaneous and uncontrolled, as if a car had farted or a preacher had burped. I looked up. The boy feigned innocence, but his laugh had said it all. Why so grim? What does this have to do with me?

According to one of my teachers, "Life is a tragedy for those who feel, a comedy for those who think." Normally I liked such adages, liked their cadence and finality, the unexpectedness of the wisdom they were grounded in. I liked this one enough to write it down. But after the assassination, as I pondered the saying, I realized that the boy who burst out in laughter in study hall found life comic all right, but he was not one to waste time in thought. Most people did both: they thought and they felt. Did that mean that they alternated in their conceptions of life? Or did they think and feel at the same time and in such a manner that such moments as these reminded them that experience was not reducible to a clever caption or phrase? It was a riddle, life. It was a riddle from the start. Like death, it still was.

BY THE START OF THE EVENING FUNERAL SERVICE, the skies looked foreboding. The forecast was for rain. Since my grandfather's service was to be conducted at a Buddhist temple, Mother had prepared us in advance, had given us specific instructions on the procedures she remembered from her childhood. I found it curious that the first funeral I was to attend should be Buddhist rather than Christian.

When my turn came, I bowed before the altar, a preliminary bow, then took one step forward into a deeper bow with my hands placed together in an attitude of prayer. I took a pinch of incense from one bowl and placed it into a second. Then I repeated the bowing protocol in reverse. The chanting of the black-robed priests and the ringing of chimes permeated the incense-laden air.

Outside it started to rain. As if on cue, Aunt Mary broke down, cried out beseechingly, her wail echoing through the temple. She was inconsolable, despite Uncle Dave's efforts to comfort her. It took her some time to regain a measure of composure. Grandpa had lived to ninety. To the very end, he remained a stranger to Bryan and Laura and me, none of us being able to converse in Japanese. We did not refer to him as *jii-chan*, as other Sansei children often did when referring to their granddad. Near the end of his illness, Grandpa's wiry musculature had turned thin as joss sticks and he had become incontinent.

Throughout the service, Mother maintained a stoic calm. I felt proud of her for maintaining her dignity, for preserving her self-respect, while respecting the grief of others, including her Ne-san, who occupied—was forced to occupy—the family's center stage through the lean years, the harsh times.

On the drive home, the rain intensified. Father pulled the car into the garage, and Mother quickly retreated to the bathroom, where she found a seat on the edge of the bathtub. She did not turn on the light. Now, in the dark grip and solitude of the bathroom, she gave in. She gave in to what she had been holding back through the evening and the days and all the time leading up to the funeral.

Her grief convulsed, heaved, choked, throbbed. It was immense, measureless, an unremitting, ragged wave beneath which she sat, broken. Father came to her side, placed his arm around her, rocked her gently as one would rock a child, the pair of them shrouded in black, wordless on the narrow ledge of the bathtub, sorrow teetering as if on the lip of time.

For years I had consoled myself with the thought that Mother was the angriest person I had ever known. *That* was the being I had to contend with, I reminded myself. Of course, her thought was better. *What have you ever had to go through?* Every time Mother had expressed this thought, she had uttered it with scorn. What had I gone through in life compared to her? How could a soft life even begin to appreciate the grueling hardships faced by parents and grandparents? A bubble could appreciate a nail only in the instant it burst.

It was natural that for so long I had thought my mother was driven mainly by bitterness and rage. But now, watching her, I sensed that anger was not after all the driving force behind her rancorous actions and harsh words. It was not anger but loss. Everything Mother had done in life referred to it. It had no bottom, and at this moment no start and no end. To understand this much about her was wondrous, humbling, in its own way comparable to the seeker being granted a whisper of enlightenment before reaching the summit of the hill.

Why should she ever have apologized to me for losing her temper? Should one apologize for suffering loss? Give her credit. Mother had tried. She had tried her best to mold her children into an acceptable shape to inhabit successfully the world she had hoped she was helping to create. She had sacrificed too. Not things, not trips, not even time. But personal desire, its very possibility.

It was self-sacrifice then, just as constant watchfulness meant self-sacrifice now. So what if Mother constantly chastised and corrected? From her point of view, what good mother did not? Someone had to monitor movement, supervise the difficult trek into the future. A good Nisei mother did that. A mother who sacrificed her private wants even before they materialized as wants. A mother convinced that time was no ally but who nevertheless endured. Endured not rocklike against the face of the cliff but in furious daily panic, the lungs struggling for the next breath, despair whistling like a sirocco, gaining an advantage until momentarily beaten back, momentarily quelled.

It would be terrible if you died, but worse if you caused the death of another. Mother had never truly believed one loss to be more acceptable than another.

Not the loss of her own child. Nor its reverse—the loss of another's. It was never a matter of choosing between them, between water and blood, not really, and I always knew that much. What I had not realized until now was how she had intended her words to cast a spell of protection against each dire possibility, a spell of protection over the whole, even if it meant—especially if it meant—quashing self-fulfillment even before it gained definition as desire. Her manner of giving was peculiar, but her intention was at last clear.

Outside, the rain continued. It pounded hard against the windows and the roof, heavy and hurtful, as if demanding entry. Through the night it poured. At some point it would lighten. I went to bed, certain that the rain would lighten, just as I felt certain that Mother's tears would subside, but not knowing just when.

PART VI

REQUIEM FOR YESTERDAY

28

GONE HEART MOUNTAIN

OF THE PHYSICAL RECORD, LITTLE REMAINS. At least, compared to what once was. The wood from the tar-paper-covered barracks was sold off when the camp closed for good in late 1945, months after the end of the war. The barbed wire was repurposed. The machine guns resting atop the guard towers vanished, as one by one the towers came down. But in the distance a structure still rises from the ground. It shows some age, having endured seventy-five years and more of brutal winters, of relentless dust and wind, of withering summer monotony. It pokes up from the ground, bleak yet enduring, like the weathered thumb of a god. In actuality, it is the chimney for the hospital boiler house.

Officially named the Heart Mountain Relocation Center, the internment camp was completed in 1942 under the supervision of the Army Corps of Engineers, who hired local laborers, many of them unskilled, to erect the buildings. Located some fifty miles east of Yellowstone National Park and about fourteen miles north of the town of Cody, by 1943 the camp held nearly eleven thousand internees. Had it been incorporated as a city, it would have constituted the third-most populous in all of Wyoming. Except that even after the war ended, the state prohibited the camp's "residents" from buying property or voting.

Today, visitors can wander through the former campgrounds, scattered parts of which have been preserved or restored. They can inspect a barrack. Their cell phones can snap pictures of the root cellar and the site once excavated for a swimming hole. Often, these visitors arrive in caravans, sometimes on pilgrimage. The Honor Roll Memorial commemorating military veterans enlisted directly from the Heart Mountain camp draws a crowd, the solemnity broken only by the occasional murmur of people chancing upon familiar surnames. Could that one be related to someone they once knew in middle school?

As for the mountain, that is a different matter. Rising more than eight thousand feet above the stark terrain, Heart Mountain is magisterial, a big, rugged geological crust composed of limestone and dolomite, more than three hundred million years old. If ever there was blood coursing through its rocky veins, it must have long ago congealed, perhaps in tribute to the slower, more patient entreaties of erosion. But the mountain continues to loom overhead—grand, unmoving, imperturbable, as if simultaneously inhabiting two tenses, the past destitute and the present perpetual. Through its unflinching gaze, it might easily have observed a barbed-wire city, its residents pinched together like so many criminal seedlings until orders came for their random dispersal during the all-clear.

A GRADUATE OF THE OTIS ART INSTITUTE, Estelle Ishigo was particularly adept at capturing both the austere beauty of the mountain and the ordinary activities occurring within the grounds of the concentration camp. Like other camp artists, she had to improvise at first with pencil stubs and bits of charcoal and with paints fashioned from clothing dyes and plants. It takes skill to capture the quotidian, even more skill to capture its fleeting indignities, and more yet to convey the invisible scars left from being wrenched from homes and possessions, from neighbors and coworkers and friends, and from the hopes and plans for succeeding generations.

One of Ishigo's most famous depictions is of a pair of children reclaiming their kite from a barbed-wire fence. Another is entitled *Children Scavenge through Barrels*, and still another depicts the forfeiture of privacy in *The Showers in the Women's Wash House*. Her painting *Gathering Coal* shows internees buffeted by a winter storm, which renders both sky and earth identically severe. Poorly dressed, their hair and tattered jackets windblown, the anonymous figures struggle to collect scraps of coal to feed their furnaces. In the background appear portions of barracks like the worn hulls of wooden ships. The figures in the foreground risk toppling over with the next wintry blast.

The fact that Ishigo displayed professional talent came as no surprise to the internees at Heart Mountain. After all, her father was a professional painter and her mother a San Francisco opera singer. But not everyone in camp remembered Estelle Ishigo for her skill as an artist. They remembered her because she was born Estelle Peck, and she was white. She married a Nisei man named Arthur Ishigo in 1928, and her parents disowned her. Her wealthy, cultured parents disowned her. In the cauldron of Estelle Ishigo's interracial marriage, blood had by no means proved thicker than water.

As a newlywed, Florence Funakoshi saw her marriage to Katsumi Uba as both a sacred bond and an emotional anchorage. Florence did not have the benefit of professional training as an artist or a writer. But for several months, from January 1 to July 17, 1944, she maintained a diary. Housed in a stippled black leather binding with the words "1944 Year Book" etched onto the surface, it remains the only surviving day-to-day record of her life in camp. The entries take note of a "beastly blizzard" on March 21, the first day of spring, and of an ensuing camp blackout two days later. They include scattered accounts of various mundane activities—on March 4, Florence went to her sister Mary's barrack "to learn how to make teriyaki," and on March 20, she "cut Toshi's hair" in the morning and in the "afternoon, sewed."

But the diary devotes much more attention to Florence's expressions of love for her husband and to her frequent avowals of physical fatigue.

Saturday, January 1, 1944
The new year dawned and all that I am aware of is that I love my husband dearly—perhaps too much and unwisely. God, please grant me the wisdom to see, the tolerance to understand.

Monday, January 3, 1944
Today I slept a whole lot, didn't do my work. Far too exhausted.

Florence's love for and dependence upon her husband intensified after Katsumi received permission to leave camp to "scout out" potential cities for the couple to resettle in. During his thirty-four-day sojourn, Katsumi stopped at the Amache camp in Colorado to check in on his sister Miyeko and then proceeded to Minnesota to see his sister Fukiko. Traveling mainly by bus or train, he investigated possibilities for resettlement in city after city, including Minneapolis, Chicago (where he stayed with his brother Hideo), Cincinnati, and Kansas City, while also undergoing medical treatment for a hand injury, followed by an episode of blood poisoning. Back at Heart Mountain, his 1-A draft classification arrived in the mail.

Saturday, January 29, 1944
No letter again!—Oh! Gee! What can the matter be?
    I figured it best that I cry my eyes out and try to get the pent-up feelings out of my system.

Monday, January 31, 1944
Two letters from Kats!!! Bless the lad—he's well!

I have learned something about fortitude. It's given me a taste of what our lives can be if he should be called into the service. It's lonesome, yes. But a purpose that has honor—can be comforting to one's loneliness.

God, if you should take from me my husband's love, I shall know I did wrong. Please keep me as thy will. My own mother has helped me through the years thus far.

On February 27, Katsumi returned to Heart Mountain. He and Florence were thrilled to see each other once again. Yet unexpectedly, within days, they experienced a brief falling out. The backdrop was Florence's constant fatigue. The diary leaves the reader with the suspicion that her fatigue may have been related, at least in part, to an undiagnosed depression brought on by the conditions of camp life and by the uncertainties of the couple's future.

Wednesday, March 8, 1944
Today I didn't go to work. Kats was tolerantly patient of me. In my own analysis—I feel that it's just an outgrowth of being in camp so long. I feel rusty. Very much. The fact that our future has no plan— must lead to this feeling of frustration.

Thursday, March 9, 1944
Kats would be very provoked if he should learn of what I am thinking. I'm tired—just so terribly tired of leading this camp life. I wish I had some outlet. I am not as happy as I could be. His entire attitude toward my cold is one of patient tolerance—not much on genuine sympathy.

Wednesday, March 15, 1944
At night I got mad at a small thing Kats said—about my constantly being tired. After that I didn't speak to him much. Went to bed with the heavy silence still pervading. However I kissed him goodnight.

Thursday, March 16, 1944
This morning one of the most important things happened to me. When I told Kats what I was mad about the night before—he told me "I couldn't take it." I won't say I was[n't] shaken up because I was. He continued saying my behavior confirmed a suspicion of his.

Well, God—I guess this is part of your doing, too. I asked to have wisdom, grace, dignity, kindness and goodness for Kats' sake. You are laying the groundwork. Please give Kats some of your infinite patience.

In late May, the couple was granted permission to exit the camp, and by mid-July, Florence's diary entries ceased. A lone surviving entry from an un-recovered 1943 diary succinctly attests to a "complete dislike for camp—its degenerating influences, the lack of dignity in living, the lack of privacy." That fragmentary entry concludes with these words: "I only hope that one day we can exit beyond that barbed-wire fence so I can collect my soul. What they [have] allowed me to have in camp is only the carbon copy."

AS FOR ESTELLE AND ARTHUR ISHIGO, they managed to return to the West Coast after the war ended, despite the government's earlier efforts to pressure former internees to stay far, far inland. As a white American citizen, Estelle had not been obliged to join Arthur in a desolate internment camp. But she did. She had chosen to remain with him. For better or for worse, through sickness and in health. Till death.

For a time after the war, they lived in a trailer park near Terminal Island, due east of San Pedro and southwest of Long Beach, where Issei had established a thriving fishing community and had helped develop the canned tuna industry before the war. The Uba family, when they were not harvesting strawberries during the summers, had regularly traveled to Terminal Island for holidays back then. Fishermen and community leaders from Terminal Island were among the first Japanese to be arrested and incarcerated following the attack at Pearl Harbor. Estelle and Arthur found work at a fish cannery but struggled to make a living. In 1957, Arthur died.

In 1984, Estelle was discovered living alone, destitute, both her legs amputated from gangrene. Her Japanese American friends from the Heart Mountain Relocation Center tended to her and proved instrumental in having her 1972 book, *Lone Heart Mountain*, republished. The book is a firsthand account of life in camp, and it includes anecdotes, reflections, and observations, as well as numerous drawings, sketches, and paintings reproduced in black-and-white.

Filmmaker Steven Okazaki produced and directed a documentary entitled *Days of Waiting: The Life and Art of Estelle Ishigo*, which was released in 1990. Estelle did not have an opportunity to view the film. She died shortly before its completion. The film went on to win an Academy Award.

In one of her pencil drawings, a triptych depicting men and machinery involved in the construction or repair of a horseshoe-shaped building, Ishigo depicts in the upper panel an oversized brick chimney enveloped in scaffolding. It may well be the chimney to the hospital boiler house, for it is not one of the smaller chimneys serving the barracks. But the drawing is untitled. Whatever the case, it provides an eerie complement to the old, weathered chimney that remains, while provoking a before-and-after meditation on the dreams of youth reduced to ash, on the years like smoke sent spiraling into air.

29

MAGIC MIRRORS, FABLES FOR CHILDHOOD

To provide the right kind of nourishment, Mother's habit was to feed her naughty boy a scrap of wisdom—"*You* need to take a long look in the mirror!" I did literally as told. For in truth, mirrors had always fascinated me, the stories they hid, the stories they revealed.

In the famous tale "The Mirror of Matsuyama," a daughter sees the pure, selfless soul of her dead mother, to whom the mirror was originally given. Looking into the mirror helps keep the daughter steadfast, maintains her in kindness and devotion through years of hardship and mistreatment. Eventually, it is discovered that the mirror's image of purity is that of the girl herself, a discovery that enlightens the father and transforms the cruel stepmother. In reality, few cruel stepparents are transformed by anything of the sort. And not everyone possesses a pure soul from the start. Still, purity is something to aspire to.

On the other hand, the *ungaikyō* in Japanese folklore is a mirror that manipulates reflections such that humans see a monstrous version of themselves. The long gaze into this possessed mirror means that viewers will see the side of themselves they labor to keep hidden and out of public sight. But what if the ungaikyō reveals an essential, primary expression of oneself? Then the best one can hope for is to work conscientiously to maintain a pleasing mask.

I experimented with different faces in the mirror—long faces, sour faces, happy faces. In the story "One Thousand Mirrors," a cheerful dog, upon entering a mysterious house, encounters the reflections of a thousand other cheerful dogs and vows to return each day. But a growling dog encounters a thousand hostile, snarling faces and quickly decides to leave such a dismal abode, never to return.

The story contains a good lesson, even though it is difficult to keep smiling into a mirror for long. It is hard to keep doing anything. They say you cannot keep crying if you stare long enough into the mirror. Try it if you feel sad. Eventually, the face reconsiders the facts, grows curious about the operations of the tear ducts, its levers and gears. You cannot sustain laughter either while looking steadily at yourself. Or self-pity, which the mirror is quick to remind you is tedious and boring.

If I had had my own mirror story, it would have gone like this. Once there was a child whose mother loved him so deeply that she predicted for him a future of wealthy palaces, glorious fame, and matchless stature, all of which he utilized to make life better for all the subjects in the realm. Her prediction was unrealistic, but she was so determined that it come true that she scolded and beat the boy daily as if to instill its certainties deep into his flesh. Day after day, when the boy looked in his mirror, he saw a figure scarred and hopeless, a figure filled with frustration and rage.

The boy grew to be a man, and the man grew old. One day he found the mirror covered in dust in an attic. He wiped the dust and grime off the old mirror and peered into it once again. He saw a young face, which he recognized as his own. When he looked away and then back to the mirror, he saw an older face, which also was his own, yet quite different. He repeated the action, and each time a still recognizable yet remarkably different face appeared.

Finally, he saw a face long in years, which belonged to a man who had attained neither a throne nor great fortune. But the face no longer bore traces of scars, no longer looked ravaged with anger. Instead, it was a face declaring a faith in small acts of kindness and marked with traces of chagrin, as if wondering why it had taken so many years to learn such a simple lesson.

The man looked at the mirror a final time, and when he did, he saw a second face, that of his mother, very old and feeble and wracked with pain, for she had prayed bitterly hard to the gods night after night and year after year that her son's destiny be fulfilled.

In her hands, she held a baking instrument with a flat blade. It was a spatula laden with icing, for she had baked many delicious things to celebrate his anticipated success. When the man was still a boy, his mother had allowed him to consume leftover icing, his tongue reaching for the sweetness on the front and back and carefully along each side.

The icing coated a wish, a wish often lost sight of because of the more urgent wishes that daily pressed upon the mother as she sought to raise her child, but one mustering strength for that very reason. The wish was for her child to be happy.

The man reached into the mirror and withdrew the spatula. He took it just as he used to do as a child, exposing the sweetness on each side, taking care to let none of it go to waste.

FROM THE TIME I WAS YOUNG, I found all mirror stories entertaining and instructive, even when I was not sure that I had fully absorbed their lessons. It would have been nice to believe that mirrors were accompanied with sets of instructions or that a trusty mentor resided on their other side. That would have helped. But either way, a mirror has a more active function than merely to keep one immobile and stuck in place.

I recalled a trick I learned after I had mastered the basic alphabet. I took a pencil and proceeded to print letters on a piece of paper—but going right to left and, with a bit of practice, backwards. When I was done, I turned the paper to face the mirror, and as if by magic, six letters appeared, an identity clear and distinct. Out of nothing they appeared, six letters, each one rounded, evenly spaced, legible, and assured, as if all along they had been proceeding forward, guided by a capable hand.

30

EGG AND ROSE

Mother's words astonished me.

It was the day before Father's funeral. His suffering had been un-remitting, ever since the stroke left his brain broken, words unrecoverable. For four years, Mother had attended to him, convinced that there was not enough money to hire help. It was not true, but saving and saving rather than spending reassured her. Now and again she had grumbled to herself that Father had not prepared better for such contingencies. For four years she had pinched pennies. But every day she had attended to his needs.

She took me aside as the funeral plans were finalized. Her intentions were good, I suppose. She took me aside to warn me that during or after the funeral there might be moments when people chatted, smiled, even laughed. It was human nature, she informed me solemnly. So don't be offended if people do not wear sad faces all night long.

I looked at her. Was she serious? I was thirty-seven years old, a father of two. Seven years ago, Janice and I watched helplessly as our eight-day-old son died in the neonatal intensive care unit. That was the same year the Nazis planned their march through the streets of Skokie. That was the year the movie *Close Encounters of the Third Kind* came out, and two grieving parents wept quietly in the theater when the small, ghostly aliens stepped from their spacecraft. Did Mother really believe that she was offering sage advice about human behavior? How, even in serious situations, humans slipped into casual conversation, smiled and laughed, how they acted like humans?

It was not just her condescending tone that caught me off guard. Like a lot of people, she thought that a PhD in English simply meant that I was really, really good at grammar. No, what left me shocked was the realization that after all these years, Mother understood nothing of substance about her own son.

Mother died in 2002 at the age of eighty-two, having outlived Father by eighteen years. Year by year she became more socially withdrawn from the Japanese American community but for a long time remained active in volunteer work with organizations directed by hakujin. After acquiring her driver's license, she had commuted to the Hollywood chapter of the USO. Later, she had volunteered as a museum docent for the Los Angeles County Natural History Museum and for the Science and Technology Museum. Over the years, she battled angina and endured angioplasties and three separate heart valve operations. In her sixties, she successfully battled another recurrence of cancer.

Laura, who has suffered from a multitude of her own chronic ailments, lived with her. Laura has used her doctorate in psychology to teach and to author three landmark books on Asian American mental health and psychology. Bryan, a lifelong bachelor and longtime government employee, still lives in Idaho. He took an early retirement, and several times a year, he visits Los Angeles before driving home. His cars are equipped with gadgets and the latest safety features, which are essential for his long drives. And in any case, he no longer travels anywhere by plane.

When the funeral director asked me what music to play at Mother's funeral, I handed him a CD containing Pachelbel's Canon in D, with a suggestion to play it on a loop. It seemed like a classical piece Mother would have liked. Relatives attended the brief service, including Uba relatives from as far away as Denver. I marveled, always marveled, at the unstinting generosity of my blood relations. When I greeted my cousin Grant, who had served as president of his medical school class at USC, I immediately recalled the numerous times he had quietly donated blood for my father following the stroke. During Mother's funeral service, I uttered a few words of appreciation, but I did not deliver a lengthy eulogy. Mainly, I expressed gratitude for those who had come from far away.

The divorce had occurred years earlier, but Janice and her mother were in attendance. My girlfriend Chi was instrumental in helping me make the arrangements in Chinatown for the dinner following the service. She had to attend to her own restaurant too. Gregarious, occasionally tempestuous, on the surface Chi seemed utterly different from Janice. But both were exceptionally hardworking, smart, generous, kind. By now, I had come to believe that kindness and generosity were the most important human traits to possess. Those—and forgiveness.

LIKE ANY SEVEN-AND-A-HALF-YEAR-OLD, I knew better, but the night before Fort Leonard Wood's annual Easter egg hunt, I imagined gigantic birds covered with spots, with stars like asterisks, with Saturnian rings, swooping through the park while clutching brilliantly colored eggs. John James Audubon had neither categorized nor painted these birds, but they produced multitudes of eggs they were willing to surrender to the children.

From aloft, they dropped the eggs. *Plop, plop, plop,* they fell to earth one after another, but they did not explode into pieces. Instead, they bounced like rubbery balls, seeking good places to hide. The next day, from their hiding places high in the leafy canopy, the mothers held their breath and watched the human children, dozens of them, mostly from the army base, assembled noisily behind the starting line.

Bryan and I were the only Orientals participating, the only children, in fact, who were not Caucasian. I felt self-conscious, but my brother and I always started out as the only two kids who looked different, and here at least there were two of us. Father wore civvies. He held Laura in the crook of his arm so that she could see what was going on. A man in an official-looking hat warned several boys not to push. In the near distance, the domes of Easter eggs were clearly visible, their bright happy colors like flares resting on patches of grass or snuggled between the roots of trees. These were the easy finds.

Searching for the brightly painted eggs Father hid around the house in Skokie was a fun memory, a safe memory. The day before, Mother would help us paint and decorate each egg. Half of a hardboiled egg was dipped in a red food dye, then turned around so that the other half was dipped in a food dye of a contrasting color. For zigzag effects or bands of color, the eggs were suspended in delicate wire holders with wire handles. I fought through the unpleasant odor of vinegar and participated happily in decorating the eggs.

On Easter morning, we kids raced to discover the eggs—not just the eggs we had painted but ones that had miraculously multiplied overnight. These were the Easter Bunny eggs. There were many good hiding places. Tucked in a fold of curtain, slipped inside the hollow of a victory cup, nestled in a Yuban can or left crouching beneath a cereal bowl on the dish-drying rack, they eventually were found out, one and all. A few were located in conspicuous places. Behind a table leg or in an elbow of the arm chair. Bryan and I took advantage of Laura's youth and inexperience. Father helped guide her to a few select hiding places. Bryan was formidable, an able hunter, who moved swiftly through the rooms, overturning things at random. *Careful!* Mother warned.

This Easter egg hunt was different. It was an all-out competition, a race for success. The man in the hat suddenly cried out, "Go!" Instantly, waves of legs cascaded across the park, eyes peered in multiple directions, hands reached madly over the ground. The scramble was on! Many had brought their own Easter baskets as containers. Having lost sight of my brother, I edged shyly away from the starting line, the last one to move. People were going lickety-split, the parents of some of the children rushing to hold the gathered eggs and to direct their children toward others. Look, look, here, over here! And c'mere, will ya?

After a while, I spied an egg on the ground, somehow overlooked, and walked toward it. As I bent down and reached for it, a boy raced up, scooped the egg from the ground, and hurried away. Already that boy had collected many eggs of various colors in his basket, which he swung confidently, without bothering to tally his catch. Eggs were rapidly vanishing. The ones in plain view at the start were all gone. Now it was getting harder to locate them.

Finally, near a random tuft of grass I spotted an oval tip. This time I reached quickly, securing the egg before anyone else might take it away. It was just one egg, a blue one, and partly cracked. Everyone was slowing down now, the easy finds already secured, with only the well-hidden eggs left. Some children reached as high as they could into the overhanging boughs, which drooped downward, as if guilty with bounty. Some kids wandered out of bounds, until the adults steered them back.

One portion of the grassy field had been sectioned off for softball, with the bases defined by patches of dirt. It was flat, unpromising. As I scanned the area approximating second base, I noticed the smallest protrusion, nothing more than a wrinkle in the ground. I tapped around it with my foot. The dirt slipped away, and there it was, the corner of an egg. Digging with my hands, I soon uncovered more of the oval shell. This egg I scooped up quickly, lest some spy swoop in and steal it. It was a whole egg, uncracked, come to life. A brilliant gold egg. Now I had one egg for each hand.

"Hey, he got one!" It was another adult. He was pointing at my find. Before the egg hunt began, the man wearing the hat had mentioned the two special "golden eggs" hidden among the dozens of others. Somehow I had managed to find one of the special eggs. The pace of the hunt slowed even further, as fewer eggs were left to be found. Eventually, the Easter egg hunt was declared over. Shyly, I took my only two eggs to my parents. *Lookit.* Bryan had located several eggs, although not nearly as many as most of the other children had done.

The director of the egg hunt called on the kids who had managed to find a golden egg to step forward. There were so many kids and grownups there. My parents gently pushed me to the front, and a man announced, here's a golden egg! He held it up for everyone to see and admire. Instead of returning the egg, he reached into a large box and withdrew an enormous Easter basket. There were marshmallow bunnies, jelly beans, round chocolate eggs, and sweet hard candies encased in strawberry wrappers. They rested atop a blanket of artificial Easter grass. Hollow at the bottom, the basket nevertheless looked impressive. It was enclosed in shiny foil and topped with a gigantic green bow.

I experienced a burst of pride. This was a splendid prize, one of only two to be handed out that day. Oh, that mound of dirt near second base had failed to deceive me, all right. I had known how to look for the big prize in the least likely place! As the crowd dispersed, families moving back toward their cars, a lady came up to me and cried out, "Congratulations!" I managed a shy thank-you. What a nice lady.

When another lady paused to offer her congratulations, Father replied, "Well, he only found two." I shrank in embarrassment.

The sun had come out, and suddenly I felt assaulted by its intense heat. It was typical Japanese self-effacement. Japanese, even Japanese born and raised in America, did not trumpet their children's success. Especially not in front of Caucasians. It was bad form. Instead, they modestly demurred, deflected, sometimes openly denied any excellence on the part of their own child. *Oh no, he was lucky! He's not good at it!* Receiving public praise from others for one's own children was like boasting about oneself. *She did not do well at all. You are too kind.* In public, one needed to be humble, not brash. Quiet, not loud.

I glanced at the other kids, their baskets brimming with eggy plenitude. The boy who had swiped the egg I had almost claimed paraded by, his basket containing what must have been a thousand eggs. It came as a jolt, then, the truth. That boy had won his glory by being swift and aggressive. I had merely gotten lucky. Many kids had rushed right by the little dirt mound near second base. If one of them had kicked up the dirt, even by accident, that one would have discovered the hidden treasure, and I would have been left with just the one blue egg with spindly cracks crawling across its shell.

The smallest pinprick had shattered my thin pretense of success, which proceeded to drain from me in yolky haste. Bryan would have handled things better. Although only managing to collect five or six eggs himself, he did not care. He had no particular fondness for hardboiled eggs. His salivary glands at work, Bryan glanced at his little brother carrying the big basket. Yes, he would be sure to share the goodies. Mother would see to that. In our family, we always had to share. My brother could not eat chocolate because of allergies. But the marshmallow bunnies and the jelly beans looked like fair game.

As our family walked along, something unexpected occurred. We were passing several houses, not military-issue homes, just modest bungalows occupied by local townspeople. One had a dirt yard protected by a chain-link fence. A kid, just a squirt, maybe two or three, pressed his face against the fence. He was shirtless, dressed only in a pair of white briefs. His cheeks were pink. Mystified by the parade of strangers, the child reached through the chain-links as if trying to grasp the meaning of the moment through his hands, his wispy blond hair keeping rhythm with the uncontrolled movements of his reaching. On the porch behind him sat his mother, watching. People passed by. We all smiled at the tyke. So cute. Mother turned to me and murmured, "Give him your egg."

My egg? My only one?

"Go ahead," she urged. But it was not an order.

We stopped. It was only fifty yards or so to the car, but it seemed far away. Approaching the fence, I took my blue egg and proceeded to coax it into the child's outstretched fingers. Walking in the unsteady fashion of barefooted toddlers, he clutched the egg as he retreated to the porch. He was not wearing briefs after all. It was a white diaper. He showed the prize to his mother, who waved a quick thank-you. I felt good. I had not wished to part with my only egg, but now I was glad I had followed Mother's suggestion.

That was when a second unexpected thing occurred. A girl who had been walking with her parents a few yards away approached. Her dress had picked up dirt smudges from the egg hunt. I had never seen the girl before, but evidently she was adept at tracking down Easter eggs, for eggs of various hues filled her basket. As her parents looked on, she took an egg from the top of her basket and extended it to me. They had seen the whole incident with the toddler.

For an instant I reeled, almost overcome with bashfulness. For one thing, I did not speak to girls except my sister, which did not count against me. Fortunately, the girl did not utter a word. Instead, she reached in my direction with the egg. The eyes of so many people seemed focused on me. What to do? It was a girl! Before the situation could turn even worse, I accepted the egg. There! We reached our car and we piled in. For a moment, I forgot about the Easter basket. I examined the egg. It was red as a raspberry. It was not cracked.

"You should have thanked her," said Father.

"I did," I insisted.

FROM THE START, Jack Robinson was the shiniest comet shooting through the skies above Pasadena and soon enough through parts beyond. At least, once the neighbors adjusted to having a Negro family move onto their segregated block. He excelled at baseball, at basketball, at track, at tennis, and sportswriters swore that he was even better at football. Renowned for his athletic feats at Pasadena Junior College, Jack would go on to star in four sports at UCLA. By the time he broke the color barrier in major league baseball in 1947, he would be known as Jackie Robinson.

During the war, Jack Robinson's mother continued to work as a maid for the wealthy white family in Pasadena. But Joe Funakoshi, who performed odd jobs and gardening tasks for the same family, disappeared. Having neither the inclination nor the aptitude for learning a foreign language, Joe could not explain in English precisely where he and his family were about to go. Nevertheless, he parted on friendly terms with Mallie Robinson.

At Pasadena Junior College, Jack Robinson had become the Big Man on Campus several years before the Japanese Americans were forced to pack up and leave. Having availed herself of a college continuation opportunity, young Florence Funakoshi attended PJC as a part-time student. One day, between classes, Jack strolled by the famous reflection pool that graces the front of the college. In his hand he carried a single red rose. Exactly why he carried the rose and to whom it was actually intended were never made clear. What was clear was that he was intercepted first by one girl and then by another. Pretty girls. Girls with charms. He waved greetings, evidently forgetting for the moment that any rose in his hands was, socially speaking, a potential firework with a short fuse.

"Oh, Jack, is that rose for me?"

"Dear Jack, how thoughtful!"

Caught in the vise of celebrity, as well as in the snares of two crafty Minervas, Jack Robinson had to be nimble and he had to be quick.

Nearby stood Florence Funakoshi, the bashful, petite Japanese girl he had met through his mother's and her father's humble work at the Pasadena mansion. Florence stood silently nearby, not daring to extend a greeting over the confident voices of the girls vying for Jack's attention. But suddenly he took notice of her, standing there, almost hidden amid a throng of her Nisei girlfriends.

"It's for her!" Jack proclaimed, rushing toward Florence and grandly extending the rose.

Caught off guard, Florence accepted the gift. She managed a thank-you, fearing for a moment that her face had turned as deep a crimson as the rose. She turned away from the disappointed rivals. If those girls said anything behind her back, she preferred not to hear it. Anyway, as she reminded herself, she knew Jack Robinson personally. They were practically friends.

EPILOGUE

In Pursuit of Deer

DAWN IN THE INTERNMENT CAMP
AT HEART MOUNTAIN
(WYOMING, 1942)

Someone clever has carved a deer
from a scrap of wood
and set it on a table or shelf
inside a shabby room among a file
of barracks, along a street of sleep.
In its miniature dawn, its hues
are gradually revealed,
its legs regain their poise,
its eyes open. Someone clever
has set a mountain in the backyard
beyond the barracks and morning's incipient din,
to loom above the density of human emotions,
to relieve the clutter of stars overhead.
And—just now it beckons to the deer.

WERE A DIRECT LINE POSSIBLE, the site of the Japanese American internment camp at Rohwer, Arkansas, could be said to lie less than 300 miles south of Fort Leonard Wood and maybe 60 miles southwest of the tiny municipality in Mississippi where the trial for the accused murderers of Emmett Till took place. Till, a fourteen-year-old Negro from Chicago's South Side, was savagely beaten and slain, allegedly for flirting with a white woman. This was 1955.

During the war, a white deer hunter observed a group of Japanese American internees performing supervised labor in the woods outside the Rohwer facility. The hunter shot and wounded two of the workers, later asserting that he mistook them for a pair of deer. The accused killers of Emmett Till, whose decomposed body was found in the Tallahatchie River, were acquitted by an all-male, all-white jury. Spotted by a passerby while having blood washed from his pickup truck, one of the accused had claimed it was blood from a deer.

A SIGN in a California store window after the attack at Pearl Harbor read

JAP

HUNTING LICENSES

BELOW THE MESSAGE, the words **Sold Here** were crossed out. They were replaced with one word.

FREE

George Uba is Emeritus Professor of English at California State University, Northridge (CSUN), where he served as Chair of the Department of English and was a founding faculty member and Acting Chair of the Department of Asian American Studies. He is the author of *Disorient Ballroom*, a volume of poetry, and recipient of CSUN's Nathan O. Freedman Outstanding Faculty Award.

Velina Hasu Houston, ed., *But Still, Like Air, I'll Rise: New Asian American Plays*

Josephine Lee, *Performing Asian America: Race and Ethnicity on the Contemporary Stage*

Deepika Bahri and Mary Vasudeva, eds., *Between the Lines: South Asians and Postcoloniality*

E. San Juan Jr., *The Philippine Temptation: Dialectics of Philippines–U.S. Literary Relations*

Carlos Bulosan and E. San Juan Jr., eds., *The Cry and the Dedication*

Carlos Bulosan and E. San Juan Jr., eds., *On Becoming Filipino: Selected Writings of Carlos Bulosan*

Vicente L. Rafael, ed., *Discrepant Histories: Translocal Essays on Filipino Cultures*

Yen Le Espiritu, *Filipino American Lives*

Paul Ong, Edna Bonacich, and Lucie Cheng, eds., *The New Asian Immigration in Los Angeles and Global Restructuring*

Chris Friday, *Organizing Asian American Labor: The Pacific Coast Canned-Salmon Industry, 1870–1942*

Sucheng Chan, ed., *Hmong Means Free: Life in Laos and America*

Timothy P. Fong, *The First Suburban Chinatown: The Remaking of Monterey Park, California*

William Wei, *The Asian American Movement*

Yen Le Espiritu, *Asian American Panethnicity*

Velina Hasu Houston, ed., *The Politics of Life*

Renqiu Yu, *To Save China, To Save Ourselves: The Chinese Hand Laundry Alliance of New York*

Shirley Geok-lin Lim and Amy Ling, eds., *Reading the Literatures of Asian America*

Karen Isaksen Leonard, *Making Ethnic Choices: California's Punjabi Mexican Americans*

Gary Y. Okihiro, *Cane Fires: The Anti-Japanese Movement in Hawaii, 1865–1945*

Sucheng Chan, *Entry Denied: Exclusion and the Chinese Community in America, 1882–1943*